The Ancient Mediterranean World

The Ancient Mediterranean World

From the Stone Age to A.D. 600

Robin W. Winks
Late of Yale University

Susan P. Mattern-Parkes
University of Georgia

New York   Oxford
OXFORD UNIVERSITY PRESS
2004

Oxford University Press

Oxford   New York
Auckland   Bangkok   Buenos Aires   Cape Town   Chennai
Dar es Salaam   Delhi   Hong Kong   Istanbul   Karachi   Kolkata
Kuala Lumpur   Madrid   Melbourne   Mexico City   Mumbai
Nairobi   São Paulo   Shanghai   Taipei   Tokyo   Toronto

Published by Oxford University Press, Inc.
198 Madison Avenue, New York, New York, 10016
www.oup.com

Library of Congress Cataloging-in-Publication Data
Winks, Robin W.
    The ancient Mediterranean world : from the Stone Age to A.D. 600 / Robin W. Winks,
Susan P. Mattern-Parkes.
    p. cm.
    Includes bibliographical references and index.
            ISBN 13 978-019-515563-1 (pbk.)
    ISBN 0-19-515562-9 — ISBN 0-19-515563-7 (pbk.)
        1. Mediterranean Region—Civilization. I. Mattern-Parkes, Susan P. II. Title.

DE71.W57 2004
930′.09822—dc22   2003058493

Printed in the United States of America
on acid-free paper

Contents

Maps, Boxes, and Chronological Tables

Maps

Boxes

Chronological Tables

---

*Box contains illustrations.

Preface
The Value of History

History is a series of arguments to be debated, not a body of data to be recorded or a set of facts to be memorized. Thus controversy in historical interpretation—over what an event actually means, over what really happened at an occurrence called "an event," over how best to generalize about the event—is at the heart of its value. Of course history teaches us about ourselves. Of course it teaches us to understand and to entertain a proper respect for our collective past. Of course it transmits to us specific skills—how to ask questions, how to seek out answers, how to think logically, cogently, lucidly, purposefully. Of course it is, or ought to be, a pleasure. But we also discover something fundamental about a people in what they choose to argue over in their past. When a society suppresses portions of its past record, that society (or its leadership) tells us something about itself. When a society seeks to alter how the record is presented, well-proven facts notwithstanding, we learn how history can be distorted to political ends.

Who controls history, and how it is written, controls the past, and who controls the past controls the present. Those who would close off historical controversy with the argument either that we know all that we need to know about a subject, or that what we know is so irrefutably correct that anyone who attacks the conventional wisdom about the subject must have destructive purposes in mind, are in the end intent upon destroying the very value of history itself—that value being that history teaches us to argue productively with each other.

Obviously, then, history is a social necessity. It gives us our identity. It helps us to find our bearings in an ever more complex present, providing us with a navigator's chart by which we may to some degree orient ourselves. When we ask who we are, and how it is that we are so, we learn skepticism and acquire the beginnings of critical judgment. Along with a sense of narrative, history also provides us with tools for explanation and analysis. It helps us to find the particular example, to see the uniqueness in a past age or past event, while also helping us to see how the particular and the unique contribute to the general. History thus shows us humanity at work and play, in society, changing through time. By letting us experience other lifestyles, history shows us the values of both subjectivity and objectivity—those twin conditions of our individual view of the world in which we live, conditions between which we constantly, and usually almost without knowing it, move. Thus, history is both a form of truth and a matter of opinion, and the close study of history should help us to distinguish between the two. It is important to make such distinctions, for as Sir Walter Raleigh wrote, "It is not truth but opinion that can travel the world without a passport." Far too often what we read, see, and hear and believe to be the truth—in our newspapers, on our television sets, from our friends—is opinion, not fact.

History is an activity. That activity asks specific questions as a means of arriving at general questions. A textbook such as this is concerned overwhelmingly with general questions, even though at times it must ask specific questions or present specific facts as a means of stalking the general. The great philosopher Karl Jaspers once remarked, "Who I am and where I belong, I first learned to know from the mirror of history." It is this mirror that any honest book must reflect.

To speak of "civilization" (of which this book is a history) is at once to plunge into controversy, so that our very first words illustrate why some people are so fearful of the study of history. To speak of "Western civilization" is even more restrictive, too limited in the eyes of some historians. Yet if we are to understand history as a process, we must approach it through a sense of place: our continuity, our standards, our process. Still, we must recognize an inherent bias in such a term as "Western civilization," indeed two inherent biases: first, that we know what it means to be "civilized"and have attained that stature; and second, that the West as a whole is a single unitary civilization. This second bias is made plain when we recognize that most scholars and virtually all college courses refer not to "Eastern civilization" but to "the civilizations of the East"—a terminology that suggests that while the West is a unity, the East is not. These are conventional phrases, buried in Western perception of reality, just as our common geographical references show a Western bias. The Near East or the Far East are, after all, "near" or "far" only in reference to a geographical location focused on western Europe. The Japanese do not refer to London as being in the far West, or Los Angeles as being in the far East, although both references would be correct if they saw the world as though they stood at its center. Although this text will accept these conventional phrases, precisely because they are traditionally embedded in our Western languages, one of the uses of history—and of the writing of a book such as this one—is to alert us to the biases buried in our language, even when necessity requires that we continue to use its conventional forms of shorthand.

But if we are to speak of civilization, we must have, at the outset, some definition of what we mean by "being civilized." Hundreds of books have been written on this subject. The average person often means only that others, the "noncivilized," speak a different language and practice alien customs. The Chinese customarily referred to all foreigners as barbarians, and the ancient Greeks spoke of those who could not communicate in Greek as bar-bar—those who do not speak our tongue. Yet today the ability to communicate in more than one language is one hallmark of a "civilized" person. Thus definitions of civilization, at least as used by those who think little about the meaning of their words, obviously change.

For our purposes, however, we must have a somewhat more exacting definition of the term, since it guides and shapes any book that attempts to cover the entire sweep of Western history. Anthropologists, sociologists, historians, and others may reasonably differ as to whether, for example, there is a separate American civilization that stands apart from, say, a British or Italian civilization, or whether these civilizations are simply particular variants on one larger entity, with only that larger entity—the West—entitled to be called "a civilization." Such an argument is of no major importance here, although it is instructive that it should occur. Rather, what is needed is a definition sufficiently clear to be used throughout the narrative and analysis to follow. This working definition, therefore, will hold that "civilization" involves the presence of several (although not necessarily all) of the following conditions within a society or group of interdependent societies:

1. There will be some form of government by which people administer to their political needs and responsibilities.
2. There will be some development of urban society, that is, of city life, so that the culture is not nomadic, dispersed, and thus unable to leave significant and surviving physical remnants of its presence.
3. Human beings will have become toolmakers, able through the use of metals to transform, however modestly, their physical environment, and thus their social and economic environment as well.
4. Some degree of specialization of function will have begun, usually at the workplace, so that pride, place, and purpose work together as cohesive elements in the society.
5. Social classes will have emerged, whether antagonistic to or sustaining of one another.
6. A form of literacy will have developed, so that group may communicate with group and, more important, generation with generation in writing.
7. There will be a concept of leisure time—that life is not solely for the workplace, or for the assigned class function or specialization—so that, for example, art may develop beyond (although not excluding) mere decoration and sports beyond mere competition.
8. There will be a concept of a higher being, although not necessarily through organized religion, by which a people may take themselves outside themselves to explain events and find purpose.
9. There will be a concept of time, by which the society links itself to a past and to the presumption of a future.
10. There will have developed a faculty for criticism. This faculty need not be the rationalism of the West, or intuition, or any specific religious or political mechanism, but it must exist, so that the society may contemplate change from within, rather than awaiting attack (and possible destruction) from without.

A common Western bias is to measure "progress" through technological change and to suggest that societies that show (at least until quite recently in historical time) little dramatic technological change are not civilized. In truth, neither a written record nor dramatic technological changes are essential to being civilized, although both are no doubt present in societies we would call civilized. Perhaps, as we study history, we ought to remember all three of the elements inherent in historical action as recorded by the English critic John Ruskin: "Great nations write their autobiographies in three manuscripts, the book of their deeds, the book of their words, and the book of their art."

The issue here is not whether we "learn from the past." Most often we do not, at least at the simple-minded level; we do not, as a nation, decide upon a course of action in diplomacy, for example, simply because a somewhat similar course in the past worked. We are wise enough to know that circumstances alter cases and that new knowledge brings new duties. Of course individuals "learn from the past"; the victim of a mugging takes precautions in the future. To dignify such an experience as "a lesson of history," however, is to turn mere individual growth from child into adult into history when, at most, such growth is a personal experience in biography.

We also sometimes learn the "wrong lessons" from history. Virtually anyone who wishes to argue passionately for a specific course of future action can find a lesson from the past that will convince the gullible that history repeats itself and therefore that the past is a map to the future. No serious historian argues this, however. General patterns may, and sometimes do, repeat themselves, but specific chains of events do not. Unlike those subjects that operate at the very highest level of generalization (political science, theology, science), history simply does not believe in ironclad laws. But history is not solely a series of unrelated events. There are general patterns, clusters of causes, intermediate levels of generalization that prove true. Thus, history works at a level uncomfortable to many: above the specific, below the absolute.

If complex problems never present themselves twice in the same or even in recognizably similar form—if, to borrow a frequent image from the military world, generals always prepare for the last war instead of the next one—then does the study of history offer society any help in solving its problems? The answer surely is yes—but only in a limited way. History offers a rich collection of clinical reports on human behavior in various situations—individual and collective, political, economic, military, social, cultural—that tell us in detail how the human race has conducted its affairs and that suggest ways of handling similar problems in the present. President Harry S. Truman's secretary of state, a former chief of staff, General George Marshall, once remarked that nobody could think about the problems of the 1950s who had not reflected upon the fall of Athens in the fifth century B.C. He was referring to the extraordinary history of the war between Athens and Sparta written just after it was over by Thucydides, an Athenian who fought in the war. There were no nuclear weapons, no telecommunications, no guns or gunpowder in the fifth century B.C., and the logistics of war were altogether primitive, yet twenty-three hundred years later one of the most distinguished leaders of

American military and political affairs found Thucydides indispensable to his thinking.

History, then, can only approximate the range of human behavior, with some indication of its extremes and averages. It can, although not perfectly, show how and within what limits human behavior changes. This last point is especially important for the social scientist, the economist, the sociologist, the executive, the journalist, or the diplomat. History provides materials that even an inspiring leader—a prophet, a reformer, a politician—would do well to master before seeking to lead us into new ways. For it can tell us something about what human material can and cannot stand, just as science and technology can tell engineers what stresses metals can tolerate. History can provide an awareness of the depth of time and space that should check the optimism and the overconfidence of the reformer. For example, we may wish to protect the environment in which we live—to eliminate acid rain, to cleanse our rivers, to protect our wildlife, to preserve our majestic natural scenery. History may show us that most peoples have failed to do so and may provide us with some guidance on how to avoid the mistakes of the past. But history will also show that there are substantial differences of public and private opinion over how best to protect our environment, that there are many people who do not believe such protection is necessary, or that there are people who accept the need for protection but are equally convinced that lower levels of protection must be traded off for higher levels of productivity from our natural resources. History can provide the setting by which we may understand differing opinions, but recourse to history will not get the legislation passed, make the angry happy, or make the future clean and safe. History will not define river pollution, although it can provide us with statistics from the past for comparative measurement. The definition will arise from the politics of today and our judgments about tomorrow. History is for the long and at times for the intermediate run, but seldom for the short run.

So if we are willing to accept a "relevance" that is more difficult to see at first than the immediate applicability of science and more remote than direct action, we will have to admit that history is "relevant." It may not actually build the highway or clear the slum, but it can give enormous help to those who wish to do so. And failure to take it into account may lead to failure in the sphere of action.

But history is also fun, at least for those who enjoy giving their curiosity free reign. Whether it is historical gossip we prefer (how many lovers did Catherine the Great of Russia actually take in a given year, and how much political influence did their activity in the imperial bedroom give them?), the details of historical investigation (how does it happen that the actual treasures found in a buried Viking ship correspond to those described in an Anglo-Saxon poetic account of a ship-burial?), more complex questions of cause-and-effect (how influential have the writings of revolutionary intellectuals been upon the course of actual revolutions?), the relationships between politics and economics (how far does the rise and decline of Spanish power in modern times depend upon the supply of gold and silver from New World colonies?), or cultural problems (why did western Europe choose to revive classical Greek and Roman art and literature instead of turning to some altogether new experiment?), those who enjoy history will read almost greedily to discover what they want to know. Having discovered it, they may want to know how we know what we have learned and may want to turn to those sources closest in time to the persons and questions concerned—to the original words of the participants. To read about Socrates, Columbus, or Churchill is fun; to read their own words, to visit with them as it were, is even more so. To see them in context is important; to see how we have taken their thoughts and woven them to purposes of our own is at least equally important. Readers will find the path across the mine-studded fields of history helped just a little by extracts from these voices—voices of the past but also of the present. They can also be helped by chronologies, bibliographies, pictures, maps—devices through which historians share their sense of fun and immediacy with a reader.

In the end, to know the past is to know ourselves—not entirely, not enough, but a little better. History can help us to achieve some grace and elegance of action, some cogency and completion of thought, some harmony and tolerance in human relationships. Most of all, history can give us a sense of excitement, a personal zest for watching and perhaps participating in the events around us that will, one day, be history too.

History is a narrative, a story; history is concerned foremost with major themes, even as it recognizes the significance of many fascinating digressions. Because history is largely about how and why people behave as they do, it is also about patterns of thought and belief. Ultimately, history is about what people believe to be true. To this extent, virtually all history is intellectual history, for the perceived meaning of a specific treaty, battle, or scientific discovery lies in what those involved in it and those who came after thought was most significant about it. History makes it clear that we may die, as we may live, as a result of what someone believed to be quite true in the relatively remote past.

We cannot each be our own historian. In everyday life we may reconstruct our personal past, acting as detectives for our motivations and attitudes. But formal history is a much more rigorous study. History may give us some very small capacity to predict the future. More certainly, it should help us arrange the causes for given events into meaningful patterns. History also should help us to be tolerant of the historical views of others, even as it helps to shape our own convictions. History must help us sort out the important from the less important, the relevant from the irrelevant, so that we do not fall prey to those who propose simple-minded solutions to vastly complex human problems. We must not yield to the temptation to blame one group or individual for our problems, and yet we must not fail to defend our convictions with vigor.

To recognize, indeed to celebrate, the value of all civilizations is essential to the civilized life itself. To understand that we see all civilizations through the prism of our specific historical past—for which we feel affection, in which we may feel comfortable and secure, and by which we interpret all else that we encounter—is simply to recognize that we too are the products of history. That is why we must study history and ask our own questions in our own way. For if we ask no questions of our past, there may be no questions to ask of our future.

Robin W. Winks

Acknowledgments

Susan Mattern-Parkes wishes to thank the book's editors, Peter Coveney and Linda Harris, and anonymous readers for the Press for their invaluable contributions. In particular, the suggestions of Michael Gaddis of Syracuse University have resulted in major improvements to the text. I would also like to thank my husband, Adam Parkes, for his thoughtful comments and unflagging support. The book's remaining faults are, of course, entirely my own.

ONE

The First Civilizations

What Is History?

Muses who live on Olympus, tell me now
who were the leaders and commanders of the Greeks,
For you, being goddesses, were there, and know all;
but we have heard only the rumor, and know nothing.

(Homer, *Iliad*, 2.484–487)

As the Greek poet Homer sang the story of the Trojan war 2,800 years ago, he saw himself as a messenger—the conduit of a tradition. His poem was not something he created himself; in his view, divine inspiration offered him and all poets a window on the past. He told of the things that were important to himself and his audience: war, feud, and violent combat; heroes and their genealogies; victory and death. His *Iliad*, the inspiration for the first prose histories in Greek, played a large part in defining what it meant to be Greek for more than a thousand years.

What is history? A simple answer to this question might be: the study of the past. But of which past? Should we write, like Homer, about wars and kings? Or should we focus on anonymous groups of ordinary people (women, farmers, soldiers)? Should history tell of revolutions, assassinations, and conquests? Or should it describe everyday realities? Can history be about ideas, and if so, which ones—political ideas, such as concepts of citizenship? Or social ideas, such as marriage?

Our choice, like Homer's, will depend on our own interests and on the interests of the audience we hope to reach. Both of these will reflect the needs and values of our culture. Homer's *Iliad* described the legendary, first Greek national venture—the Trojan war—in a poem that took shape as the Greeks were beginning to develop a sense of themselves as a people. This was one of the functions of his work. Other histories serve different purposes; the way they present the past, and how they choose to present it, will depend on what the historian is trying to accomplish.

In the West, the most influential works that established history as a discipline were written by the Greeks in the fifth century B.C. The word "history" takes its origin from the Greek writer Herodotus, who used the word *historia*, which meant "inquiry," to describe his study of the recent war between the Greeks and Persians. The root meaning of "history," then, refers to a method—to the *investigation* of the past. Once the historian has decided which aspects of the past to study, how does he or she go about reconstructing them?

One way is to read histories produced by other scholars, whether modern or ancient. But the authors of these works have already gathered and interpreted the evidence of the past to suit their own purposes. They may not tell us what we want to know, if our interests are different. For this reason, the real work of ancient historians is to locate and interpret the kind of raw evidence from antiquity that will shed light on the problems they want to investigate.

This means, first of all, looking beyond histories to other kinds of written works. For example, dramas and novels—which often focus on love, marriage, and the family—can illuminate aspects of everyday life that no historical source can reveal. Texts are not the only sources available to the historian, however. Archaeological excavations of houses and settlements can show us where and how people lived, what they ate, and how they made a living. Countless other types of evidence survive from antiquity: inscriptions on tombstones; shopping lists, receipts, and personal letters written on broken pot sherds or on papyrus (an ancient form of paper); legal codes regulating everything from homicide to taxes to the inheritance of property; monuments celebrating imperial victories; medical texts describing symptoms of disease and ancient forms of therapy. This book offers a basic narrative outline of ancient history and a guide to some features of ancient culture and society— but doing history, rather than just reading about it, means using primary sources* like those just described to reach original conclusions.

The Origins of Civilization

Most people realize that the Western world as we know it is a recent phenomenon. Just one hundred years ago, our great-grandparents lived without the technological and scientific advances that define the modern lifestyle: conveniences such as the automobile, the telephone, and indoor plumbing, or the vaccines and antibiotic medicines that make life much safer than it once was. But we may not realize that civilization itself—such innovations as agriculture, writing, weaving, and permanent architecture—is a recent development. Anatomically modern humans (*homo sapiens sapiens*) lived on earth for at least

---

*A primary source is the *evidence* that the historian uses to prove a conclusion—for example, the comedies of Aristophanes, written in the fifth century B.C., are a primary source for ancient Athenian politics. A secondary source is another scholar's study of the material, such as modern books and articles about Aristophanes or ancient Athens. Some sources can be either primary or secondary: Edward Gibbon's *Decline and Fall of the Roman Empire*, published in 1776, would be a secondary source for a study of the Roman Empire, but a primary source for a study of Gibbon.

| *Doing History* |

CHRONOLOGY

Chronology means "the study of time." Chronology has always been a part of the task of history. The earliest histories produced in Western culture—the Hebrew Bible and the historical works of classical Greece—sought to assign dates to the events they described. The Greeks used several methods, including lists of Athenian officials and of victors in the Olympic games and the reigns of the kings of Sparta. The Jewish historians of the Bible were so careful to indicate the number of years lived by all the important figures in its complex genealogical system that it is possible (with a few complications) to calculate the exact age of the earth as represented in Jewish mythology. The Jewish calendar still dates events from the traditional first year of creation, 3761 B.C.

Other cultures developed their own chronological systems. For example, the traditional Chinese calendar counts years in cycles of sixty, each associated with a different animal; the years are numbered sequentially from 2637 B.C., when the calendar was invented. The Muslim calendar dates all events from the *hijra*—the flight of Muhammad from Mecca to Medina in A.D. 622.

The Western world dates events from the traditional year of Christ's birth, a method that became widespread in Europe in the seventh and eighth centuries. The terms B.C. (before Christ) and A.D. (*anno domini*, "in the year of the lord") refer to this system. Western chronology uses a 365-day calendar based on the one devised by Julius Caesar in the first century B.C., but other traditions use different calendars with shorter or longer years, so that tables or mathematical calculations (or a simple computer program) are usually needed to convert dates from one system to another.

Sometimes, historians substitute the terms "C.E." and "B.C.E."—"common era" and "before the common era"—for B.C. and A.D. in order to avoid the appearance of privileging a Christian, European chronological method. However, since these terms may create the misleading impression that dating events by Christ's birth is a practice "common" to other traditions, they have been avoided here.

100,000 years before building the first cities five thousand years ago. In a sense, civilization as a way of life is still in the experimental phase. We do not know whether it will be as successful in the long run as the hunting-and-gathering existence that sustained our ancestors for most of human history.

The period before the widespread use of metals, when most tools were made of stone, is called the Stone Age. It is divided into two main periods, the **Paleolithic** or "old stone" age, which begins with the earliest artifacts*, and

---

*An **artifact** is an object produced by human manufacture or modified by humans.

the **Neolithic** or "new stone" age, which begins with the invention of agri-culture. These terms refer to technical innovations (stone tools, farming) rather than to absolute dates. Both the Paleolithic and the Neolithic began and ended at different times in different places. The earliest known stone tools have been recovered from Ethiopia; they were produced by a hominid* called *homo habilis* and date to about 2.5 million years ago. In the Mediter-ranean region, the earliest Paleolithic sites (in Israel, Morocco, and Spain) date to about 1 million years ago; the tools at these sites were produced by populations of *homo erectus,* a hominid that evolved later than *homo habilis.* The Neolithic period began as early as eleven thousand years ago in the Near East but did not reach other areas of the Mediterranean region until much later.

The Archaeological Record

No written records survive to tell historians about the Stone Age, since writ-ing did not appear anywhere in the Mediterranean region before about 3300 BC.† When studying early societies without writing, we must rely on artifacts (of stone, metal, or other durable material) and the skeletons of humans and animals for information. Archaeological excavation—digging into the ground to unearth bones, artifacts, and the remains of dwellings—can give us deep insight into life at a specific site. Survey archaeology, which looks at remains that survive on the surface of the ground over a wide area, gives a better idea of general settlement patterns. Scientists can examine seeds and pollen samples from archaeological sites to learn about the climate, natural environment, and food sources of ancient peoples; bones can reveal clues to their owners' diet and activities and the diseases that affected them during their lives.

In recent years, new techniques have been developed to help date the remains unearthed by archaeologists, although more traditional methods remain important. Analysis of an excavated site's **stratigraphy**—the layers in which the finds were deposited—helps archaeologists to determine the rela-tive age of finds, since more recent layers are normally closer to the surface of the ground. Other techniques can help assign absolute, rather than relative, dates to finds. Some of the most important are radiocarbon dating, which can be used on organic matter (such as bones) and is reliable to about forty thou-sand years ago; and, after the invention of pottery, the changing styles of pot-tery fragments found in association with other artifacts.

Other methods developed in the last few decades have greatly aided the study of artifacts too old for reliable radiocarbon dating and are especially important for the Stone Age. Electron spin resonance dating can be used on tooth enamel and some other crystalline materials and can date fossils several

---

*A **hominid** is a creature closely related to modern humans.
†The long period of the human past before writing was invented is sometimes called "prehistory."

millions of years old. Thermoluminescence dating can be used on any artifact that was heated to high temperatures when it was made or, for example, when a site was destroyed by fire. But all dating techniques have important limitations and problems; our image of ancient societies, especially those without writing, is revised frequently as new discoveries are made and old finds are reexamined and assigned new dates.

Even for periods with a substantial written record, such as the imperial Roman period, archaeology is a valuable source of information. It can tell us more about the lives of ordinary people than literary sources, which usually are produced by the upper classes and reflect their point of view. But it is important to remember that even cultures with few archaeological remains were not necessarily simple and unsophisticated. Materials such as wood and textiles do not survive well in the archaeological record; more importantly, the rich oral culture of myth and ritual that characterizes preliterate societies often does not survive in any form.

The First Modern Humans

In the Paleolithic era, the most important feature of the climate was a series of glaciations, or "ice ages," during which world temperatures declined and sea levels dropped as ice covered much of the world's surface. The last of these ice ages ended about ten thousand years ago; we do not yet know whether another will succeed it, although this seems likely.

About 100,000 years ago, anatomically modern humans begin to appear in the archaeological record. Scholars debate whether they arose in one place only or evolved separately in several locations. A controversial but widely accepted theory sometimes called the "Out of Africa" hypothesis holds that the common female ancestor of all humans today lived in Africa about 150,000 years ago. (This theory is based on mitochondrial DNA analysis, which examines the DNA of microorganisms that live inside us all and are inherited only from our mothers.) In this scenario, anatomically modern humans evolved in Africa and spread from there to Asia and Europe, where they replaced the earlier hominids they encountered.

Some of the earliest traces of *homo sapiens sapiens* have been found in the Mediterranean region; remains from two sites in Israel are 100,000 years old. Another species of humans—*homo sapiens Neanderthalensis,* or "Neanderthal man,"—had inhabited Europe for more than 200,000 years and arrived in the Near East at about the same time as modern humans. These two species coexisted for a long time, but by about thirty thousand years ago all the Neanderthals had disappeared. The reasons for this are unknown but may be related to technological advances among populations of modern humans.

Toward the end of the Paleolithic, about forty thousand years ago, these humans began to manufacture finer and more efficient tools and weapons, to live or travel in social groups of a hundred or more, and to produce music, paintings, and art objects. The most spectacular remains from the later Paleolithic are the cave paintings found in France and Spain. The earliest of these, from the Chauvet Cave in southern France, are at least thirty thousand

This Paleolithic painting from the caves of Lascaux in France dates to about 15,000 B.C. While animals are portrayed with vivid grace and realism in cave paintings, humans are depicted more schematically, like the bird-headed stick figure (perhaps a shaman) in this scene. Hunting is an important theme in many cave paintings; the bison in this picture has been wounded by a spear. (Art Resource, NY)

years old. (Surviving paintings are located deep inside the caves, sometimes in nearly inaccessible spots, but anthropologists believe Paleolithic humans also produced art in the open air, which has not been preserved.)

But the innovation that paved the way for civilization was an economic one that did not occur until much later. Throughout the Paleolithic period, hominids and humans subsisted on wild foods—that is, they hunted or scavenged for meat, they fished, and they collected plants and shellfish. In the Neolithic period, humans started to produce their own food by farming and raising domesticated animals. Over time, this development had important consequences for every aspect of human life. But the Neolithic revolution did not occur anywhere until about eleven thousand years ago. For 90 percent of its history, our species hunted and gathered wild foods for subsistence.

The Beginnings of Agriculture

Why did some human populations begin to farm? Many scholars point to the environmental conditions at the end of the last ice age, between thirteen thousand and ten thousand years ago. This period, called the **Mesolithic** or "middle stone" age, was one of climatic instability that required humans to adapt to environmental changes. As sea levels rose and many species became extinct, some humans broadened the range of plants and animals on which they relied for food. For example, some exploited fish, shellfish, and marine mammals (even whales) much more intensively; others focused on specific kinds of food that were especially abundant. The remains of permanent houses, cemeteries, and shellfish middens (enormous piles of shells) suggest that many populations began to lead a more sedentary life.

In the Neolithic, perhaps as a result of these changes, some species of plants and animals became domesticated. Humans selected the individuals with the most desirable traits—grain stalks with bigger seeds, sheep with thicker wool, and so on—and bred from them to produce more plants and animals with the same traits.

As humans domesticated their food sources, they also took steps to nurture and protect them: sowing seeds by hand rather than letting them scatter naturally, plowing and irrigating to help them grow, fencing in animals to protect them from predators or keep them from running away. They changed subsistence strategies from foraging to agriculture.

The earliest evidence of agriculture comes from the Near East, especially the so-called fertile crescent.* Here, some grains, legumes, and animals were domesticated as long as eleven thousand years ago (about 9000 B.C.). In Europe, farming is attested in parts of Greece and Bulgaria beginning about 5500 B.C.; but it did not reach western Europe until later.

We do not know exactly why humans first began to domesticate and cultivate wild foods. Perhaps, humans who had become settled in one area did not want to migrate as the climate warmed; instead of moving to where their preferred sources of food were more abundant, they sought to increase the availability of these foods in their own area. Another possibility is that mortality decreased in some communities as they became more settled, leading to population explosions that caused people to look for ways of increasing the food supply. Some agricultural techniques may have developed gradually over a long period of time, as people intervened more and more in the

---

*The fertile crescent is that part of the Near East in which agriculture is possible, with or without the aid of irrigation; it is not especially "fertile" when compared to many other areas of the world, but only when compared to the very arid desert regions of the Near East. The arms of the crescent are the Levant (the Mediterranean Sea's eastern coastline) and Mesopotamia (the area between the two rivers Tigris and Euphrates, in modern Iraq); the two arms meet in what is now southern Turkey. See map, p. 14.

In Mesopotamia, writing developed from a system of accounting by clay tokens that was widespread in the Neolithic Near East. This clay envelope and tokens from Susa, in Iran, date to about 3300 B.C.   (Réunion des Musées Nationaux/Art Resource, NY)

wild environment, for example, by corralling the animals they hunted or weeding out plants they did not like. When crises occurred, they responded by exploiting these techniques more intensively.

Over time, agriculture resulted in important changes in the way people lived. As a result of a diet richer in grain they probably accumulated more body fat, which increased fertility in women and led to larger, denser populations. In an agricultural economy it is easier to acquire and store a surplus beyond what is necessary for survival; this allowed some people to control more resources than others—to become rich—and these economic inequalities led to social inequalities and more complicated social systems. Surpluses could also be used to support members of the community—craftsmen, musicians, or priests, for example—who did not need to spend all their time farming or foraging for subsistence; thus agricultural societies tended to become more culturally sophisticated. A large surplus might support a labor force for a major project, such as an irrigation system or a monument. Such projects imply not only economic resources but also leadership—some individuals began to assert authority over others in the community.

One of the most important innovations of the Neolithic period was a new way of recording information. Agriculturalists needed a way to keep track of the goods they stored, especially as society became more stratified and elites collected goods from others to redistribute to their families and dependents. Archaeologists at numerous sites throughout the Near East have discovered small clay tokens, often in simple geometric shapes, that were used to signify quantities of grain and livestock and, later, manufactured goods and abstract economic units such as a day's work. Later, these tokens would evolve into the first system of writing.

The Neolithic revolution did not happen all at once. Agriculture and foraging are not mutually exclusive ways of living, and for a while people practiced both. And while farming began in the Near East about 9000 B.C., it did not reach Britain until 4000 B.C.; a few small populations of foragers remain even today. But compared to the Paleolithic period, social, economic, cultural, and technological changes have taken place at an astounding rate since the invention of agriculture. This may have been the most important event in the history of our species.

The shift to agriculture should not necessarily be viewed as simple "progress." As we have noted, social inequality is part and parcel of the complexity that resulted from Neolithic innovations. There is also good evidence that agriculture made life harder in many ways. For example, it requires much more work than hunting and gathering. Studies of Neolithic human skeletons also show that agricultural societies were more vulnerable to infectious disease, no doubt because they tended to have denser, more settled populations than hunters and gatherers. Archaeologists have also found more evidence of malnutrition in these populations, perhaps because of their dependence on a single crop which might fail. As a result, life expectancy was shorter in early agricultural societies than it was for foragers.*

A New Complexity: Some Neolithic Sites

Jericho. A number of early Neolithic sites in the Near East, dating from about 7000 B.C. to 5000 B.C., show the first signs of more social and cultural complexity. One of these sites is Jericho in Israel, later made famous in the biblical book of Joshua. Here a stone perimeter wall, ten feet thick and twelve feet high, with a tower twenty-six feet high, was constructed around 8000 B.C. It enclosed an area of about ten acres, with a population of perhaps two thousand people. This is the earliest known example of public architecture (buildings used by the whole community instead of by individual families) and the earliest large group labor project.

Çatalhöyük. Çatalhöyük is one of the largest and most famous of several early Neolithic sites in Turkey and Syria. It covers about thirty-two acres and was a substantial settlement by 6300 B.C.; archaeologists estimate that the population of the village may have been between five thousand and ten thousand at its maximum. Nearby, the Hasan Dag volcano produced an abundant

---

*See Mark Nathan Cohen and J. Armelagos, "Paleopathology at the Origins of Agriculture: Editors' Summation," in *Paleopathology at the Origins of Agriculture*, Orlando, FL: Academic Press, 1984, pp. 585–601.

The circular tower inside the walls of Jericho is 26 feet high and dates to about 8000 B.C.
(Scala/Art Resource, NY)

supply of obsidian, a glassy volcanic rock that is both beautiful and well-suited for making sharp tools and weapons. It was a rare commodity traded throughout the Near East, and it is probably this economic advantage that accounts for the early settlement and large size of Çatalhöyük.

This site provides a good example of a population that relied both on wild and domestic foods for subsistence: While the remains of cultivated grains have been found at Çatalhöyük, studies of the villagers' teeth show that wild legumes and roots formed the main part of their diet. They also tended domesticated cattle, sheep, and goats.

The village consisted of a conglomeration of mud brick houses sharing adjoining walls. The houses were all about the same size (about sixteen-by-sixteen feet) and had the same plan: one large room with a smaller, adjoining room perhaps used for storage. The villagers entered the houses through holes in the roof.

There is no conclusive evidence of public buildings or of districts serving specific functions (such as a religious or administrative center). While it was

The mud brick houses of Çatalhöyük were built in agglomerations with adjoining walls; open spaces served as pens for domesticated animals. (The Çatalhöyük Project)

once thought that some buildings were religious shrines, archaeologists now question this identification. The village seems to have been formed mainly or entirely of private houses and open spaces where animals were kept. Some houses contained more sophisticated architectural features (such as pillars, moldings, or wall paintings) and more artifacts than others, indicating that the population was socially and economically stratified (that is, some families had higher socioeconomic status than others). Some of the artifacts, such as polished obsidian mirrors, must have been made by specialized craftsmen. But in general Çatalhöyük lacks the more structured organization of space and of society that later characterized the first cities.

The people of Çatalhöyük buried the bones of the dead beneath the floors of their houses, where skeletons of all types—men, women, children, and infants—have been found. Because people of all ages were buried in the same way, which is unusual in premodern societies, we are able to get an idea of the village's **demography**—the statistical makeup of its population. The average age at death was thirty-four for adult men, thirty for adult women. Each woman had about four children, of whom nearly half died before adulthood. A few people lived beyond the age of sixty. Many of the villagers suffered from anemia (low red blood count), caused by malnutrition or disease.

Çatalhöyük has produced a wealth of artifacts, including dozens of varieties of flint or obsidian tools and weapons, polished obsidian mirrors, fine bone objects such as needles and hairpins, and pottery. Art objects include statuettes of men, women, and animals; some of the female statuettes may depict goddesses. Among the most interesting and unusual remains are the

Stonehenge, on the Salisbury Plain in southern England, is the most famous and spectacular of over a thousand stone circles that survive from Neolithic Britain, Ireland, and Brittany. (Photo by Susan P. Mattern-Parkes)

paintings that decorate some interior walls. They depict a range of themes from simple geometric patterns and handprints, to scenes of hunting or religious festivals, to a landscape with a town in the foreground and an erupting volcano in the background. A few portray headless corpses—perhaps the bodies of criminals—being devoured by vultures.

Stonehenge. Stonehenge in southern England is an example of a very different type of Neolithic site; in its way, it is no less complex than Jericho or Çatalhöyük. It is one of the largest and best-preserved of over a thousand Neolithic stone circles in the British Isles and Brittany (northwestern France). Four thousand years ago, the builders of this monument moved sixty enormous sandstone blocks, each weighing between twenty and fifty tons, a distance of eighteen and a half miles from their source—no simple feat even today—and stood half of them upright in a circle nearly one hundred feet in diameter. They then raised the remaining thirty blocks sixteen feet off the ground and rested them horizontally on top of the uprights. Inside the circle, more **megaliths** (literally, "large rocks") were erected to form a pattern radiating outward from the center, where a single sandstone block once stood. Although only about half of these megaliths remain today, they still make an awesome impression on the observer.

The Stonehenge monument is not only large; it was also constructed with a great deal of precision. For instance, the horizontal blocks (called "lintels") of the outer ring were carved in a subtle curve so that they would make a perfect circle when joined together, and the plane they form is almost exactly level, although the ground slopes slightly. The builders adapted woodworking techniques to create a secure, exact fit between the stone lintels and the uprights.

Why would the people of Neolithic Britain invest so much time and labor in this megalithic monument? Some features of Stonehenge suggest that it had a ritual significance having to do with death and time. The finished stone ring was oriented toward the midsummer sunrise; other, earlier parts of the monument were aligned to the northernmost and southernmost risings of the moon in midwinter, which oscillate on an eighteen-and-one-half-year cycle and would have required prolonged astronomical observations. A ring of fifty-six pits contained cremated human remains. Whatever its ritual function, the monument probably also served to lend cohesive focus to the community, as an organized labor project and a gathering-place for festivals.

The Iceman. One of the most spectacular Neolithic finds is the "Iceman," discovered by hikers in the Austrian Alps in 1991. He is technically called "Similaun man" after the glacier in which he was encased, which preserved not only his body but also the clothes he was wearing and the equipment he was carrying. He died about 3300 B.C., probably of exposure; he had been injured recently and his ribs had been broken. An earlier rib fracture had healed; the Iceman's bones also show evidence of periods of malnutrition or serious illness. Tattoos on his legs and torso may have been a kind of medical treatment (like acupuncture). His clothes were made of several types of animal skin; he carried a backpack, a hip pack, and about twenty items, including a small copper axe (the earliest evidence for copper in this area), a six-foot wooden bow, a quiver of arrows (but only two had flint tips), a flint knife, a type of medicinal fungus, and a fungus that was useful for starting fires. Scholars have debated about his social status and what he was doing on the mountain. Possibly he was a shepherd—a dangerous and isolated job in any time period—who met with an accident or bad weather.

The First Civilizations: The Eastern Mediterranean in the Bronze Age

Archaeologists use the word **civilization** to describe societies with certain features, especially a stratified and hereditary social system (one is born into a specific social class); government, including taxation, fixed laws, and organized labor; division of labor and craft specialization (instead of working primarily as farmers, some individuals achieve high levels of skill as sculptors, metalworkers, and so on); record-keeping and some form of writing; and monumental architecture (such as the pyramids of Egypt or the ziggurats of

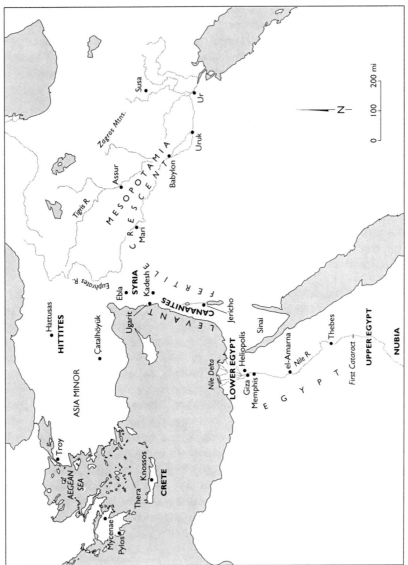

The Eastern Mediterranean in the Bronze Age

Mesopotamia). Compared to earlier Neolithic cultures, civilizations were larger, more densely populated, and more centralized.

At the root of the word "civilization" is the Latin word for "city." It is in cities that we find most of the characteristics mentioned in the preceding paragraph. But every city had to be supported by the agricultural surplus of the countryside. In the ancient economy, this meant that most people were farmers. They worked on land they owned themselves, or land that was owned by urban aristocrats or by the state; the surplus they generated was sent to the cities as taxes or rent.

Most of our evidence for life in the ancient world, however, comes from the cities. Rural sites are usually small and scattered and thus difficult to find, and literature was produced by urban elites. It is important to remember this bias in the evidence when studying ancient civilizations.

The Bronze Age

Around 3500 B.C., copper began to be used widely instead of stone for tools and weapons. (In some places, copper was used much earlier; for example, it appears at Çatalhöyük beginning around 5500 B.C.) By 2500 B.C. most Mediterranean populations had switched to bronze, an alloy of copper and tin. Since the mid-nineteenth century, scholars have used the term "Bronze Age" to refer to the period when bronze was the primary material used to make weapons and tools. The beginning of this period roughly corresponds with the rise of the first civilizations. It lasted until about 1200 B.C., when an era of destruction threw much of the Mediterranean world into a dark age. Afterward, around 1000 B.C., iron—which is more common than copper or tin and harder and more durable when carburized (a complicated process of repeatedly heating to high temperatures)—became the material of choice for weapons and metal tools. Although the classification of ancient societies according to this aspect of their technology now seems arbitrary, the term "Bronze Age" remains a convenient way of indicating the earliest period of civilization up to the destructive events of 1200 to 1100 B.C.

Mesopotamian Civilization

"Mesopotamia" means "the land between the rivers"—in this case, the rivers Tigris and Euphrates that flow through modern Iraq to the Persian Gulf. Throughout the Bronze Age, the center of Mesopotamian civilization lay in the southern part of this area. It is hard to determine how far it extended at any time. Kings captured and lost cities in wars that are barely known to us; some sites have not been excavated well enough to determine their cultural orientation. In general, sites in the south have been better excavated and have produced more documentary evidence than northern sites, so scholarly attention tends to focus on them.

Civilization did not arise in southern Mesopotamia because it was an unusually fertile area. In fact, the climate was (and remains) hot and dry; trees were scarce, and until oil became important in the modern economy the land was poor in natural resources. Farming was only possible with the aid of irrigation. The communal organization required to dig the canals that brought water from the rivers to the countryside partly accounts for the early growth of cities in Mesopotamia.

The Written Sources.　Mesopotamia was the first civilization to develop writing. Their system is called **cuneiform** because scribes used a sharpened reed to impress shapes like a wedge (*cuneus* in Latin) into clay tablets. Because clay is very durable, especially when baked hard (for example in a fire), many thousands of these tablets survive.

Cuneiform writing evolved from the system of tokens used for accounting throughout the Neolithic Near East. As central institutions—temples and palaces—began to collect goods as taxes, the need for sophisticated account-ing practices grew. Mesopotamian scribes found it more efficient to draw pic-tures of the tokens on clay tablets than to manufacture and store the tokens themselves. The earliest written documents recorded quantities of goods, but cuneiform writing quickly developed the complexity necessary to record a wide range of material, including literary works. Gradually it evolved from a **pictographic** system of signs representing concepts into a mostly **phonetic** system—a set of symbols that represented the sound combinations (such as *mu, na,* or *sum*) of the language it was recording. The ancient Mesopotamians called the language of the earliest cuneiform tablets "Sumerian," and schol-ars refer to the writers of the language as "Sumerians."

Sumerian is not related to any known living or ancient language. Scholars can read it because, although people apparently ceased speaking in Sumerian around 2000 B.C., it was taught in schools as a classical language (like Latin today) until the first century B.C. Dictionaries, vocabularies, and bilingual texts were produced to teach Sumerian to speakers of Akkadian, the other major language spoken in early Mesopotamia, which used the same writing system. Akkadian is a Semitic language related to Arabic and Hebrew. Because scholars can read Akkadian, they have been able to reconstruct the Sumerian language using the bilingual texts and study aids written in Akkadian.

Although until about 2300 B.C. documents were written in Sumerian only, speakers of Sumerian and Akkadian seem to have lived side by side since the early third millenium B.C., and some early kings of Mesopotamian cities had Akkadian names. For this reason it is impossible to separate Sumerian from Akkadian civilization.

A huge variety of cuneiform documents survive. Writing originated as a way to keep track of goods and labor, and tens of thousands of such records have been discovered. Legal documents, court records, business records, offi-cial and private correspondence, hymns and incantations, and great literary texts, such as the famous epic of Gilgamesh, also survive in large numbers.

Cuneiform documents shed light on many aspects of early Mesopotamian life that are much more difficult to trace in other ancient societies. Marriage, slavery, and household organization; property and inheritance; wages, prices, and taxes; food and farming; and other aspects of the Mesopotamian economy and society are all well-represented in cuneiform texts. In fact, it is easier to reconstruct the social and economic history of early Mesopotamia than its political history, which is confusing and obscure.

HISTORICAL PERIODS OF BRONZE AGE MESOPOTAMIA

Before ca. 3000 B.C.	Predynastic
3000–ca. 2300 B.C.	Early Dynastic
2300–2200 B.C.	Akkadian
ca. 2100–2000 B.C.	Ur III Dynasty
ca. 2000–1595 B.C.	Old Babylonian (or Amorite)
1595–ca. 1450 B.C.	Dark Age
ca. 1450–1155 B.C.	Kassites

The City.   The city lay at the heart of Mesopotamian culture and politics. Kings created empires by conquering cities, and, in boasting of the extent of their territory, they listed the cities under their rule. Cities were supposed to have been founded by the gods, and unlike some other societies, the Mesopotamians did not idealize the agrarian lifestyle but contrasted city life with the poverty and barbarism of the desert. At its height in the period of Sargon (ca. 2300 B.C.), the largest Mesopotamian city—Uruk—contained perhaps sixty thousand people and was the most populous city in the world.

The city was a central theme of the most famous literary text of ancient Mesopotamia: the epic of Gilgamesh, which survives in fragments dating back to the Old Babylonian period (and in a complete version dating to the seventh century B.C.). The hero is the king of Uruk, and the poem begins with a passage in praise of the great city's walls. The first episode of the story is the "civilization" of Enkidu, a wild man from the desert, whom Gilgamesh subdues and introduces to the pleasures of sexual intercourse, beer, and bread. Gilgamesh's relationship with the elders and people of Uruk and his development into a responsible king are also important themes of the epic.

The earliest cities arose in the southernmost part of Mesopotamia. Around 5000 B.C. farmers began building canals to carry water from the Euphrates River to the otherwise dry, sterile soil of the surrounding countryside. Irrigation created the possibility of an agricultural surplus; the canals also made trade and communications easier, which allowed resources to become concentrated in urban centers. By 3000 B.C., Uruk was already a large site covering an area of 247 acres. A temple constructed on a massive forty-foot platform at this time indicates that a central administration was collecting goods as taxes and using them to fund public buildings. The same administration was using writing to keep records of the resources it managed.

The city was defined spatially and symbolically by its defensive walls. Some city walls were several meters thick; some had massive, monumental

The ziggurat of the god Enlil at Nippur, southwest of modern Baghdad, dominates the hori-
zon. Continually occupied from about 5000 B.C. to A.D. 800, Nippur was mainly a religious
center. A long series of kings funded the construction of sacred buildings like this one to help
legitimize their rule.   (The Oriental Institute, University of Chicago)

citadels and gates; and some were surrounded by moats. The practical function of the walls was to protect the people of the city and its environs in time
of war. Cities could be captured by siege—the enemy might starve the inhabitants by preventing the influx of supplies or assault the gates with battering-
rams or construct wooden scaffolds or ramps to climb over the walls.

Aside from the walls, the most prominent public building in any city was
the temple. Temples were built on high platforms in the city center; by 2000
B.C., they had developed into striking, pyramidal ziggurats, which were visible in the landscape for a long distance and dominated the city's "skyline."

The temples were the focus of economic power in the Mesopotamian city.
They funded and controlled irrigation canals and owned large quantities of
land, flocks, and herds in the countryside; they manufactured textiles, wood,
metal, and stone products; and they employed thousands of public workers,
both male and female. The temples, then, controlled a large part of the agricultural surplus generated in the countryside; one of their main functions
was to collect and redistribute that surplus.

Temples were also the center of religious authority in Mesopotamian civilization; no evidence remains of local village shrines or of the nature-cults of
springs and hilltops that were ubiquitous elsewhere in the ancient Mediterranean world. All temples were in the city, and religious worship apparently

centered on them. Each temple was associated with one or more gods or goddesses, whose cult-statues it housed. The clothing, jewelry, and precious items dedicated to the deity over the years were also stored in the temple. The proper interpretation of omens was one of the most important functions of the temple staff; experts in divination predicted the future by interpreting dreams, by observing the internal organs of slaughtered animals, by astrology, and by numerous other techniques. Scribes generated long, systematic lists of possible omens and their meanings and produced other types of religious literature, such as hymns to the gods. Temple staff included priests and priestesses, singers of hymns and incantations, diviners, and a host of support personnel from barbers to doormen. Some temple officials, including priestesses and some of the scribes, were women.

Gradually, a center of political and economic authority separate from the temple developed in Mesopotamian cities: the palace, the home of the king. The kings served as military leaders, paid for public works such as temples and irrigation canals, heard legal appeals, and represented the city in various religious rituals. Next to the temple, the palace was the largest building in the Mesopotamian city. The palace at Mari on the middle Euphrates had more than 250 rooms and housed hundreds of people, including the king's family and household staff. But the king was not the only source of secular authority in the city. The most important form of citizen government was the assembly of citizens that heard cases and resolved a wide range of everyday disputes on issues such as divorce or murder. Many texts also refer to a group called the "elders" who formed a council of more restricted membership.

Like the temples, kings owned a great deal of land, employed a substantial number of people as household staff and laborers, and collected taxes and rents. Between these two institutions—the temple and the king—a large part of the Mesopotamian economy was "redistributive" in nature; that is, a central authority collected and distributed resources, for example, to pay for public buildings or warfare or to feed its own staff. This is different from a market economy, which is governed by the principles of supply and demand; but some parts of the Mesopotamian economy probably functioned in this way. Coinage had not yet been invented, but silver bullion was used as a medium of exchange or for accounting purposes (it is easier to trade commodities if the value of each can be expressed in silver). The Code of Hammurabi specifies fines payable in quantities of silver (see p. 25).

Dynasties and Empires.   The political history of Mesopotamia is a complicated story of conquests and upheavals—at times power in a whole region was consolidated under a dynasty of rulers (although it is often difficult to tell exactly which cities were subject to their rule), and at other times power was fragmented among the individual cities. The city—each with its own patron god, temple, and king—was always the true focus of Mesopotamian politics. Even in times when a monarch exercised leadership over many cities, each city still had its own king or governor and remained the basic administrative unit; when the central government collapsed, political power devolved onto the cities' leaders. This perhaps explains why Mesopotamian culture remained relatively stable, evolving slowly over many centuries despite frequent and dramatic changes in the region's political situation. While the general population must have fought and suffered in the wars of conquest upon which many of the Mesopotamian empires were founded, the long-term effects of these changes are more difficult to measure.

The main source for the earliest political history of Mesopotamia is the "Sumerian King List," which was composed in Akkadian around 1800 B.C.; it lists kings and the lengths of their reigns, beginning with the legendary rulers of the remote past. The document makes an interesting division between mythic and historical time: the earliest kings had unnaturally long reigns (for example, of 28,800 or 36,000 years); but these gradually become more realistic as the list gets closer to the time of compilation. The most important event punctuating the list is a flood that separates the earliest dynasty from the next—other Mesopotamian texts also refer to the myth of a great flood, which destroyed all but a remnant of the population. (Similar stories existed in Hebrew and Greek mythology, which were perhaps influenced by the Mesopotamian legend.)

The list's premise is that at any given time, one city and its rulers exercised leadership over the others. It seems likely that the authors of the document were simplifying the situation, but it is difficult to arrive at any more concrete idea of the political history of early Mesopotamia than the one it offers. In general, it seems that about thirty cities in southern Mesopotamia competed with one another for dominance.

The first king successfully to unite many Mesopotamian cities under one central government was Sargon, an Akkadian, whose reign dates to about 2300 B.C. In inscriptions that were copied and preserved by later generations, and in the legends that grew up around him, Sargon was remembered as a great conqueror. He founded a new capital, Akkad, whose location is uncertain today. He destroyed the walls of some of the most powerful cities and installed his own people as governors there and took other steps to create political unity under his rule; he appointed his daughter Enheduanna as high priestess of two important cults in the key cities of Ur and Uruk (some of the beautiful hymns she wrote survive).

Sargon's empire lasted until about 2100 B.C. before dissolving, perhaps as a result of tribal incursions from the north. Briefly, a Sumerian dynasty from Ur, today known as the "Ur III dynasty," reunited much of the territory once ruled by Sargon. During this period, a massive government bureaucracy generated enormous quantities of administrative records. The Ur III kings also standardized weights and measures and developed a communications system of messengers and way stations. They promulgated the first legal code, which assessed fines for acts of violence and bodily injury, and they constructed the first ziggurats, monumental temples built in a stepped pyramid design.

Beginning around 2000 B.C. the Ur III dynasty gradually disintegrated and the political focus of Mesopotamia reverted once again to the cities. By 1760

Hammurabi, ruler of the city of Babylon, had once again united southern Mesopotamia under a single government. Today Hammurabi is most famous for his legal code (see p. 25). His dynasty lasted for about 150 years, and this era is called the Old Babylonian or Amorite period.

In 1595, Babylon was sacked by Hittites and the empire founded by Hammurabi collapsed. After a "dark age" of about a hundred years, the next people to rule over southern Mesopotamia were the Kassites, who captured Babylon and reestablished its hegemony over the other cities. Not much is known about the Kassites except that they were foreigners, perhaps from the Zagros mountains; too little was written in Kassite to allow firm conclusions about their language, but it was not a Semitic language like Akkadian. They succeeded in ruling for longer than any other Mesopotamian dynasty— about three hundred years. The Kassites called their kingdom "Babylonia"; they were the first Mesopotamian dynasty to imagine their empire as a geographic territory rather than a group of cities. They seem to have adapted to Mesopotamian culture instead of changing it; Akkadian and Sumerian remained the kingdom's written languages, and the Kassite kings supported traditional Mesopotamian cults and restored important public buildings. It is not clear whether their Mesopotamian subjects perceived the later Kassites as a dynasty of foreign rulers, or simply as "Babylonians."

Society and Family.   Slavery existed in every society discussed in this book, but it took many forms and was different in each. In fact, since it was such a diverse institution and since there is no one test that all scholars agree on to determine what qualifies as "slavery," there is controversy about whether some groups of people (such as the *mushkenu* discussed later in this section) should be considered slaves or not. Slaves that are bought and sold and treated mainly as property are often called **chattel slaves** by scholars today, but this was not the only type of slavery that existed. For example, certain kinds of slaves might be inherited or sold with an estate, but not independently (scholars sometimes call these "serfs"), and people enslaved to their creditors for defaulting on a debt, or women bought as concubines, might be treated differently than other kinds of slaves. In some societies the emancipation (freeing) of slaves was commonplace, or slaves might own property in a restricted sense or intermarry with free people; in others, the boundary between slavery and freedom was more difficult to cross.

Finally, slavery was not equally important in all ancient societies. In some, including classical Athens and Roman Italy, a substantial part of the population was enslaved; many or most households had domestic slaves, who performed crucial functions such as raising children; and slaves played a large role in the economy, for example, as an agricultural labor force. In other societies, slaves were relatively rare.

Slaves in ancient Mesopotamia might be owned by the king, the temple, or a wealthy private citizen. Most privately owned slaves in Mesopotamia were domestic servants. Slaves were distinguished from the free population by armbands, special haircuts, and distinctive names. They could be bought,

Art and Society

WARFARE IN EARLY MESOPOTAMIA

The Vulture Stele from Lagash.   (Réunion des Musées Nationaux/Art
Resource, NY)

The "Vulture stele" (a **stele** is an upright stone slab) from the city of Lagash,
dated to 2450 B.C., preserves an illustrated narrative of a war between Lagash
and the city of Umma, about thirty miles to the northwest along the Tigris.
Infantrymen wield axes, adzes, and spears; one group carries shields and
stands in a tight formation similar to the Greek hoplite "phalanx" (see p. 63).
In one scene the king rides in a four-wheeled chariot at the head of the army; in
another, he leads them on foot into battle. All the soldiers wear pointed helmets,
perhaps made of leather. Other texts refer to contingents of "hunters," perhaps
wielding nets.

At its largest, an army raised by a great king like Hammurabi might number about ten thousand. Little evidence survives to indicate who the soldiers were—for example, whether they were ordinary citizens or paid professionals. Hammurabi's code suggests that in his time, the state leased some land to individuals on the condition that they serve when drafted. In practice people often hired substitutes, and this eventually became legal.

inherited, and sold; but the Code of Hammurabi allows them to marry free women and in this way to have children of free status. Slaves either inherited their status from their parents, were prisoners of war, or were bought from slave traders dealing abroad. Children were also sold into slavery by their parents; most likely these were mainly poor parents who could not afford to feed them. People enslaved when they defaulted on debts would be freed when their loan was worked off; other types of slaves might be freed by their masters.

A large part of the population worked for the temples and the palaces. They formed a legally separate class of people—in the Code of Hammurabi they are called *mushkenu* (see box, p. 25); earlier sources refer to public laborers called *gurush* (for male workers) and *geme* (for females). The temple of Lagash around 2000 B.C. employed more than six thousand woolworkers, mostly women and children, but the temples also employed laborers and craftsmen of many other kinds, including farmers to work the land that they owned. Temple workers were paid mostly in food and in commodities such as wool. Some scholars have argued that they were essentially slaves owned by the state, which provided them with rations rather than wages. Others have seen state service as a sort of labor tax to which some of the population was subject, working part of the year for the state, and part for themselves. In any case, it is clear that much of the Mesopotamian labor force was controlled by the state; but what percentage of the population was involved, and how much control over their economic activities the state exercised, is debatable.

Mesopotamian houses were made of mud brick or plaster with adjoining walls, and often with a central courtyard. Rooms were small, and these courtyards may have been the centers of domestic life. Most city households were composed of monogamous, nuclear families—a married couple and their unmarried children—and some had domestic slaves. Marriage involved an exchange of property between the families of the bride and groom; fathers were expected to provide a dowry to support the daughter during the marriage, and husbands also paid a bride-price to their new fathers-in-law. Divorce could be initiated by the husband, especially on the grounds of adultery or childlessness, but not by the wife. Polygamy was legal in some circumstances, although not extensively practiced, and kings sometimes had many wives. Husbands might also have slave concubines, whose children could inherit their property in some situations; for example, childless wives might protect themselves from divorce by supplying the husband with a slave concubine to produce heirs. (This practice is also well attested in the Hebrew Bible; see p. 51.)

Traditionally, property was divided among male children on their father's death. Women were not prevented by law from owning property; daughters occasionally inherited, and wives could also inherit property from their husbands. In the Old Babylonian period, a custom arose whereby some women from wealthy families were dedicated to the service of the gods and remained unmarried, supported by a donation from their families; they were called *naditu*. In some cities they lived in segregated communities with other women. This prevented the family's wealth from being divided among too many heirs and also created a class of independently wealthy and economically powerful women. They controlled the property donated by their families, for example, by lending it at interest or leaving it to heirs of their choice—often, a younger woman from the same community. Legal documents upholding their right to do this against the objections of their brothers survive.

There is some controversy over family structure in ancient Mesopotamia. Did married couples and their children live independently, or did brothers and their wives remain in the same household with their parents? Overall, it seems that smaller, simpler families were the rule in the cities, but the situation in the villages may have been different. Some documents suggest that land in the countryside was owned jointly by the males of a family—the consent of many, related owners was necessary to sell it. Communal ownership of land could prevent property from being divided into miniscule plots over many generations and probably increased the importance of the complex family in the Mesopotamian countryside.

Science and Mathematics.   Some of the most influential intellectual achievements of the ancient Mesopotamians were in the areas of astronomy and mathematics. In both of these disciplines they strongly influenced the Greeks, and through them later Mediterranean civilization.

The Mesopotamian system of numerals dates back as early as writing itself and, like writing, had its origins in the accounts kept by temple scribes. While much of the evidence for advanced mathematical thinking dates to the Old Babylonian period, these texts may represent a tradition with much older roots. Tables of multiples, squares, square and cube roots, exponents, and other mathematical relationships between numbers survive, where the numbers have been calculated to a high degree of accuracy. Problem books show that the Mesopotamians managed complicated algebraic expressions with many unknowns; they also investigated problems of plane (two-dimensional) and solid (three-dimensional) geometry.

While many of the Mesopotamians' achievements in astronomy date to the centuries between 1100 and 400 B.C., their origins are traceable to the Old Babylonian period. Around 1700 B.C., they began to produce lists of signs in

The Written Record

HAMMURABI'S CODE

One of the best sources for the social history of Mesopotamia is the law code of King Hammurabi. This was inscribed on a stone stele discovered at Susa, where it had been carried off as plunder by tribal raiders in the thirteenth century B.C. Beneath a sculpted relief showing Hammurabi receiving tokens of kingship from the sun god Shamash, a long inscription details his regulations on a wide variety of subjects, from the price of renting a donkey to witchcraft and homicide.

Some questions to consider while reading the following selection are: (a) To what distinct legal or social categories of people does the code refer? (b) What is the status of women in the code? (c) What do you think is the purpose of this part of the code?

(196) If a man has knocked out the eye of another man, his eye shall be knocked out.

(197) If he has broken the limb of a man, his limb shall be broken.

(198) If he has knocked out the eye of a commoner (*mushkenu*) or has broken the limb of a commoner, he shall pay one mina [about five pounds] of silver.

(199) If he has knocked out the eye of a man's slave or broken the limb of a man's slave, he shall pay half his value.

(200) If a man has knocked out the tooth of a man that is his equal, his tooth shall be knocked out.

(201) If he has knocked out the tooth of a commoner, he shall pay one-third of a mina of silver . . .

(206) If a man has struck another in a quarrel, and caused him a permanent injury, that man shall swear, "I struck him without malice," and shall pay the doctor.

(207) If he has died of his blows, [the man] shall swear [similarly], and pay one-half of a mina of silver; or,

(208) If [the deceased] was a commoner, he shall pay one-third of a mina of silver.

(209) If a man has struck a man's daughter, and has caused her to miscarry, he shall pay ten shekels of silver [about three ounces] for her miscarriage.

(210) If that woman dies, his daughter shall be killed.

(211) If it is the daughter of a commoner that has miscarried through his blows, he shall pay five shekels of silver.

(212) If that woman dies, he shall pay half a mina of silver.

(213) If he has struck a man's slave-girl and caused her to miscarry, he shall pay two shekels of silver.

(214) If that slave-girl dies, he shall pay one-third of a mina of silver.

Adapted from C. H. W. Jones, *Babylonian and Assyrian Laws, Contracts, and Letters*, Edinburgh: T. & T. Clark, 1904.

the heavenly bodies (stars, sun, moon, planets) and in the weather and of the events predicted by these phenomena. By 500 B.C. they had developed the ability to tabulate periodic celestial occurrences, such as the progression of one of the planets, rising and setting at a different point in the sky each day and returning eventually to its original position. Without developing a theory of the motion of the heavenly bodies, they nevertheless used mathematics to calculate the changes in their position over time; by these calculations or by continual observation, they were able to predict events such as eclipses. This tradition of astronomical observation and calculation arose from the Mesopotamians' interest in divination from omens.

In both mathematics and astronomy, the Mesopotamians avoided the highly theoretical approach that later characterized the Greeks; much of the surviving evidence takes the form of lists and tables. While these could only have been constructed with a sophisticated understanding of some theoretical principles, the Mesopotamians chose to focus not on expounding these principles, but on the results they generated. Attempts to explain this approach as a product of a rigid, hierarchical social system are speculative and unconvincing, but it remains a distinctive feature of Mesopotamian science.

Egypt in the Bronze Age

The Gift of the Nile.   The Greek historian Hecataeus, writing in the late sixth century B.C., described Egypt as "the gift of the river." In antiquity, the Nile river was always the heart of the Egyptian economy. Every year in the summer, the river would flood, leaving a strip of fertile, black soil behind when it subsided. The cultivation of the Nile floodplain produced the agricultural surplus that sustained an extremely complex and distinctive civilization from a very early date. Beyond the banks of the Nile, however, the Egyptian desert is habitable only by nomads—it cannot sustain settled agricultural life. Throughout antiquity, the vast majority of the land's inhabitants lived within a few miles of the river. Each year the Egyptians anxiously anticipated the flood, and from an early period governments measured and recorded its depth for tax purposes. A scanty flood would mean disaster, famine, and death.

The Nile not only provided Egypt with food, but it was also highly navigable as far as Aswan, where the "First Cataract" (a rocky, unnavigable stretch) formed the original boundary of the Egyptian kingdom. The river was like a highway with the potential to connect the communities on its banks. Perhaps for this reason, Egypt was unified under a single government much earlier than any other Mediterranean civilization.

The Written Sources.   The first Egyptian texts date to the same time as Egypt's political unification, about 3100 B.C. The earliest form of Egyptian writing, **hieroglyphs** ("sacred engravings"), combined pictographic and phonetic symbols; these symbols are beautiful and elaborate, and hieroglyphic script was mainly used for inscriptions on temples and monuments.

Doing History

THE ROSETTA STONE

In 1799, one of Napoleon's officers in Egypt discovered a large piece of black basalt with a text chiseled into its surface in three scripts: Greek, hieroglyphs, and demotic. Eventually, the "Rosetta stone" proved to be the key that allowed modern scholars to read hieroglyphs. At first, they could read only the Greek. It was only two decades after the stone's discovery that French scholar Jean-François Champollion, realizing that both demotic and hieroglyphic were partly pictographic and partly phonetic scripts, was able to decipher both. Using their knowledge of Coptic, scholars were then able to read and understand the ancient Egyptian language.

Shortly after the first hieroglyphic writing appeared, the Egyptians developed another script that scholars call **hieratic;** it could be written more quickly and was useful for documents. Around 700 B.C., a new script—called **demotic**—was invented that better represented the Egyptian language as it was spoken at that time. Finally, in the third century A.D., Christian Egyptians began writing in **Coptic,** which used a modified Greek alphabet. Coptic, which is a direct descendant of the earliest Egyptian language, is still used as a liturgical (ceremonial) language in the Egyptian Christian church.

Writing was ubiquitous in ancient Egypt; in the Bronze Age as later, writing seems more pervasive here than in other parts of the ancient world. Temples and monuments were inscribed with lengthy texts in hieroglyphs; art objects were often inscribed as well. Documents and literary texts were written on **papyrus,** a reed that was processed to produce thin sheets; the sheets were often joined together into long strips that, when rolled up, formed the ancient book. In the dry Egyptian climate, papyrus can be preserved for thousands of years. A cheaper, more plentiful and durable source of writing material was broken pottery—called **ostraka** in Greek (modern scholars also use this term). But most of the papyri and ostraka that have been found in Egypt date to the Hellenistic and Roman periods; most of the written evidence for Bronze Age Egypt comes from inscriptions on stone. For this reason, we do not have the same wealth of evidence about everyday life from Egypt as we do for Bronze Age Mesopotamia; we have more formal documents such as religious texts, funerary inscriptions, and royal decrees, giving us a different picture of its civilization.

While archaeology is a crucial source for Bronze Age Egypt, there is an important problem with this evidence: The ancient Egyptian cities lie underneath modern ones, and this severely limits the amount of excavation and surface survey that is possible. The surviving archaeological evidence is weighted toward tombs, since these were normally located in the desert, out-

The Sphinx and the pyramids of Giza in Egypt were constructed by the kings of the Fourth Dynasty in the 2500s B.C. The oldest pyramid in the complex, the tomb of Khufu, is also the largest. The Sphinx was carved from a rock outcropping; its face is perhaps a portrait of king Khafre, who reigned shortly after Khufu.   (Werner Forman/Art Resource, NY)

side settled areas. For this reason, we know a great deal about Egyptian burial practices and beliefs about death, which can lead to a distorted perception of the Egyptians as a culture preoccupied with death. But the aspects of Egyptian civilization for which we have the most evidence are only part of the whole picture.

The Old, Middle, and New Kingdoms.   Egyptian political history centers on the figure of the king, sometimes called the "pharaoh" (*pr-aa* in Egyptian, a word first attested in New Kingdom times). The king was a figure central to Egyptian culture in many ways. The Egyptians themselves perceived their national history in terms of a series of kings, whom they eventually grouped into thirty successive "dynasties." Lists of pharaohs were an important type of document, and several of these survive and form the basis for the modern understanding of Egyptian chronology. The pharaohs symbolized the unified kingdom of Egypt; their headdress, for example, combined elements traditionally associated with both parts of the country. They were believed to be the incarnation of the hawk-god Horus and sons of the sun-god Re. They were, in theory, all-powerful, subject only to the idea of *ma'at*—order and justice. They were, also in theory, the owners of all the land in Egypt (although individual ownership is attested in practice). The pyramids were their tombs.

Before unification, Egypt was divided into two sections. Lower Egypt was the area around the Nile Delta—the triangular region (shaped like the Greek letter delta, Δ) where the Nile divides into many mouths before emptying into the Mediterranean Sea. Upper Egypt stretched south of the delta about 750 miles to the First Cataract. The Egyptians believed that Upper and Lower Egypt were first unified into a single kingdom in 3100 B.C. by king Menes. This partly legendary figure is also credited with founding the new kingdom's capital, the city of Memphis, and with bringing civilization and the rule of law to Egypt. The period that followed, from 2686 down to the year 2181 B.C. (these are traditional dates), is now called the "Old Kingdom." Not much written evidence remains for this remote and mysterious era of Egyptian history, but it was in this period that Egypt's most astounding monuments, the first pyramids, were built.

At Giza, near Cairo, a complex of three pyramids and the Great Sphinx—an immense stone sculpture of a creature with a lion's body and a man's head—forms one of the world's most renowned and impressive sights. They were built in the first two centuries of the Old Kingdom. The largest of the pyramids—the Great Pyramid—was one of the traditional seven wonders of the ancient world, and the only one that survives today. King Khufu (also known as Cheops, his name in Greek sources) constructed it, his own tomb, in the twenty-sixth century B.C. It is 479 feet high and built entirely of dressed stone—an estimated total of 2.3 million blocks was required. It occupied about 100,000 workers, probably for several decades. Originally filled with treasure, it was plundered in antiquity—as were all the other pyramids—so that only the king's granite sarcophagus remained. But the structure itself is eloquent testimony to the power and image of the ruler, who was buried inside it and worshipped there after his death.

The Old Kingdom dissolved under circumstances that are poorly understood; it seems that the governors of some local districts (called *nomes*) became powerful enough to challenge the established ruling dynasty. It is also possible that the increasing power of the priests of the sun-god, Re, helped to weaken the monarchy. After two centuries of political chaos called the First Intermediate period (traditionally dating from 2181 to 1991 B.C.), Egypt was reunited under the kings of the eleventh dynasty, who ushered in a period of vast building projects, expanded bureaucracy, and literary productivity. This was the classical era of ancient Egyptian literature, when genres and texts were developed that remained important in Egyptian culture through the New Kingdom and afterward.

The Middle Kingdom dissolved in another interval of political upheaval, the Second Intermediate period, during which Egypt was ruled for about a century by a dynasty of foreigners called the Hyksos. Tradition dated their expulsion and the beginning of the New Kingdom to 1567 B.C. The New Kingdom was a period of imperialist expansion southward into Nubia and northward into Syria and the Levant. In the fifteenth century, King Thutmose III led a series of fourteen military campaigns that extended Egypt's rule to the Euphrates river.

The New Kingdom was also a period of great monumental architecture, especially temples. The largest and most renowned of these is the Temple of Amen at Karnak, built in honor of the local god Amen, who in this period was worshipped together with the sun-god Re as Amen-Re. This temple was extended and renovated over a long period by a series of New Kingdom pharaohs, whose deeds were inscribed in hieroglyphs on its walls and pillars.

EGYPTIAN HISTORICAL PERIODS

3100–2686 B.C.	Early Dynastic
2686–2181 B.C.	Old Kingdom
2181–1991 B.C.	First Intermediate
1991–1786 B.C.	Middle Kingdom
1786–1567 B.C.	Second Intermediate
1567–1085 B.C.	New Kingdom

Dates given here are traditional but not necessarily correct; they trace back to the history composed in Greek by the Egyptian scholar Manetho in the third century B.C.

Society and Family.   Slaves may have been rare in Egypt until the New Kingdom, when military conquests created an abundant supply of prisoners. As in Mesopotamia, slaves might be owned by the king, by the temples, or by private individuals; they might be bought, sold, inherited, and rented out. But they had some limited legal and economic rights: They could hold property and bequeath it to their heirs, and some slaves married women of free status.

As in Mesopotamia, much of the land in ancient Egypt was owned by the king and by the temples, and a large part (perhaps a majority) of the population worked directly for them. At one site in western Thebes dating to the New Kingdom, called Deir el-Medina, a village that housed the workers who built the royal tombs in the Valley of the Kings provides a wealth of evidence about its inhabitants. Because its population worked on the desert's edge, in areas that were later abandoned, this settlement is well preserved and has even produced a large number of documents on papyrus and on ostraka. The population, at its height, was about twelve hundred. The workers were divided into two crews, each inhabiting one half of the village, who worked in shifts. Records of many private economic transactions—bartering with goods or silver bullion, which was used as money—and legal documents describing everyday crimes and disputes show that the state that employed them did not dominate all aspects of their lives.

View of Deir el-Medina from the east. The workmen who lived here built the royal tombs in the Valley of the Kings, near Thebes. The walled village is to the right of the picture; on the left is the village's cemetery. (Photo by Tom Van Eynde)

The prominence of writing in this village inhabited only by workmen, their families, and one or two of their immediate supervisors is especially striking. The names of the inhabitants were written on the doors of their houses and sometimes on columns inside the houses and on the benches of the village's cult-buildings. Scribes kept daily records of the work done by the villagers; court records, business records, and a wide variety of other documents—including school texts—also survive. The inhabitants of this village, or many of them at least, were literate.

As in Mesopotamia, the state paid public laborers like those at Deir el-Medina mainly in food, and some scholars see them as serfs or slaves receiving rations rather than wages. Even those Egyptians who did not work full-time for the state were sometimes required to provide labor for specific projects (this type of forced labor is sometimes called **corvée labor**); the wealthy could hire substitutes. It is clear that in both Egypt and Mesopotamia the state, represented by the kings and the temples, controlled a large part of the economy.

More is known about the royal family than about ordinary families in Bronze Age Egypt. Kings normally had several wives, but only one "Great Royal Wife"; the king's throne would pass to her children. Kings often married their sisters or other close female relatives, but most scholars agree that this was not normal practice in the general population at this time.

Most of the evidence for ordinary households and families comes from Deir el-Medina and dates to the New Kingdom; we do not know how well it applies to other times and places. In this village, most houses had a small reception room with an altar, the focus for a domestic cult; there was also a central room with a bench for social occasions, and one or more living rooms in the back. There were no courtyards, but the inhabitants used the roof as living space also. Monogamous nuclear families—a husband, wife, and their children—were typical. Polygamy was legal in ancient Egypt, but is only scantily attested at Deir el-Medina and may have been unusual. Divorce and remarriage were common for both men and women.

It was the Egyptian custom to divide property equally among all of a person's children at his or her death, a tradition that persisted at least through Roman times. This contrasts strikingly with the situation in other ancient Mediterranean societies, where sons inherited all or most of their parents' property. As a result, it was not unusual for women in Egypt to own land, slaves, and other property and to pursue a wide variety of economic activities. It seems, however, that men still owned or controlled most of the economic resources. At Deir el-Medina, women were involved in about 18 percent of the financial transactions of which records survive, and other evidence indicates that only about one in ten landowners was a woman.*

Warfare and Weapons.   Because the desert cut them off from other peoples and protected them from military aggression, the Egyptians did not fight as many wars as other ancient civilizations did, at least until the Second Intermediate Period, when they were conquered by the Hyksos. After the enemies were expelled, the kings of the New Kingdom embarked on a series of imperialist campaigns that expanded Egypt's borders north and east to the Euphrates river and south into Nubia. The king was Egypt's military chief, and he led the army himself.

The Egyptians were conservative about weapons technology, retaining stone and copper weapons after other civilizations had switched to bronze. From the Hyksos, however, they adopted the chariot, the composite bow, and the curved sword used by other Near Eastern peoples. In sieges, they used scaling ladders and battering-rams.

The Egyptians employed some foreign mercenaries—professional soldiers—from an early date. But the early Egyptian army was mainly composed of peasants who were drafted as the need arose. In the New Kingdom, the kings created a professional, standing army, partly drafted from the population and partly formed of volunteers and foreign mercenaries. At times, up to 10 percent of the eligible male population might be under arms. Soldiers received a share of the spoils of war; some received land for their service.

The Gods, Death, and the Afterlife.   The aspect of Egyptian culture for which the most abundant evidence survives is their treatment of death. This is for two reasons: First, tombs were normally located in the desert, and thus have escaped being built over; and second, the Egyptians buried their dead with great care, in tombs of stone decorated with inscriptions and paintings and filled with art objects.

At first, only kings were thought to have immortal spirits, but in the Middle Kingdom immortality became "democratized"—everyone could expect an afterlife in the land ruled by Osiris, king of the dead. The Egyptians believed that life continued after death in much the same way as before. Tombs were decorated with paintings and carvings of people making food

---

*Gay Robins, *Women in Ancient Egypt*, Cambridge, MA: Harvard University Press, 1993, pp. 131, 135.

and providing other services for the dead person's spirit or *ka*. They were filled with clothes, food, jewelry, and other things that the *ka* might need after death. But the body as well as the spirit continued to be important after death. Dead bodies were carefully embalmed and wrapped in linen strips ("mummified") and placed inside two nested coffins; the inner and, later, the outer coffin was shaped like a mummy and decorated to look human, with a face, hair, and jewelry painted on. Texts painted or inscribed on the tomb's walls and on the coffin ensured a smooth passage to the afterlife with the correct prayers and incantations. In the New Kingdom, some of these texts tell how the deceased would appear before Osiris and proclaim his or her innocence of crimes on earth: "I have not done evil to men. I have not ill-treated animals. I have not blasphemed the gods," and so on. The jackal-god Anubis then weighed the person's heart to test the truth of this self-defense, which would determine the deceased's fate in the afterlife.

In the Old Kingdom, only kings and nobles had elaborate tombs, but in the Middle and New Kingdoms, everyone who could afford to build and equip a tomb seems to have done so—even ordinary people such as the workmen of Deir el-Medina. The poor who could not afford tombs or mummification (the complete procedure took seventy days and required a team of professional embalmers) were buried in shallow graves in the desert, where the hot, dry sand often preserved their bodies naturally from decay.

Besides tombs, the largest and best-preserved Egyptian monuments are temples. Even in the Greco-Roman period, travelers were impressed by their great size and antiquity. In the fifth century B.C., the Greek historian Herodotus, learning that Egyptian cults and temples were far older than anything in the Greek world, believed and wrote that all the Greek gods had come from Egypt.

The Egyptian pantheon of gods is often described as **syncretistic**—it preserved many local traditions, and no set of gods dominated the others to create a single, national religion. For example, in a tradition arising in Heliopolis, the original creator-god was Atum, who produced his progeny by spitting and vomiting, but the creator-god of Memphis was Ptah, who made the universe with thought and speech. Both were important gods worshipped all over Egypt.

Some gods were worshipped in vast temples with powerful priesthoods and were patronized by the kings and associated with them; others had more limited geographic range. Evidence from Deir el-Medina shows a rich variety of religious practices in the village. Although the villagers worshipped the state cult of Amen-Re, the most important gods were the major deities of nearby Thebes, such as Hathor, the cow-goddess of love, fertility, and the desert. The villagers also worshipped the deified king Amenophis, who gave oracles; and a nature-cult of Mereseger, the spirit of a local mountain peak portrayed as a woman with a snake's head. In their homes, they worshipped household deities like the ugly, bowlegged dwarf Bes, who presided at marriages and other festive occasions, or his wife Taweret, who helped with childbirth and was portrayed as a pregnant hippopotamus.

From an early date, the Egyptian kings were believed to be the sons of the sun-god Re; the priesthood of Re had already become powerful in the Old Kingdom. Other gods became associated with Re and were worshipped together with him as a single deity: Atum, the creator-god of Heliopolis; and in the New Kingdom, Amen of Thebes. In the fourteenth century B.C., king Amenhotep IV (also known as "Akhenaten") abolished the worship of all other gods, especially Amen, and promoted the cult of a single deity, the Aten. The Aten was also the sun—but instead of being depicted as part-human, part-animal, like other Egyptian gods, he was represented as an abstract figure of the sun's radiant disk. Akhenaten's attempt to replace the worship of Egypt's ancient, traditional gods with the cult of a single, universal god of light was short-lived; at his death, the cult dissolved.

The Canaanites

Some of the earliest evidence of agriculture comes from the Levant, and several important Neolithic sites—such as Jericho, discussed earlier—developed there. As early as 3000 B.C. this region had cities with fortification walls, temples, long-range trade networks, craft specialization, and town planning. Palace archives discovered in the 1970s reveal that the city of Ebla in Syria flourished in the twenty-fourth century B.C. and dominated a wide surrounding territory; they are written in Sumerian and in a local Semitic language.

Urban sites in the Levant were mostly abandoned around 2300 B.C. but revived early in the next millenium, when sites in the region also became more culturally homogeneous. Later, the Israelites who composed the Hebrew Bible would refer to the peoples they displaced as "Canaanites," and since this word is also attested in Bronze Age sources, scholars call the peoples of the southern Levant in the second millenium B.C. Canaanites. The city of Ugarit on the Syrian coast flourished in the fourteenth and thirteenth centuries B.C.; there, a palace and a large archive of cuneiform tablets in a number of Near Eastern languages have been found. Ugarit is often considered the largest and best-preserved Canaanite site, but its population was diverse and it is questionable whether its culture can properly be described as Canaanite.

It was probably the Canaanites who developed the first alphabet—a writing system that was easier to use than other scripts because each letter represented a single sound, not a syllable or a whole word. The earliest known examples date to the nineteenth century B.C. and appear on inscriptions from Egypt, but the language they record is Semitic and they may have been the work of Canaanite workers or slaves. Ugaritic scribes used a different alphabet, possibly influenced by the one attested in Egypt.

Most Canaanite cities were destroyed in war by the Egyptians in the sixteenth century B.C., and many were depopulated again in the destructive events that ended the Bronze Age in the eastern Mediterranean (see later in this chapter). But a group of maritime cities on the coast of Lebanon (including the famous cities of Sidon and Tyre) continued to flourish for centuries;

scholars usually call these people the Phoenicians, their name in ancient Greek sources. They were adventurous sailors, traded widely with the Greeks and other eastern Mediterranean peoples, and founded colonies around the Mediterranean world, including the famous city of Carthage in modern Tunisia. The Phoenicians used a version of the Canaanite alphabet; the Greeks acquired it from them in the eighth century B.C., and the Latin alphabet used to represent the English language today ultimately derives from it.

The Hittites

Before the twentieth century, scholars mainly knew of the Hittites from references to them in the Hebrew Bible. But in A.D. 1906–1908, excavations of the ancient city of Hattusas in northeast Turkey (modern Bogzaköy) brought to light about twenty-five thousand clay tablets, in several languages. One of the languages, written in two different scripts (a cuneiform script and a hieroglyphic script), was eventually identified as the language of the Hittites. It proved to be an Indo-European language: That is, it was related to ancient Greek, Latin, and Sanskrit; most modern European languages and some modern Near Eastern languages, such as Persian and Hindi, belong to this family. Because of this, Hittite could be deciphered and read.

The Hittite kingdom emerged shortly after 1700 B.C.; its capital was Hattusas. By about 1600 the Hittites had unified much of Asia Minor under their control. After a period of crisis in the fifteenth century B.C., their empire expanded again in the fourteenth century to include nearly all of Asia Minor, as well as northern Syria and northern Mesopotamia.

At first, the Hittite monarchy was not very strong; assassinations and civil wars happened frequently. Eventually, however, a stable principle of succession was established, and in the fourteenth century the king was addressed as "My Sun" by his subjects and deified after his death. While queens never ruled as sole monarchs, they were unusually powerful in the Hittite kingdom; the queen did not lose her authority at the death of her husband, but continued to hold the title of queen until her own death.

Early in the twentieth century, some scholars influenced by ideas of racial superiority theorized that their Indo-European ancestry allowed the Hittites to conquer and dominate "inferior" indigenous peoples. Even after this hypothesis was discredited, scholars agreed until recently that the Hittites ruled as an ethnically distinct caste of Indo-Europeans over a native, non–Indo-European population. But the evidence for this interpretation is shaky. Hittite religion and mythology borrowed from other cultures; the royal family was, through marriage and adoption, ethnically mixed, and it is likely that the same was true of the rest of the Hittite ruling class. While Hittite was the official written language of the kingdom's administration, the tablets recovered from Hattusas are written in many different languages. It is not clear that the distinction between rulers and subjects was an ethnic one, or what in fact the basis for this distinction was.

In antiquity as today, the Hittites were renowned as great warriors. They were especially famous for their association with a type of chariot warfare which begins to appear in the Mediterranean region some time before 1600 B.C. The Hittites were among the first to use the new light, two-wheeled, horse-drawn chariots, designed for speed, that revolutionized warfare at this time; by 1200 B.C. the Egyptians, Mesopotamians, and Mycenaean Greeks were all using chariots to some extent. Previously, horses had not been used in battle, but chariots could outflank and outrun an infantry force. Chariot contingents were usually small, as the equipment involved was expensive and the horses required a great deal of training, but when manned with spearmen or archers, even a small force could be very effective. Sometimes, some or all of the expense of equipping the chariotry was shouldered by the king; in other societies, nobles supplied their own equipment. In either case, chariot warfare may have tended to create a social structure where power was centered on an elite group—either of professional soldiers close to the king or of aristocrats with substantial economic resources. The Hittite infantry probably outnumbered the chariotry by a wide margin, but the surviving sources do not emphasize its role in battle.

The Hittites fought every year in the spring and summer. They preferred pitched battles, where their chariotry could be most effective; they also besieged cities, although we know little about their techniques. Around Hattusas and other important cities, they constructed massive fortification walls of stone filled with rubble.

Around 1500 B.C., the kingdoms of the Near East began to communicate with one another and to influence one another more than previously. Military expansion was one reason for this. The Hittites invaded Mesopotamia and sacked Babylon around 1600 B.C., and beginning in the mid-sixteenth century, after the expulsion of the Hyksos, the Egyptians campaigned in Syria and the Levant. In these wars they conquered the Canaanites and came into direct conflict with the Hittites. But this was a time of alliance and diplomacy as well as war. From the first half of the fourteenth century B.C., clay tablets from el-Amarna in Egypt and from the Hittite capital Hattusas show regular diplomatic contact between the three great kingdoms of Babylonia, Egypt, and the Hittites. The tablets are written in Akkadian, the international diplomatic language.

Conflict between the Egyptians and the Hittites reached a climax around 1280 B.C. in the reign of the pharaoh Ramesses II: Accounts of the great battle of Kadesh in Syria, as well as the treaty that the two kingdoms concluded afterward, survive in Egyptian temple inscriptions and on clay tablets from Hattusas. After this, the Egyptians and Hittites became allies, and a Hittite princess married Ramesses II.

The Aegean

In the Bronze Age, two distinct civilizations arose in what was later the Greek homeland of the Greek peninsula and the Aegean islands. The earlier of the two was centered on Crete and today is called "Minoan" after the mythical king Minos of Knossos. The other civilization, which arose on the mainland, is called "Mycenaean" after the city of Mycenae, legendary home of king Agamemnon, which is one of the best-preserved and most impressive Bronze Age sites.

To the Greeks of later eras, the Bronze Age was an age of heroic kings and warriors who were taller, stronger, better-looking, and wealthier than the men of their own times. It was an age when monsters and half-gods roamed the earth and adventurers traveled to its outer limits, performing deeds of spectacular courage; when kings fought one another in agonizing wars and together sailed against Troy in northern Asia Minor, which they destroyed after a ten-year siege. Stories of Bronze Age heroes formed the content of Greek mythology, and these myths were the subjects of epic poetry, of tragedies, of sculpture on temples, and of paintings on vases.

Minoan Civilization. In 1899 Sir Arthur Evans, a British archaeologist, began excavations on Crete and discovered a civilization that seemed different from the Bronze Age culture of mainland Greece; it was he who gave the name "Minoan" to the people he discovered. The Minoans remain mysterious in many ways because the two writing systems they used ("Cretan hieroglyphic" and a script called Linear A) cannot be read today. While scholars are sure that the language they spoke was not Greek, it is unclear to what, if any, known language family it belonged. Also, writing does not seem to have been as important in Minoan and Mycenaean civilization as it was in ancient Egypt or Mesopotamia. Only a relatively small number of texts in Linear A survive, and these are mostly short inscriptions on seal stones and clay tablets.

The Minoans arrived on Crete around 7000 B.C.; only a few early sites— simple farming villages or cave dwellings—are known. Around 3500 B.C., the population of the island increased dramatically; metalworking and pottery appear in the archaeological record, and some sites, such as Knossos, grew into substantial settlements. These changes may reflect the arrival of a new wave of settlers, but it is also possible that they happened spontaneously within the indigenous population.

Around 2000 B.C., the Minoans began to build complex structures that archaeologists have labeled "palaces." Writing appears for the first time, to record inventories of goods stored in the palaces. In this period, Knossos grew to a city with a population of perhaps twelve thousand. The early palaces were all destroyed around 1700 B.C., probably by earthquake, and little is known about them. The civilization that Arthur Evans excavated and that is best known to us today dates to the centuries between 1700 and ca. 1470 B.C., from the rebuilding of the great palaces to an unknown disaster that left a layer of destruction in the archaeological record.

The palaces constructed at Knossos and a few other sites on Crete were complex, sprawling structures with workrooms, courtyards, ceremonial chambers, and storage facilities, indicating that they served a wide range of

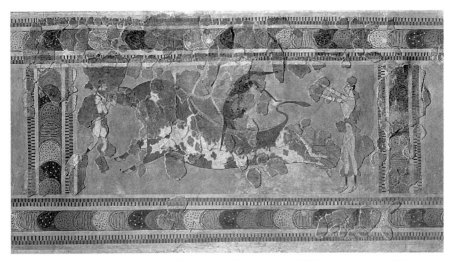

A fresco from the Minoan palace at Knossos, dating to about 1500 B.C., portrays athletes apparently vaulting a bull. This type of ritual or entertainment perhaps took place in the spacious courtyards that are found in all the Minoan palaces. (Nimatallah/Art Resource, NY)

functions. Each palace contained a large, rectangular central courtyard and another courtyard on the western side of the complex—both were probably used as assembly-places for ritual, entertainment, or perhaps political purposes.

The palaces' large number of storage rooms indicates that they collected and redistributed products from the surrounding countryside. Their workshops produced fine art objects such as ritual vases of carved stone, plaques and figurines decorated with the glazing technique known as "faience," delicately carved seal-stones that were worn as jewelry or magical amulets, and a huge variety of fine pottery. Artists also decorated palace walls with vivid frescoes depicting myths, gods, religious rituals, and scenes from nature. Some illustrate bull-leaping events which may have been an important type of ceremony or entertainment.

Nature-cults, especially sanctuaries on mountain peaks, were prominent in early Minoan religion. Here the Minoans dedicated clay figurines of people and animals, and also representations of limbs and parts of the body, probably as tokens of thanks for healing. Later, after 1700 B.C., the focus of religious ritual seems to have shifted to the palaces. The palace at Knossos is especially rich in religious decoration, architecture, and artifacts and may have functioned as a cult-center or even as a temple (although this impression may result from a tendency of archaeologists, since Arthur Evans, to find religious significance in potentially ordinary features of the palace). Here, some suites have been interpreted as sites for "epiphany rituals," in which a deity was invited to take possession of a person or object in the room. "Ritual baths" have been identified in other rooms. Images or models of bull horns and double-headed axes, found at Knossos and at other Minoan sites, have also been interpreted as religious symbols.

Most large towns were on or near the coast, and the Minoans traded widely by sea. The towns lack military architecture (such as fortification walls), and in contrast with other Bronze Age Mediterranean societies, war is not a major theme in Minoan art. But the Minoans were later legendary for their naval supremacy, and it is likely that they maintained a fleet of warships. Minoan frescoes have been found on the ancient island of Thera (now called Santorini), and traces of Minoan culture have surfaced on some other Aegean islands (these sites are sometimes called Minoan "colonies"), showing that this civilization was not confined to Crete but, after 1700 B.C., began to spread around the Aegean world.

Around 1470 B.C., many Minoan sites were destroyed by fire. The palace at Knossos continued to function for some time, but texts from the last phase at Knossos are written in a new script—Linear B, a writing system that originated on mainland Greece. The language recorded in these documents is Greek, not Minoan. It is possible that the destruction of 1470 was caused by an invasion of Mycenaean Greeks, who conquered Crete and ruled it from its principal city. The date at which the Knossos palace was finally destroyed remains controversial, but could have been as late as 1250 or 1200—if so, the fall of Knossos may have taken place as part of a more general pattern of destruction in the eastern Mediterranean at that time.

Mycenaean Civilization: The First Greeks. Between about 1700 and 1100 B.C., a separate Bronze Age civilization flourished on the Greek peninsula. Until the late nineteenth century, this civilization—like that of the Minoans— was known only through the mythology that later developed around it, and no one was sure whether these stories preserved the memory of a real society or not. But in the 1870s, Heinrich Schliemann, a German archaeologist, identified and excavated several Bronze Age sites that were later renowned in Greek mythology. One of these was Mycenae, the legendary home of king Agamemnon, leader of the Trojan expedition. It was Schliemann who named the civilization he discovered "Mycenaean," after this city.

Schliemann not only excavated Bronze Age cities on mainland Greece but also, using Homer as his guide, found and excavated Troy. Later excavations discovered Mycenaean pottery at Troy—showing that this city did have contact with Mycenaean Greece—and evidence that it had been destroyed in war around 1250 B.C. It is possible that Homer's epics and other Greek traditions about the Trojan war preserved the memory of a real event, just as they preserve the names of Greek cities that were important in the Bronze Age.

Writing from Bronze Age Greece survives, mainly on clay tablets but also painted on storage jars, in a script called Linear B. In 1952, a young English scholar named Michael Ventris proved that the language recorded in Linear B was Greek; in this sense, the Mycenaeans were the first Greeks. Writing, however, was used in a very restricted way. The clay tablets survive in much smaller quantities than those produced in ancient Mesopotamia; they contain administrative records, mostly inventories of goods in storage and tax records. No known Linear B text records a religious ritual, a legal proceeding, or a work of literature. While these documents shed light on the Mycenaean economy, they do not tell us about other aspects of Bronze Age culture. Thus even though scholars can understand the language of the Mycenaeans, in some ways they remain as mysterious as the Minoans.

The first Greek speakers arrived some time before 2000 B.C., probably traveling from the northeast. Traces of an earlier, different culture survive in the archaeological record, and in some geographic place names on the Greek peninsula, suggesting that the Mycenaeans were newcomers who intermingled with a preexisting population. How they became the culturally dominant people on the Greek mainland is unclear; scholars today tend to argue that they arrived gradually in small bands or tribes rather than in a single, conquering wave.

At Mycenae, Schliemann excavated a group of burials called "Grave Circle A," which later became his most famous discovery. Dating to about 1700 B.C., these burials are the earliest remains of the complex, sophisticated civilization that flourished and died at the site over the next six hundred years. Grave Circle A contained the bodies of nineteen individuals, including two children, buried in deep shafts dug into the bedrock beneath what later became the Mycenaean citadel. Buried with the bodies were artifacts of astounding beauty and value: delicate gold jewelry, ornaments, and vessels, elaborately carved swords and daggers; and Schliemann's most renowned finds, three gold masks, of which he named one the "Mask of Agamemnon." Many artifacts were made of materials—such as lapis lazuli, ivory, and amber—that were imported from all over the Mediterranean world and beyond.

The remains unearthed at Grave Circle A (and at another nearby group of shaft graves that was discovered later and labeled Grave Circle B) show that as early as 1700 B.C. Mycenaen culture was "civilized." Society was sharply stratified—some families had amassed enormous wealth. Trade contacts were wide, and skilled craftsmen were producing luxury items of great sophistication.

Around 1500 B.C. the Mycenaeans began to use "tholos tombs" for their aristocratic burials. These were round underground chambers cut into bedrock; the interior was lined with worked stone, and a long runway called a *dromos* led to the tomb's entrance. Some of these, such as the so-called 'Treasury of Atreus'* near Mycenae, are massive in size. The *dromos* to the Treasury of Atreus is 118 feet long and the larger of the two lintels over the doorway weighs over one hundred tons; inside, stone blocks line a chamber over forty feet high. The tholos tombs were once filled with valuable objects, but they were all plundered in antiquity and none of their treasure has survived intact. Smaller tholos tombs, and simpler chamber tombs cut into bedrock, housed

---

*In mythology, Atreus was Agamemnon's father.

the remains of people lower on the social scale. Burials of infants and children are rare; they must have been buried in ways that are not easy to detect archaeologically, or possibly were not buried at all but exposed.

Some of the most impressive remains of the Mycenaean period—the massive walls and elaborate palaces of Mycenae and other Bronze Age cities—date to late in the era, from 1400 to 1200 B.C. The Mycenaean palaces were smaller, simpler, and different in layout and architectural detail from the buildings also called "palaces" on Minoan Crete, but like the Minoan palaces, they dominated the economy of the surrounding countryside. Linear B tablets from Pylos show that the palace there collected commodities such as wool, oil, and livestock from a wide territory; some places mentioned may have been fifty miles away or more. This palace, which is the best preserved of all the Mycenaean palaces, contained a large courtyard and rectangular *megaron* (a room with a hearth and four interior columns, possibly used as a throne room), which was once elaborately decorated; also storerooms full of storage jars and pantries housing a huge quantity of pots and drinking jars; an archive, where Linear B tablets were stored; and other rooms that appear to be bathrooms and living quarters. Workshops where artisans repaired chariots and manufactured armor, bricks, weapons, luxury items, pottery, and other goods were also incorporated into the palace.

Mycenaean palaces were often constructed on high ground, either for social reasons (to symbolize the higher status of the ruling class) or for military reasons (to make the site more defensible). Toward the end of the Mycenaean period, some of the largest cities constructed massive fortification walls up to twenty-five feet thick, made of huge, unworked boulders (called "Cyclopean" architecture because the vast, crude stones recall mythical giants like Homer's Cyclops). They also used large ashlar blocks (stone worked into rectangular slabs).

The Collapse of Bronze Age Civilization

Around 1200 B.C., disaster struck the eastern Mediterranean world. In Asia Minor, Greece, Crete, Syria, and the Levant, layers of destruction punctuate the archaeological record of most important sites, as cities were sacked and burnt. Some places were reoccupied on a smaller scale; others were abandoned.

Scholars are uncertain what happened. From Egypt, a temple inscription describes how the pharaoh Ramesses III (ruled 1198–1166 B.C.) defeated a "conspiracy of islands" that had already destroyed the Hittites and a number of other nations; modern scholars have dubbed the list of peoples that follows the **sea peoples.** A desperate letter from the king of Ugarit, dating to about the same time, appeals for help against an assault by sea. In Greece, the fortification walls constructed at a growing number of sites toward the end of the Mycenaean period, and the water supply systems that were built at Mycenae, Pylos, and other cities at that time, may indicate an increasing military threat. It is likely that tribal migrations bringing displaced peoples—the

The Lion Gate of Mycenae, monumental entrance to the fortified citadel of the city. The wall around the gate is constructed of ashlar blocks. The lintel over the gate weighs 18 tons.
(Erich Lessing/Art Resource, NY)

"sea peoples"—into conflict with the Near East's long-established civilizations partly explain the destructive events of circa 1200 B.C. However, this theory does not explain all the evidence, nor does it explain what caused the migrations. Some scholars argue that a prolonged drought led to violence and plundering, the abandonment of settled land, and the destruction of some cities; others see a long-term decline rather than an sudden one, the result of disrupted trade networks. Another line of reasoning looks to military technology, arguing that new infantry weapons made chariot warfare obsolete and led to the downfall of military systems that were based on it.

Whatever the explanation, crucial changes took place at this time. Hittite civilization and the civilization of the Mycenaean Greeks essentially came to an end; both areas were plunged into a long dark age. Egypt repelled the

This relief from the Assyrian city of Nimrud dates to about 730 B.C. The Assyrians assault a city with archers and a battering ram and scale its walls with ladders. The bottom of the relief shows the brutal slaughter of the captured city's inhabitants. (The British Museum)

invaders of circa 1200, but by 1100 B.C. the kingdom entered into a long period of crisis and disunity (the Third Intermediate Period) lasting over five hundred years, until Egypt was finally conquered and reunified by the Persians.

While Mesopotamia, like Egypt, was spared the direct consequences of the crisis of 1200 B.C., this area also suffered a period of instability. In 1155, the Kassite dynasty collapsed after half a century of conflict with the Assyrians. After the fall of the Kassites, Babylonia endured more foreign invasions, from the Assyrians and other enemies, until eventually the kingdom was absorbed by the Assyrians.

The Assyrians' capital was Assur, on the northern Tigris. They were an aggressive and militaristic people adept at military engineering, sieges, and the use of cavalry and notorious for the brutality with which they suppressed revolts. They sometimes annihilated whole cities in slaughters they depicted on relief sculpture in gruesome detail or deported native populations in massive numbers after a conquest. They ruled Mesopotamia until the late seventh century B.C., when a revolt reestablished the kingdom of Babylonia under king Nabopollassar and his more famous son, king Nebuchadnezzar, who renovated the city of Babylon in spectacular style. In his reign, the "Processional Way"—a major street leading to Babylon's Ishtar Gate—was lined with the vivid blue glazed bricks and golden lions now visible in the Pergamon Museum in Berlin; the gate itself was embellished with bulls and dragons. Nebuchadnezzar also constructed the lost "Hanging Gardens of Babylon," one of the ancient world's seven wonders. He is best known today, however, for conquering Jerusalem in 597 B.C., and destroying the city and deporting its inhabitants in 587—the **Babylonian exile,** which shaped so much of early Hebrew literature. Babylonia was finally conquered in 539 by the Persian monarch Cyrus the Great, who restored the Jewish captives to their homeland.

By 500 B.C. the entire Near and Middle East, from Asia Minor, Syria, and Egypt all the way to modern Afghanistan and Pakistan, was subject to the immense empire of the Persians. Their history will be reviewed in more detail in the next chapter.

Israel and Judah

Unlike the Egyptians or the Mesopotamians, the early Israelites did not build great cities or impressive monuments or rule over a large territory, nor were they one of the first peoples to become "civilized." But their cultural influence on Western civilization was more profound than that of any other society except the Greeks. This is partly because of an extraordinary body of writings, the Hebrew Bible (what Christians call the Old Testament). The books of the Bible relate the history, ancestry, mythology, and laws of a people called Israel. Most of all, they tell the story of Israel's relationship with its god, Yahweh, from his bargain or "covenant" with Abraham, the ancestor of all Israelites, through the vicissitudes of Israel's history. The Bible explains history in terms of this relationship—especially, disasters result from Yahweh's anger at Israel's failure to uphold the covenant and obey his laws. While we have little sense of how the ancient Mesopotamians or Egyptians defined themselves as a people, the Bible provides a fundamental understanding of what it meant to be an Israelite. It helped to sustain a strong sense of cultural cohesion among a relatively small and, at times, widely scattered or aggressively persecuted ethnic group over thousands of years.

Myth and History

The origins of the Western historical tradition—in the Hebrew Bible and in the works of the first Greek historians—bring scholars face-to-face with the problem of distinguishing "myth" from "history" and even of deciding on a definition of those two terms. Defining the difference as one between fiction (myth) and fact (history) is too simplistic. History is by nature an interpretation of reality, not a direct reflection of it, and while the tradition of objectivity—of providing an unbiased view of past events—has been important in historical writing since antiquity, true objectivity is impossible. Everything from the decision about what aspects of the past to study, to the nuances of how the information is presented, reflects the historian's response to the needs of his or her society—the audience for the text. These needs might include support for a system of moral values, justification of a class structure, or the creation of a sense of cultural or ethnic identity—a sense that the history being written is "our" history. In this way, history serves many of the same functions as myth. Stories of gods and heroes, the deeds of famous

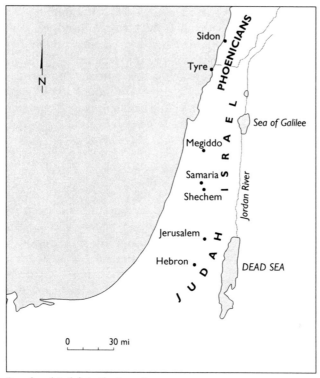

Israel and Judah in the Iron Age

ancestors, their genealogies, their visits to various places—all of these elements of mythology have important cultural purposes even if they do not reflect a literal truth. Both history and myth should be read as reflections of the society that produced them as well as guides to the past that they record.

While the difference between history and myth is not simply that between fact and fiction, it is in some ways reasonable to make another distinction: between oral and written sources. Myths may sometimes be written down, but they have another, independent life as oral traditions—stories passed down through generations. Oral traditions are much more fluid than written ones because there is no single, authoritative text that fixes the "correct" version of the story. They change quickly over time, and thus tend to reflect the context in which the story is being told as well as preserving some memory of earlier eras. Different social groups or people in different geographic areas may tell different versions of the story; usually several, contradictory versions of a myth exist at the same time.

"History" normally refers to a written text. An author has collected and organized the available material—some might be oral, and some might be documentary—and created a fixed version of it that does not change very much over time (although some changes are introduced whenever the text is copied, and somewhat different versions of a text may circulate). Usually, historians try to create a coherent, consistent story, although they do not always succeed in this effort. The story that the historian produces will depend on his or her views, assumptions, and methods of collecting evidence—which, in turn, will mainly reflect the influence of the culture in which the historian lives. Once written down, however, the text is frozen and mostly impervious to the influence of later cultural changes—although every generation (and every individual) will read the text in a different way, the text itself does not change and thus provides a more reliable reflection of the past than oral tradition.

The Hebrew Bible

In a sense, the Hebrew Bible—at least, the parts that tell the story of Israel's origins and of the kingdom founded by Samuel and destroyed by Neb-uchadnezzar—is the Western world's first history; unlike later histories, however, it was not written by a single author in a short period. The canon of the Hebrew Bible took shape over a long time; the latest work in it (Daniel) was written in the second century B.C. (on the "canon" see the box on p. 47). What were the first books to be written, when were they composed, and what preexisting sources did their authors use? Unfortunately, none of these questions is easy to answer. The first five books of the Bible, called the **Torah** (the "law"; also called the Pentateuch), which contains a narrative of early Israelite history and an exposition of the law that Israel received through Moses, is the section whose composition has been studied most extensively. Jewish tradition attributed all five books to the hero Moses, but even in antiquity scholars questioned whether he could have written some of the material they contain. From the late eighteenth century until recent times, many scholars have accepted the "documentary hypothesis," which identifies four narrative strands, each composed by a different author at a different time. Two (called J and E, for the different names—Yahweh/Jehovah or Elohim—that they used for God) told a mythical-historical narrative from the creation of the universe to Moses' death; two others (called D for "Deuteronomical" and P for Priestly) provided the legal and genealogical material. But most scholars today agree that this hypothesis is too simplistic. Each strand relied on sources that pre-dated their composition, and inconsistencies within each strand indicate that they may have been the work of several authors, not one. Epic poems and songs, genealogies, and legal traditions that were mostly transmitted orally all gradually evolved into a written text.

It is extremely difficult to date any part of the Torah. Some of its source material may have originated as early as 1200 B.C., but it did not take shape as a cohesive text until much later. Most of the narrative of Israel's early history seems to have coalesced by 600 B.C., and the legal part—approximately half—of the Torah had taken shape by 400 B.C., but some changes were added even later. The result is a very complex document that fitted the social and cultural needs of the people who produced it, but also preserved some memory of earlier times. Because it took so long to form and was the work of a

| *Doing History* |

THE CANON

Canon literally means "a rule" and sometimes refers to body of works (or *corpus*, which means "body" in Latin) that are transmitted together and considered authoritative in some way. The formation of a canon is a selective process; usually other, similar works—or different versions of the same works—circulated at the time that the canon was being formed, but were excluded from the corpus. At some point, for reasons that are not always well understood, the canon closes—no new works are admitted. The Hebrew Bible (sometimes called the "Tanakh" in Judaism), the Christian Old Testament (which contains a slightly different list of books or order of books), and the New Testament are all canons of this type; besides these, another good example of a canon from antiquity is the Hippocratic Corpus, a collection of Greek medical works dating to the classical period (see p. 92).

Because the essential feature of canonical works is authority, groups can disagree over what belongs in or out, sometimes even after the canon has closed—one group will accept one canon and another will favor a different one. For example, the Septuagint—a version of the Bible in Greek, used by the Jews of Alexandria in Egypt—contains books not found in the Hebrew Tanakh. Protestant Christians refer to these books as the **apocrypha** or "hidden" books (the word "apocrypha" also has a more general meaning, denoting any Jewish and Christian writings that were excluded from the canon). Catholics include most of these books in the canonical Old Testament, but refer to them as "deuterocanonical," literally, the "second canon."

In a looser sense, the word "canon" can refer to any authoritative tradition in literature, art, or music, or any other cultural product. For example, people often refer to the canon of authors that shapes education in English literature—the list of "classic" authors such as Shakespeare, Austen, and Joyce. Ideas about what belongs in or out of the canon may vary among groups or even among individuals—but the concept of some kind of canon, some list of works that everyone should know or study, is important in most societies.

For a good discussion of canons, see Shaye D. Cohen, *From the Maccabees to the Mishnah*, Philadelphia: Westminster Press, 1987, chapter 6.

whole culture rather than any single individual, the Torah retains some of the repetitions and inconsistencies that characterize oral, rather than written, sources.

Early Israel

The Torah begins with the story of Yahweh's creation of the world and the expulsion of its first humans, Adam and Eve, from a primeval paradise for disobeying his commands. It goes on to tell of his anger at the decadence and corruption of later generations, and the resulting flood that annihilated all but a remnant of the human population. The Torah then narrates the wanderings of the patriarch Abraham, ancestor of all Israelites, who was born in the great Mesopotamian city of Ur and migrated to Canaan, and the story of his descendants, including his grandson Jacob (also called Israel), whose twelve children became the ancestors of Israel's twelve tribes. During a period of drought and famine, Jacob's family migrated to Egypt, where their descendants were oppressed by the Egyptian kings. Finally, a hero named Moses led the Israelites out of captivity and back to the Holy Land. On the way, in the Sinai desert, Yahweh communicated through him the details of Israelite law that the Torah relates.

The Torah dates Abraham's departure from Ur to the twenty-first century B.C. and the Exodus ("journey out") from Egypt to the mid-fifteenth century, but as yet no independent evidence for the existence of Israel at that time has been found. It is not clear whether the sojourn in Egypt is a historical reality. Perhaps more important than this unanswerable question is the recurring theme of exile that shapes the Hebrew Bible—the exile from paradise, the exile in Egypt, and, finally, the exile in Babylonia, when some Jews were deported after the conquests of Nebuchadnezzar in 587 B.C.

Archaeology suggests that new settlements began to arise in the previously sparsely populated highlands of the southwestern Levant at the close of the Bronze Age—about 1250 B.C. By collecting water in cisterns plastered with asphalt and by terracing the hillsides (that is, cutting into them to produce stepped levels of flat ground), the settlers were able to farm this inhospitable land; they also kept herds of sheep and goats. It is not clear where the settlers came from: They may have been farmers from the surrounding lowlands who expanded their agricultural territory into the hill country; or semi-nomadic herdsmen who were already living in the hills may have changed their way of life, creating sedentary villages and beginning to farm the land; or they may have been newcomers to the region, as the biblical tradition suggests. Whatever their origins, archaeologists believe that these settlers were the early Israelites. It is at about this time (around 1200 B.C.) that Israel is first attested in a written source apart from the Bible—an Egyptian inscription lists Israel along with Canaan and other peoples of the Levant conquered by the pharaoh Merneptah.

The Monarchy and the Babylonian Exile

The Bible dates the first, famous kings of Israel—Samuel, David, and Solomon—to the late 1000s and early 900s B.C. and relates how they expanded the new kingdom's boundaries all the way to the Euphrates in the east and the Red Sea in the south. Jerusalem became Israel's capital city, and Solomon especially is supposed to have undertaken major construction projects there—a wall around the city, a palace, and the Temple that became the center of Jewish ritual. According to the Bible, the united kingdom of Israel split in two in the late tenth century: The northern part of the population resented the burden of providing labor for Solomon's building projects and seceded to form the separate kingdom of Israel around 925 B.C. David's descendants continued to rule in the south, now called Judah.

The Bible relates how the two kingdoms fought intermittently until Israel was destroyed in 722 B.C. by the Assyrians, who incorporated its territory into their empire and deported many of its inhabitants. Judah remained independent until it in turn was conquered by the Babylonian king Nebuchadnezzar in 597. Ten years later, he destroyed Solomon's temple and deported some of Judah's population to Mesopotamia, where they remained until the Persian king Cyrus conquered the area and allowed them to return in 538. This episode is sometimes called the "Babylonian captivity" or "Babylonian exile."

The history of the kingdoms of Israel and Judah is told in the books of the Bible that are sometimes called the "historical" books: Joshua, Judges, Samuel, and Kings. As with the Torah, modern historians approach this evidence with some caution and debate how literally it should be construed. Some argue that archaeological evidence of impressive walls, palaces, and monumental gates at some settlements supports the tradition of a great kingdom of Israel under Solomon and David. Other scholars interpret this evidence differently or challenge its dating and point out that archaeological attempts to locate Solomon's building projects in Jerusalem or to confirm that it was an important city in the tenth century have met with little success. These scholars question whether the unified kingdom of Israel ever existed and characterize the history of united Israel as a legend of a golden age. In this view, there had always been two kingdoms; the northern region became a populous, multiethnic kingdom with impressive cities and a developed state in the ninth century B.C., while Judah remained a rural and pastoral hinterland. But after the fall of Israel to the Assyrians in the late eighth century, Judah entered a period of political, economic, and cultural development. Because the Bible took shape in Judah during this period and reflects the views and ambitions—including territorial ambitions—of its kings and people, it portrays Israel as a corrupt, idolatrous splinter state and Judah as the original heart and capital of an earlier, greater kingdom of Israel.

Society and Family

Society in the kingdoms of Israel and Judah was more rural than in Mesopotamia or Egypt. There is archaeological evidence for cities and a centralized state (although the dating and details of the area's political evolution are open to debate) and for the centralized collection or production of grain and olive oil in some cities. Nevertheless, the state did not control as much of the economy as it did in the great Bronze Age civilizations; the agricultural household remained the basic economic unit. Houses were typically two-story structures with three or four ground-floor rooms; the lower level was used to shelter livestock and store produce, while the family lived upstairs. The self-sufficient, multi-functional design of Israelite houses suggests that each household produced most of the food needed to sustain it and would sell or trade any surplus.

Some houses were bigger and some were smaller—indicating some social differentiation—but the range of sizes is relatively limited and there is no evidence of large, many-roomed mansions except for a few royal residences. It seems that wealth was more evenly distributed in Israel than in some other ancient societies. Poverty, however, always threatened the typical agricultural family—one or two bad seasons might force a father to sell his children or himself into slavery or to hand over his property to a creditor. In theory, the Torah protected these people by dictating that land must revert to its original owner every fifty years in the "jubilee" year.

For the social structure of the Israelite family we mostly depend on the evidence from the Hebrew Bible, but because of the complicated and ill-understood nature of its composition, it is difficult to know how accurately it reflects reality. The household imagined in the Hebrew Bible is composed of a father, his sons, his sons' wives, their children, their domestic slaves, and their livestock; authority centers on the "patriarch"—the male head of the household. Archaeological evidence from houses is difficult to interpret and could be consistent with complex, multi-generational families where the sons remained in the household after marriage or with "nuclear" families that tended to contain only one married couple, with their children, servants, and animals.

In the Bible, husbands pay a bride-price when they marry, which goes to the bride's father, not to her. Biblical example allowed polygamy, which was still practiced in the Roman period, and divorce could be initiated by the husband, but probably not by the wife. Women might marry very young—in the Bible, girls marry in their early teens. Marriages were arranged by the parents, and brides may have had little voice in the choice of their partners. Traditional roles for women were indoor, household activities such as cooking or weaving, although the Bible also portrays women tending flocks and helping with work in the fields. While women probably exercised some power in the household—despite the traditional primacy of the patriarch—their role in public life was less prominent. Women could not, for example, be priests, although the Bible mentions a few female prophets, judges, and queens.

Sons normally inherited from their fathers, with the eldest son receiving the largest share, but younger sons and daughters also received a share. If a father had no son, his daughter could inherit the entire estate but she was required to marry within the father's kinship group. Widows could inherit from their husbands, but the law did not guarantee this, and in the Torah widows and orphans are especially vulnerable, requiring charity and protection.

Slavery is well attested in the Bible, although it is difficult to tell how pervasive it really was. The Torah recognizes two separate categories of slaves: those of foreign origin and Hebrews enslaved by poverty or debt. In theory, Hebrews could not be enslaved permanently but had to be released every seventh year. Slaves were perceived as a part of the household rather than simply as property or sources of labor; for example, the law required that male slaves be circumcised like their masters and that slaves rest on the Sabbath like other members of the household. As in Mesopotamia, masters sometimes adopted their children by slave concubines as heirs (the case of Jacob, whose twelve sons included four by slave concubines, is the most famous).

Religion and Law

Throughout the Hebrew Bible, Yahweh demands that Israel worship no other god but him. This is part of his covenant with Abraham and his descendants. However, the Bible also tells of episodes where the Israelites lapsed and did worship other gods, such as Baal, a local deity. Archaeology confirms that Yahweh was worshipped together with other gods (especially his consort, Asherah) and that domestic or "popular" cults survived throughout the period of the monarchy. (The memory of a domestic cult is preserved in the story of Rachel from Genesis, who steals her father's "household gods"—*teraphim*—when she runs away with Jacob.) This pluralism was the more normal pattern in antiquity, and it is not clear when the Israelites began to associate themselves with a single deity. In the Bible as it eventually took shape, however, monotheism—the worship of a single god—is a fundamental part of Israel's identity; they were the chosen people of Yahweh, the creator of the universe.

Yahweh's cult centered on the Temple in Jerusalem, traditionally constructed by Solomon in the tenth century B.C. and reconstructed in the fifth century after the Babylonians destroyed it. Priests of the Jerusalem temple traditionally descended from Aaron, Moses' brother, and belonged to the tribe of Levi. In the legal sections of the Torah, they are responsible for carrying out rituals, celebrating festivals, and, most of all, administering the sacred laws that bound Israel to Yahweh. Many of the Torah's laws regulate the ways in which Israelites can be alienated from, and reintegrated into, the community: For example, a long section of Leviticus classifies certain foods (such as pork) and bodily fluids (especially blood and semen) as "unclean," and those who have contact with them must be purified before they can resume their place in society. People and things disfigured by blotchy affections (such as skin disease—leprosy was endemic to ancient Palestine—or mildew) are also classed as "unclean." These taboos separate the pure from the impure just as Yahweh's chosen people are separated from the others around them (cf. Lev. 20:25–26). Abiding by the law became one of the main tests of Jewish identity.

Since the legal sections of the Torah probably evolved later than the narrative parts, it is not clear when the laws took shape—possibly not until the sixth or fifth century B.C., perhaps in response to the destruction of the Temple and the deportation of a part of Judah's population. This catastrophe may have prompted the exiles to seek new ways of identifying themselves as a people— and to seek this sense of identity partly in sacred law.

One final feature of Israelite religion besides the worship of Yahweh, the Temple, and the law deserves discussion here. The period of the monarchy, exile, and restoration was also the age of prophets. Prophets were independent, charismatic figures who were often powerful voices of social and religious reform. They were visionaries who believed they were personally called by Yahweh to remedy the evils of their times. They tended to take the side of the poor and oppressed against that of the rich, the kings, and the priests, whom they perceived as hopelessly corrupt. They insisted that Israel's past disasters resulted from the wrongdoing of its people and warned that Yahweh would abandon or punish them for continued offenses. The prophets predicted that Israel would be rewarded for repentance and reform with victory, peace, and prosperity. With their focus on the history and destiny of Israel as a people, and on its relationship to Yahweh, they, like the priests, helped to create a sense of ethnic cohesion.

At no time in antiquity or since have the Jews been a homogeneous people—there were social and cultural divisions among them, a point we shall return to when we discuss Second Temple Judaism (p. 108). But the Biblical tradition offered the possibility of perceiving oneself not as a member of a specific family, clan, tribe, class, or sect, but as an Israelite or a Jew. This sense of ethnic identity does not occur spontaneously or naturally; it must be constructed, and the Bible offers fascinating evidence for how this construction might take place.

SUMMARY

Around 3000 B.C., the rise of civilization in parts of the Near East revolutionized human history. Before that date, humans had for a long period—the Paleolithic age—lived in small nomadic groups, hunting and gathering for subsistence. Then in about 9000 B.C., agriculture was invented in the Near East and eventually spread to Europe, as humans domesticated both plants and animals and began to live in permanent settlements. Agriculture allowed for the accumulation of an economic surplus—humans were able to produce more food than was needed for mere survival; eventually, that surplus became the foundation of civilization.

The Mesopotamians and the Egyptians were the first to develop civilizations. They built large cities with crowded, dense populations and impressive public buildings. They developed writing and used it for accounting, works of literature, edicts and decrees, and a wide variety of other purposes; many of these documents survive today and shed light on all aspects of ancient society, from the deeds of kings to the lives of ordinary workers. A central administration—either king or temple—owned much of the land, collected taxes, and controlled the labor of large parts of the population. The state used these resources to fund the construction of great monuments and other major public works, to wage wars of conquest, to pay specialized craftsmen to produce luxury items, and to worship the gods with festivals, rituals, and dedications.

In the Aegean, civilization arose somewhat later than in the Near East. Mycenaean civilization developed on mainland Greece, while Crete and some Aegean islands were the homeland of Minoan civilization. While they were culturally distinct and used different languages, both Mycenaean and Minoan civilizations centered on palaces that collected resources from the surrounding countryside. In antiquity, these civilizations were remembered in Greek myths about the "age of heroes."

Around 1200 B.C., an era of crisis and widespread destruction affected much of the eastern Mediterranean; both Mycenaean and Minoan civilization were destroyed, and Egypt and Mesopotamia were weakened in more indirect ways. In the era that followed, the new kingdoms of Israel and Judah formed and were conquered and temporarily absorbed by Mesopotamian empires. Oral traditions about Israel's early history later evolved into the Hebrew Bible.

TWO

Greek Civilization: Hellas and Hellenism

The Greeks may at first seem more familiar than the Egyptians or Mesopotamians because so many Western ideas trace back to them: ideas about government and politics, art and architecture, literature and philosophy. The concept of democracy, the nude figure in art, and the Western approach to history as a discipline all trace back to the Greeks.

But while many aspects of Greek culture have been influential over time, it is also part of the historian's job to recognize the ways in which the Greek world was different from the modern one. Consider one famous Greek monument, the Parthenon of Athens. This building may look familiar for several reasons: It has become the symbol of classical Greek civilization, which is perceived as part of the Western heritage. Nineteenth- and twentieth-century Western architects admired classical Greek styles and periodically revived them, so that many modern public buildings resemble the Parthenon in a superficial way. The Greeks also developed aesthetic theories of correct proportions and compensation for optical illusions that were applied to the Parthenon and seem modern today.

But it is also possible to view the Parthenon in another way. It was constructed entirely of marble blocks, some of them very large. Each piece had to be transported several miles from Mount Pentelicus to the northeast of the city, then precisely carved to fit into the spot where it would be located. In this sense the Parthenon is a megalithic monument more similar to Stonehenge than to modern buildings constructed in utilitarian fashion of brick, wood, or concrete. It is familiar and foreign at the same time. Despite their cultural influence, the Greeks were not necessarily more "like us" than other premodern societies. Their dazzling cultural sophistication impressed and influenced all who encountered them, but a modern observer transported back to classical Athens might find it a strange, primitive environment.

The Parthenon of Athens was constructed between 447 and 432 B.C. Like the other buildings on the acropolis, a hill that was the city's most important sacred precinct, it was didicated to Athena. It is a sophisticated example of the Doric order of Greek architecture. (*Photo by Susan P. Mattern-Parkes*)

The Dark Age

After the fall of Bronze Age civilization around 1200 B.C., many Mycenaean sites were abandoned or declined dramatically in population. In contrast to the tombs, palaces, and citadels of Greece's early kings—some of which remain astounding sights even today—the architecture of the Dark Age that followed is much simpler. The Greeks lost the art of writing; their memories of the Bronze Age evolved over the centuries as oral traditions and continued to evolve after writing was rediscovered in the eighth century B.C. It is no wonder that, in their minds, the Bronze Age took shape as an era of myth. Their Bronze Age heritage, and the mysterious and devastating destruction of early Greek civilization, was the background for the later evolution of Greek culture.

Population Decline and Dark Age Culture

After the collapse of Mycenaean civilization, the population of the Greek peninsula declined steeply. The number of known Dark Age sites is very small compared to Mycenaean sites, and the Dark Age settlements that have

IMPORTANT DATES AND PERIODS IN GREEK HISTORY

ca. 2000–1200 B.C.	**Mycenaean Age**
*1184 B.C.	Fall of Troy
ca. 1200–800 B.C.	**Dark Age**
ca. 800–480 B.C.	**Archaic Age**
776 B.C.	First Olympic games
594/3 B.C.	Solon's archonship
508/7 B.C.	Reforms of Cleisthenes
480–323 B.C.	**Classical Age**
480 B.C.	Battle of Salamis: Greeks defeat Persians
447–432 B.C.	Construction of Parthenon
431–404 B.C.	Peloponnesian War
399 B.C.	Trial of Socrates
338 B.C.	Battle of Chaeronea: Victory of Philip II of Macedon
331 B.C.	Foundation of Alexandria
323 B.C.–31 B.C.	**Hellenistic Age**
323 B.C.	Death of Alexander the Great
31 B.C.	Battle of Actium: Octavian defeats M. Antonius and Cleopatra VII

An asterisk (*) indicates that the date is traditional.

been found are smaller in size—even the largest of them probably had populations of less than five hundred. Perhaps as a result of harsh conditions on the mainland, many Greeks migrated across the Aegean Sea to the western coast of Asia Minor, which the Greeks called **Ionia.**

The end of the Mycenaean period was also the beginning of the Iron Age in Greece. Around 1050 B.C., iron began to replace bronze for weapons and utensils. (Later, its duller, heavier, and harder character compared to bronze inspired the poet Hesiod to use the term "Iron Age" to describe his own era of decline from the glorious age of heroes.) The art of writing was lost in the Dark Age, and Greeks no longer built structures in stone.

Lefkandi

The main exception to the overall impression of poverty and isolation in the Dark Age is the cemetery complex at Lefkandi on the island of Euboea. Some of the graves excavated there contained art objects and jewelry imported from Cyprus and the Near East. Archaeologists also discovered a large building with a surrounding colonnade, in which the remains of an adult man and woman were buried together with four horses and a variety of rich grave goods, including some in gold and silver. Clearly, this couple had a great deal of status in their community. The building itself was constructed of mud brick and timber, the same materials used for other structures of the time, but it is very large—measuring 164 feet long and 46 feet wide, it is by far the largest known building from the Dark Age. But Lefkandi remains an exceptional Dark Age site. From the rest of the Greek world, material remains are few, artifacts are simple, and evidence of trade with other areas of the Mediterranean world is scanty.

Homer and Oral Poetry

Nevertheless, it is in the Dark Age that the exceptionally rich mythic culture of the Greek world first developed. The oral traditions of this culture would normally be lost to us forever; but in the early Archaic period (ca. 800 B.C.), parts of this tradition crystallized in two great poems, the *Iliad* and the *Odyssey*, attributed to a poet named Homer. The poems recount episodes in the legendary ten-year war between the Greeks and Trojans. They are early examples of the genre of poetry called **epic**. In antiquity this word merely referred to the type of six-footed meter Homer used, but today it signifies a poem that tells the great deeds of heroes or gods.

In the *Iliad*, the Greek hero Achilles withdraws from the war in anger when king Agamemnon seizes his favorite concubine, the captive Briseis. But when his best friend Patroclus attempts to take his place in the fighting and is killed, Achilles turns his anger against his killer, the Trojan hero Hector. The poem emphasizes the importance of honor, vengeance, and feud in the society Homer imagines—including blood feud, as Achilles seeks to avenge his friend's death. But it also suggests a society in which conflicts could be resolved peacefully through gift exchange and where assemblies, courts, and other communal institutions existed side-by-side with an individualistic code of honor.

The *Odyssey* tells the story of Odysseus, king of Ithaca, whose journey home from Troy after the war becomes a ten-year ordeal after he angers the sea-god Poseidon. Odysseus encounters monsters such as the primitive, man-eating Cyclops and is seduced by an array of female characters, such as the witch Circe, who turns his crew into pigs. At home, a horde of suitors besieges his faithful wife Penelope; in the end Odysseus returns to slaughter them all in a bloody climactic scene. But while the *Iliad* emphasizes the public feuds of warrior heroes, the *Odyssey* offers more insight into private and domestic life. Odysseus' own household comprises his wife and son, female domestic slaves and male agricultural workers, and "guests" to be entertained and showered with gifts. Good guests offered gifts in return, cementing friendships that could last generations.

The original composer of the poems was probably not literate (legend related that Homer was blind, and thus could neither read nor write). While it is likely that the poems took shape around 800 B.C., it is not clear when they were actually written down; this was perhaps not until much later. The written texts also continued to evolve and did not take their current form until the second century B.C., when they were edited by the great scholars of Hellenistic Alexandria (see p. 113).

Certain features of the poems long puzzled scholars, especially Homer's repetition of phrases and sometimes of whole passages—for example, descriptions of sacrifices or scenes of arrival or departure. These kinds of repetition do not make sense in a composition that is intended to be read; they are more characteristic of oral works, such as songs. In the 1930s a scholar named Milman Parry changed the way we understand Homer when he observed illiterate bards in Serbia who sang epic poetry. He found that they composed their poems by drawing on a vast stock of standard phrases, themes, and stories, which they wove into songs before the eyes and ears of their audience. He realized that Homer must have been doing something similar. Homer's poems crystallized a fraction of the mass of poetic material that was available to him: the complex mythology that had grown around the memory of the Bronze Age, each story with innumerable large or subtle variants; and an array of heroes, gods, monsters, and minor divinities. Homer also drew on a host of specific words and turns of phrase suitable to the poems' meter—in fact, an entire language that was specific to epic poetry. The unwritten mass of epic tradition from which his poems were formed was the most important legacy of the Dark Age. In a society without writing, culture was transmitted through bards like Homer.

The Archaic Age: Hellas and the City

Beginning around 900 B.C., grave goods from some sites in central Greece show that trade with non-Greek peoples and especially with the Phoenicians began to revive; economically and culturally, Greece became inextricably entwined with the rest of the eastern Mediterranean world. The Greeks were using a version of the Phoenician alphabet by about 740 B.C. Some of the myths that the poet Hesiod records in his *Theogony*, or "birth of the gods" (ca. 700 B.C.), echo themes in Hittite and Akkadian texts. Egyptian monumental architecture and stone sculpture probably influenced the development of the Greek temple and of Greek sculptures of *kouroi* and *korai* (see later in this chapter). But while the Greeks, like all civilizations, were profoundly transformed by their contacts with others, they in turn transformed the ideas and techniques that they learned in distinctly Greek ways.

Demographic revival accompanied cultural revival. Around 800 B.C., the population of the Greek peninsula began to increase: Not only does the number of known settlements rise, but the population of previously settled areas like Attica increased dramatically as well. This trend continued throughout the Archaic period until, in the Classical Age, Greece was populated more densely than at any time afterward until the late nineteenth century.

Perhaps partly because of the strain that the rapidly expanding population placed on land, the Greeks began to found "colonies" in new areas of the Mediterranean world. Greek cities emerged in southern Italy, on Sicily, and on the coast of the Black Sea. The Greeks even settled in places as distant as the Crimean Peninsula in what is now Ukraine, Emporium in Spain, and Cyrene in modern Libya.

Hellas

The Greek word for "Greece" was and is **Hellas.** The word and the concept emerged in the archaic age, when Greek communities began to trace their descent to a common mythical ancestor, Hellen. Later the historian Thucydides would observe, correctly, that Homer did not use "Hellas" in this sense.*

Who was a Greek, a "Hellene"? The question is a complicated one, like all questions of ethnic identity. The Greek word *ethnos* meant "tribe" or "people"; the Romans used the Latin words *gens* and *natio* to express the same concept. But what does it mean to belong to a "people" (or a "tribe" or "nation")? In the nineteenth and early twentieth centuries, scholars believed that ethnicity was easy to define and identify. People who spoke the same language, practiced the same religion, and produced similar art objects shared an ethnicity and a presumed biological kinship. But in the mid-twentieth century some scholars began to see problems with this approach.†Peoples who were culturally very similar could perceive themselves—and be perceived by others—as different; while others who were culturally diverse perceived themselves as one people. Researchers began to see ethnicity less as an objective reality and more as a way that people describe themselves. But although ethnicity is a social construct rather than a natural and immutable thing, it is nevertheless real. The ways in which people define themselves and others shape their social interactions and can even lead to violence and war.

The Greek definition of Hellas was not geographic. It did not mainly refer to a specific area, such as the Greek peninsula or the Aegean basin; Hellas was wherever Greeks could be found. In the archaic period, Greeks mainly defined the Hellenic community in terms of a supposed kinship relationship, descent from Hellen. Language was also important from an early stage, and the word **barbaros** ("barbarian"), which eventually came to signify any non-Greek, imitated the nonsense sound of a foreign language to the Greek ear.

But the idea of Hellas was still nascent in the archaic period. For example, although the Greeks partly appealed to a common language to define Hellenism, they also recognized that not all Hellenes spoke the same kind of

---

*The word translated as "Greeks" in the quotation that begins this book is Homer's *Danaoi,* which is one of several terms he uses to indicate the Greek army.

†The work of Fredrik Barth, in *Ethnic Groups and Boundaries: The Social Organization of Cultural Difference,* London: Allen & Unwin, 1969, has been especially influential.

Archaic and Classical Hellas

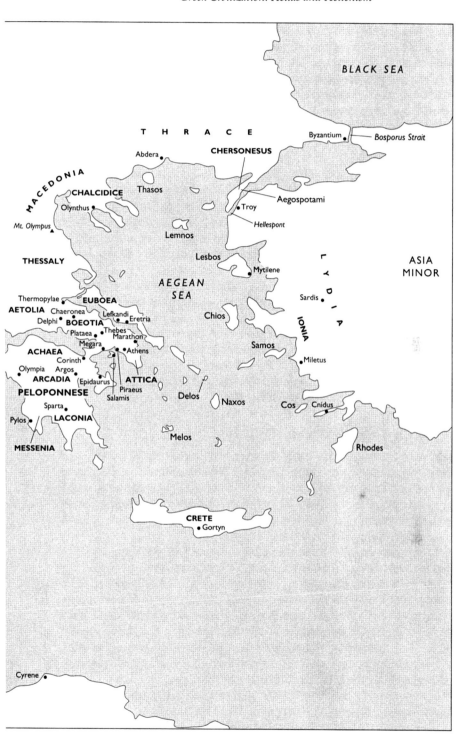

Greek. They identified four main dialects of their language; modern scholars count four or five (not the same ones), and it is not clear that speakers of different dialects could understand one another well or at all. On an even more local level, practically every city spoke its own variant of its dialect and had its own alphabet, its own system of weights and measures, its own army, and its own laws. The focus of one's identity might be a city, or a regional ethnic group, not to mention one's family, clan, or even social class; archaic Greeks may have only dimly perceived themselves as Greek.

But in the archaic period some cultural institutions evolved that were common to Hellas as a whole. The great "Panhellenic" sanctuaries arose in this era; they were religious sites visited by all Greeks, sponsoring festivals and competitions in which all Greeks participated. They include Olympia in the western Peloponnese, where the first athletic competitions were held (according to tradition) in 776 B.C., and the famous sanctuary and oracle of Apollo at Delphi, which was considered the "navel" or center of the Greek world.

There were other distinctly Hellenic traditions of the archaic period. Homer's epics were recited widely in the Greek world; they were not composed in any one dialect, but in a unique poetic language that combined elements of several dialects. The Trojan war came to be perceived as the first Panhellenic venture, a glorious event in which all Greeks had participated.

Some traditions in architecture and in sculpture transcended the boundaries of city or region. The hoplite style of warfare and organization into communities called *poleis* also characterized the Greek way of life.

War and the City: The Rise of the *Polis*

The Greek word for "city" was **polis.** To the Greeks, the idea of the city did not mainly suggest a geographic location, or monumental architecture (although both of these played a part in how the *polis* was imagined), but a community—a group of citizens. These were not only the people living within the city's walls, but also those who farmed the surrounding land within the city's territory. These citizens *were* the city.

The *polis* that developed by the end of the archaic period was strikingly egalitarian in some ways. Citizens were ruled by other citizens, not by a king or a hereditary aristocracy, according to the rules of what the Greeks called a **politeia.** This word may be translated as "constitution," but it also meant "body of citizens," reflecting the idea that all citizens had a share in the government of the city. Political institutions usually included a board of annually elected officials, a council of some kind (often of elders or ex-magistrates), and, most importantly, an assembly of the full citizen body. Citizenship became the most important status distinction in the *polis*.

But who were the citizens? The Greeks made a strong connection between citizenship and military service: Those who defended the city in war also had full rights of participation in its constitution. Women could not be citizens in this sense, nor could anyone below the warrior class. Every city had its own army, and in a sense, the army *was* the city. In archaic Greece, this meant that the heavy-armed infantryman, the *hoplite* (see below), was the typical citizen of the *polis*.

The concept of the city as it eventually developed included the idea of the equality of all citizens, but these egalitarian ideas evolved slowly. In the early Archaic period, some cities were still ruled by narrow elites, and constitutions reserved many privileges (such as the right to hold certain offices) for the highest economic classes. But eventually the Greeks' distinctive idea of citizenship resulted in broader-based, more egalitarian governments as lower-class citizens struggled for political equality, and eventually succeeded in their aims.

Why did the Greeks develop this unique institution of the *polis*? Some scholars have argued that new developments in weaponry resulting in the hoplite style of infantry warfare led to the egalitarian structure of Greek cities. However, it seems more likely that changes in technology followed social and military changes instead of causing them. On the other hand, economic factors were probably important in the development of the *polis*. As in early Israel, the Greek economy was decentralized and its basic unit was the family farm. The landowning peasant who was the backbone of the Greek economy became the warrior-citizen of the archaic *polis*.

Hoplite Warfare. The characteristic style of warfare in archaic Greece was infantry warfare. Infantrymen were called **hoplites** after the type of heavy shield that they used (the *hoplon*). The design of the shield's grip was such that it protected half of its owner's body and extended outward to protect half of the body of the man standing to the owner's right. It was designed for use in a rigid formation called a **phalanx.**

The full panoply, which developed over centuries, included the shield, a bronze helmet that covered the head and face, a heavy bronze corselet, bronze greaves that protected the knees and shins, and an iron-tipped spear used for thrusting at close quarters. Hoplites also carried a short sword as a back-up weapon. This equipment was cumbersome, and useful only in pitched battles on flat ground.

Hoplites were usually required to furnish their own armor. The normal qualification for hoplite status was a property qualification—they were landowners. But hoplite armor, while not cheap, was not exceptionally expensive either; most landowners in a given *polis* probably belonged to the hoplite class. The hoplite style of warfare reflects the importance of the landowning peasant in the Greek *polis* and the egalitarian ideas behind the *polis*—all hoplites had similar equipment and fought side-by-side.

How Big Was a Typical City? In the Archaic period, the landowning, hoplite class formed the citizen body of most *poleis*. Later, the Greeks would call this type of constitution **oligarchy,** meaning "the rule of the few," but this label is somewhat misleading as the "few" might be a large number (perhaps even a majority) of the city's adult male residents. However, citizenship was

This vase dates to about 630 B.C. and is an early depiction of hoplite warfare. The two armies face each other in phalanx formation; the unique grip of the hoplite shield is illustrated in the foremost figure on the left. (Scala/Art Resource, NY)

exclusive as well as inclusive: Those disqualified from citizenship included slaves, the landless poor, and resident aliens or **metics.** (The population of metics was probably small in most cities, but very large in Athens.) Women were excluded from political participation, although they might share in the social status and religious privileges of citizen birth.

Population statistics are very rare in ancient Greek sources. Athens, the city that we know most about, may have had fifty thousand male citizens at its height in the mid-fifth century B.C. The general population (including citizens and non-citizens) of Attica, the territory of Athens, may have been as high as 300,000, but that is just a guess. And Athens was by far the largest Greek city in the classical period. It is likely that the citizen population of the average city numbered in the hundreds or low thousands.

The Spartan **Politeia.**   The city of Sparta came to embody the ideal of the hoplite *polis*, although it was unusual in several ways. The literary sources on early Sparta are problematic because most of them date to the Classical period or later and reflect the influence of Sparta's image as an ideal warrior state preserving conservative values. Archaeological evidence for archaic Sparta is scanty and difficult to interpret.

In the early Archaic period, the Spartans conquered the nearby territory of Messenia and reduced its inhabitants to the status of **helots.** The helots were owned collectively by the Spartan state; they farmed the land and provided a quota of produce to their masters, the Spartan citizens. The helots greatly outnumbered the citizens, and occasional violent revolts punctuated early Spartan history. In response, the Spartans developed the political institutions and way of life that made them renowned throughout the Greek world for their *eunomia,* or "good laws." Although they attributed their *politeia* to a mythical lawgiver named Lycurgus, it probably evolved gradually over the course of the Archaic period.

Two kings served mainly as generals leading the army. The Spartans were unusual in having a hereditary kingship (not to mention a double kingship); in other Greek cities, such as Athens, the "king" was an elected official. The rest of its political institutions resembled those of other *poleis.* The chief magistrates were five "ephors" elected annually in the assembly of Spartan citizens, by acclamation (shouting). A council of elders over the age of sixty, who were also elected and who held office for life, prepared business for the assembly and had some judicial powers. All Spartans were in theory eligible for election to the ephorate and also the council, although in fact the council was an aristocratic body in which a few leading families predominated.

In theory, all Spartan citizens were not only equal but alike—they called themselves *homoioi,* which means "similar." They were full-time warriors who devoted themselves to military training, while the helots worked the land and provided them with food. Private life and the family were subordinated to the warrior state. From the age of seven, boys were organized into "packs" and subjected to harsh discipline and a state-run education in the traditional subjects of music, gymnastics, and military exercises. From the ages of twenty to thirty they lived in barracks, even if they were married. For their entire adult lives, until the age of sixty, they continued to eat at the barracks, which were called *syssitia*—literally, mess-halls or eating clubs. Membership in one of these mess-halls required a monthly contribution of produce and was the main criterion of Spartan citizenship.

Spartan women were famous (or notorious) for having more freedom than the women of other cities. Ancient sources record with amazement that girls received an education similar to that of boys, emphasizing physical training and dancing, and even exercised naked like boys. Spartan women of the Archaic period were prominent among the victors in the special women's footrace at the Olympics. Unlike women at Athens, many Spartan women owned land.

This is the image of the Spartans that dominates the literary sources of the Classical period and later. The reality did not necessarily conform to the ideal. There is evidence, for example, that some Spartans were wealthier than others (that is, not all Spartans were economically "similar") and that an aristocracy of noble families existed. But archaeology may corroborate the idea that that an austere warrior society arose and choked what was previously a rich and varied culture. In the early sixth century B.C., the poet Alcman wrote graceful, imaginative lyrics for choruses of young girls. Figured pottery and fine bronze vessels were produced by skilled craftsmen, and Spartans were prominent on the Olympic victor-lists. All of these aspects of culture—poetry, figured pottery, fine bronzework, and athletics—were in decline by the end of the Archaic period. Nevertheless, the archaeological record is difficult to read, and scholars today debate whether changes in Sparta's material culture were related to a new, more austere regime.

Tyranny and Democracy in Archaic Athens.   Our main source of information about the government of archaic Athens is a document called *The Constitution of the Athenians*, written some time in the fourth century B.C. and attributed to the philosopher Aristotle (although he probably is not the real author). Because few other sources for sixth-century Athens survive, it can be difficult to reconstruct the details of what happened and the conditions that led to change, but the basic outline of events is reasonably clear.

In 594 B.C., in a period of social crisis, a reformer named Solon held the chief magistracy at Athens, called the **archonship.** In his poetry, Solon described his reforms as a compromise between the demands of the rich and those of the poor. He abolished enslavement for debt and liberated the *hektemoroi*, probably sharecroppers or serfs. Solon also made constitutional reforms, organizing the Athenian citizens into four property classes. He allowed even the lowest class of poor or landless **thetes** the right to vote in the assembly and the law-court (although he restricted the right to hold high office to the richest classes). From this time forward, Athens was unusual in having no property requirement for citizenship; free birth from a citizen father was the only requirement.

Solon's changes did not put an end to violent conflict at Athens. A few decades later, in 560 B.C., a leader named Pisistratus emerged at the head of one of three warring factions in Attica; he perhaps represented the interests of the lower citizen classes. He briefly seized power, but was expelled, only to return again in 546 B.C. In 525 he died, and his sons, Hippias and Hipparchus, ruled after him.

Greek sources label Pisistratus and his sons **tyrants.** This was a foreign word signifying individuals who ruled over Greek cities, and in fact many cities, not just Athens, went through a period of one-man rule in the late seventh and sixth centuries B.C. Whether they ruled well or badly, whether they seized power or inherited it or were appointed by a higher authority (such as the Persian emperor; see p. 75), the Greeks called these rulers tyrants, not kings: The idea of a king ruling over a *polis*, which was generally governed by its citizen body, was an anomaly. For this reason and because tyrants were often associated with arbitrary and cruel behavior, the word had negative connotations. Very little is known about most of the tyrants, and it is difficult to generalize about the reasons they came to power; these were perhaps different in each city.

The Constitution of the Athenians describes Pisistratus' rule as mild and beneficial to the common farmer; he established traveling judges to bring justice to the countryside and gave loans to impoverished peasants. The Athenian economy boomed, as black-figure pottery from Attica came to dominate the market, and coinage was first introduced to Attica at this time. The tyrants were also responsible for great public building projects and the elaboration of city festivals. Legend told that the first tragedies were performed under Pisistratus at the City Dionysia, a festival in honor of the god Dionysus. On the hill called the Acropolis, he or his sons built a new temple to Athena Polias, the goddess who presided over Athens' most important religious event, the Panathenaic festival. The Pisistratids may have constructed another, larger temple on the site later occupied by the Parthenon. Southeast of the Acropolis, they began an enormous temple to Olympian Zeus that was not completed until Roman times.

Pisistratus and his sons ruled until 510 B.C. In 514 Hipparchus was assassinated in a conspiracy led by two lovers named Harmodius and Aristogiton, and in 510 aristocrats of the exiled Alcmaeonid family expelled Hippias with the help of the Spartans. Then in 508 B.C., another round of constitutional changes took place under the leadership of a reformer named Cleisthenes, himself a member of the Alcmaeonid clan.

Later, the Athenians would look back to Cleisthenes' reforms as the beginning of what they called **democracy** at Athens. "Democracy" means "rule of the people"; the **demos,** like "the people," in English, was either the whole citizen body or the poorer classes specifically. Athens' *politeia* had contained some democratic elements since Solon—especially the participation of the thetes on jury-courts and in the assembly. Under Cleisthenes the constitution became more democratic, and in the Classical period, Athens was the largest, most powerful, and probably most radical democracy in Hellas.

Cleisthenes changed the way citizens were organized; he retained Solon's four economic classes, but he abolished the political organization of citizens into four tribes. He replaced them with ten new tribes, each composed of a number of "demes," small communities to which each citizen belonged. His intention was perhaps to create more social equality by breaking up old kinship structures. Cleisthenes also replaced Solon's "Council of 400"—a body which we know little about—with a "Council of 500" to which each deme contributed one or more members (based on its population). The Council prepared business for the assembly and handled the city's finances. Cleisthenes also may have invented the odd institution of **ostracism:** In a special assembly, each citizen would write on an ostrakon (pot sherd) the name of someone to be expelled from the city; the "winner" had to leave Athens for ten years. Many ostraka inscribed with the names of Athenian statesman survive; handwriting analysis shows that some of them were mass-produced by a few people and distributed to the crowd.

Literature and Culture in Archaic Hellas

In the Archaic period as later, myth infused most of Greek literature. Around 700 B.C., the poet Hesiod composed his *Theogony*, which traces the genealogy of the gods from primeval Chaos to Zeus, Hera and the other deities that

ruled from Mount Olympus. His poem attempts to synthesize and rational-
ize what must have been a complicated mass of mythical traditions—to produce his fairly coherent account, he must have resolved contradictions and
rejected variants in the stories he used. Although Hesiod still relied on traditional, mythic explanations of the natural world, he applied critical methods
to the material.

Hesiod also wrote *Works and Days*, a **didactic** or "teaching" poem that sets
down rules for the small farmer. This work is an important source for the
social and economic history of the Archaic period, as it describes life on a typical family farm.

The fascinating genre of **lyric** poetry also flourished during the Archaic
period. Lyric poetry is difficult to define—like epic, it was performed to
music, but it used different types of meter and might be sung by an individual or danced by a chorus. Its subjects are widely varied and reflect the contexts in which it was performed (religious festivals, marriages, funerals, and
private parties) as well as aristocratic life and values. Themes range from war
and politics, to myth and the gods, love and sex, and athletics; the poet Pin-
dar, who wrote in the early fifth century B.C., celebrated and idealized the athletes of the great Panhellenic competitions.

One of the most important themes in archaic poetry is love. While some
early archaic poets romanticized heterosexual love, later authors wrote of
homosexual love between mature men and youths—the passionate and
erotic* dimensions of love that they celebrated were to be found here, and not
in heterosexual love leading to marriage. The ideal love object was an adolescent, but still beardless, youth—as in the case of female *parthenoi* (discussed later in this section), sexual desirability is associated with a fleeting
time of life. The asymmetrical relationship between a mature, active pursuer
and a young, passive love object remained central to the Greek idea of erotic
love throughout the Classical, Hellenistic, and even Roman periods.

Although we know the names of several female poets of the Archaic age,
the only one whose works survive is Sappho, who wrote on the island of Les-
bos toward the end of the seventh century B.C. Little is known about her
except what she reveals in her poetry—and even this is difficult to interpret,
because ancient (and modern) poets do not necessarily write about real experiences. Nevertheless, careful analysis of her work can illuminate its social
context. Her poems were composed for choruses of young girls—**parthenoi**[†],
girls of marriageable age but not yet married. They came from far and wide
to learn to sing and dance in Sappho's chorus before returning to their home-
lands to be married. Her aristocratic pupils hoped to emerge as graceful, tal-
ented, and cultivated women and desireable mates. But dancing in Sappho's
chorus was also an important rite of passage; living apart from men and
bonding with their peers, the dancers prepared to take their place as adult

---

*The word "erotic" derives from **Eros,** which in Greek signified either the young
god of sexual desire or sexual desire itself.

[†]*Parthenos* is sometimes translated as "virgin."

The Written Record

THE YOUNG WOMEN OF SAPPHO'S CHORUS

A large body of Sappho's work circulated in antiquity, but little remains today. This fragmentary poem survives on a parchment dating to the sixth century A.D. A close reading offers insights about the members of Sappho's chorus—where they came from, for what purpose, and how they felt about one another.

The elaborate simile comparing the poem's subject to the moon is typical of Sappho's poetry, which takes its most powerful imagery from the natural world.

At Sardis
she often remembers us here
and how we lived

To her you were like a renowned goddess
and she enjoyed your dancing most of all.

Now in Lydia she is outstanding among women,
just as the rose-fingered moon when the sun has set

surpasses all the stars, and its light spreads
equally over the salty sea
and the many-flowered fields;

in loveliness the dew gathers,
and the rose blooms, and the delicate thyme
and the flowering honey-clover.

Though she wanders abroad, she often remembers
gentle Atthis,* and her tender heart
is consumed with longing. (Sappho, fragment 96)

---

*Another girl in Sappho's chorus, mentioned in several of her poems.

---

women in society. The poems suggest that emotional bonds among the girls, and between the girls and Sappho, could be intense and even erotic in nature—some of the poems have sexual overtones.

Sculpture.　From several different parts of the Greek world, statues of young men, naked and beautiful, life-sized or larger, attest to one of the most important developments in archaic art: the large-scale nude sculpture. From a narrower area and in smaller numbers, statues of clothed young women—sometimes life-sized but often smaller—also survive; these statues offer an opportunity to compare artistic views of the male and female body.

Art historians call the male sculptures **kouroi** (sing.: *kouros*), which is simply a word for "young man." In antiquity, they would be found in cemeteries, as grave-markers, or near temples as dedications to the gods. The statues are strangely anonymous. Their faces seem to be ideal types rather than portraits; they carry no items or "attributes" that would help identify them; they

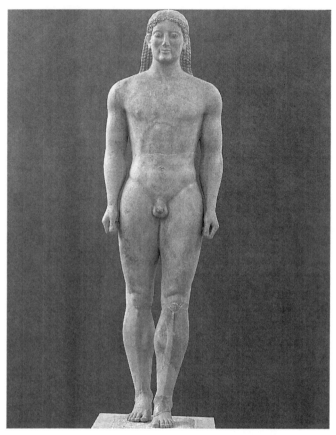

The Anavyssos or "Kroisos" kouros, from Attica, dates to about 530 B.C. It was a grave marker. The inscription on its base read, "Stop and mourn at the tomb of dead Kroisos, whom clamorous Ares slew in the front line." (Erich Lessing/Art Resource, NY)

are always young, regardless of the age of the deceased. They always stand in the same pose, arms at their sides, striding with the left foot forward, staring straight ahead, their hair arranged in long, straight braids, their facial expression a mysterious "archaic smile." In a way, they capture the spirit of the Archaic age—representing the idealized young warrior or athlete and the standard of homoerotic beauty.

Freestanding sculptures that portray young girls—**korai,** "maidens"—survive in smaller numbers; most come from the Acropolis of Athens, where they once stood among the religious dedications that crowded the sacred precinct. Damaged in the Persian War (see p. 75) and deliberately buried, they are very well-preserved; traces of paint even remain on some *korai*.

Like *kouroi, korai* are young and probably represent an ideal of beauty. But they are less anonymous than *kouroi*; they vary slightly in pose, and some

This kore *from the Athenian acropolis dates to about 520 B.C. She pulls her skirt tight around her legs with one hand and raises her other hand to display an unknown object. (Scala/Art Resource, NY)*

korai hold objects that may identify them as individuals (for example, by associating them with a goddess such as Athena or Persephone) or give a sense of context to the sculpture. *Korai* are clothed, and much artistry is devoted to the portrayal of the drapery that enfolds them. This emphasis on clothing probably reflects the conventions of Greek society, which accepted male nudity in public but jealously guarded the sexuality of respectable women and girls. The way in which the bodies of some *korai* are outlined under tightly drawn skirts suggests they had an erotic appeal—but one that was more coy than that of the *kouroi* and depended on their costume rather than their nudity. The sculptures offer us another image of the young, marriageable *parthenos* who is the subject of Sappho's poems.

Architecture.   The stone temple has its origins in the Archaic period. Temples were the earliest monumental buildings constructed in ancient Greek cities; the temple gave the city a religious center, a focus for the festivals and cults that helped give social cohesion to the city.

Greek temples were rectangular in shape, surrounded by columns and a low flight of steps on all four sides, and had a pitched, tiled roof. By tradition they faced east. Each temple housed its god's **cult-statue**—the image of the god that occupied the main interior room (cella). Offerings to the god by hopeful or grateful worshippers were displayed in and around the temple. The festivals, sacrifices, processions, and contests with which the gods were worshipped took place in the open air, in the religious space around the temples, not inside them.

The temple was the first, and remained one of the most important, distinctly Hellenic forms of architecture. But different styles of temple were built in different regions. In the Archaic period two main styles or "orders" of temple evolved. Greeks on the mainland built temples in the **Doric** style—simpler than the **Ionic** style, which is named for the region (Ionia) in which it arose. Ionic temples had more slender columns and elaborate decoration than Doric temples. In the West, the Greeks of Sicily and southern Italy built temples in the Doric style, but with variations particular to their region.

The temple was a focus for Greek art, especially sculpture. Votive offerings placed in or near the temple could take the form of *kouroi* and *korai*, plaques with relief sculpture, or statuettes (but the Greeks dedicated a huge variety of items to the gods, from tools and weapons to clothes and baked goods). The temple itself was often decorated with sculpture, especially the gable or **pediment**.

Philosophy.   In the sixth century B.C., a new way of thought arose in parts of the Greek world—the beginning of what the Greeks later called **philosophy**, which means "love of wisdom." Philosophers began to investigate nature in a new way, without invoking the traditions of myth and its vast, complicated array of gods. Although they did not deny the gods' existence, the philosophers thought about them in more abstract ways—rejecting the gods of mythology, who looked and acted like humans. Some archaic philosophers wrote down their arguments, in verse or in prose, but their works survive only in the fragmentary quotations of later wtiters.

Philosophy especially flourished in the city of Miletus, in Ionia. It was perhaps the influence of Eastern civilizations—especially Mesopotamian civilization and its traditions in astronomy and mathematics—that inspired the first Greek philosophers. Thales of Miletus is the earliest of the Ionian philosophers, and one of the most mysterious, since he apparently did not write down any of his ideas. Legend told that he predicted an eclipse (scholars date this event to 585 B.C.) and calculated the height of the Egyptian pyramids by measuring their shadows. He is said to have argued that the world floats on water, and that water is the fundamental element from which the universe was created.

The temple of Apollo at Corinth was constructed around 540 B.C. to replace an even older building. The relatively flat, sharply angled column capitals are typical of early Doric temples. (Scala/Art Resource, NY)

Perhaps the most influential philosopher of the Archaic period was Pythagoras, who was born on Samos, on the Ionian coast, but moved to the city of Croton in Italy around 530 B.C. Like Thales, he wrote nothing, and because an especially vast body of legend later grew up around him, it is difficult to separate his ideas from those of his followers in later generations. One of his genuine contributions was the idea of "metempsychosis," the transfer of the soul to another body after death, an idea that may have reached Greece from India; the Greeks themselves believed that he was inspired, in this and in many other things, by Egyptian culture. Unlike the other early philosophers, Pythagoras was a charismatic, religious figure. He could work miracles, such as being in two places at once. He advocated a disciplined way of life, with restrictions on diet, clothing, and behavior, that distinguished his followers from ordinary Greeks, and he established a "school" or tradition of learning that long outlasted his lifetime. The discoveries in geometry, number theory, and music that later generations attributed to him were probably made by his followers in the Classical period.

The Classical Age: The Empire and Culture of Athens

In 480 B.C. an event occurred that had profound effects on ancient Greek history and culture: the naval defeat of Xerxes, king of Persia, who had invaded Greece with a great force. As a result of this victory, the city of Athens, which led the Greek resistance, built an empire; a new, broader form of citizenship—democracy—took shape; the idea of Hellas, and of the foreigner or barbarian, crystallized; and the story of the war was told in the first work to be called "history"—the work of Herodotus.

In the eyes of later generations, the culture that flourished in fifth-century Athens represented the height of Greek civilization. It could be argued that the Archaic period was more important because institutions such as the *polis*, the temple, and the tradition of epic poetry all evolved then, or that Hellenistic developments in philosophy or medicine were ultimately more influential. But since antiquity both Greeks and non-Greeks have seen in the literature, art, and architecture of classical Athens the fullest expression of Greek culture.

The Persian Empire

In the fifth century B.C., the entire Near East from Asia Minor, Syria, and Egypt all the way to modern Afghanistan and Pakistan was united under the rule of the Persians. At the time, their empire was the largest in world history.

The Persians' homeland was in the southeastern Zagros Mountains, in modern Iran. They spoke an Indo-European language, the ancestor of modern Persian, which they wrote using a cuneiform script. Only a few written sources in Old Persian remain, however; these are mainly monumental inscriptions. The administration used other Near Eastern languages, including Aramaic and Elamite, for its records and documents, and many of these survive. Excavations of important Persian cities, such as Susa and Persepolis near the Persian Gulf, also provide valuable information on the Persian Empire. Sources in Greek and Hebrew, especially Herodotus, record some details of its early political history, but it is not clear how accurate these writings of outsiders really are.

The Persians rose to power under the leadership of King Cyrus II ("the Great"), who ruled from 559 to 530 B.C. Early in his reign, he conquered the Medes, whose empire or hegemony reached from their capital, Ecbatana (modern Hamadan in Iran) as far west as central Asia Minor. Cyrus went further and conquered the kingdom of Lydia, which controlled western Asia Minor (including the Greek cities of Ionia). In 539, he conquered Babylonia; it was he who allowed the Jewish exiles living there, as well as exiles of other nationalities, to return home. His son and successor, Cambyses, conquered Egypt, the last of the great Near Eastern kingdoms.

The next king, a usurper named Darius, expanded the empire westward, to Thrace and some Aegean islands; he also campaigned unsuccessfully in the Black Sea region against tribes that the Greeks called "Scythians."

The Persian Empire was organized into provinces ruled by governors, or **satraps**. The Persians were flexible in the way that they administered their empire. In general, they allowed local power structures, as well as native laws and customs, to remain intact. As much as possible they worked with these institutions, not against them, to control their subjects and extract taxes from them. Local Greek aristocrats ruled over the Greek cities of Ionia as "tyrants," with Persian support.

The Persian Wars

In 499 B.C., in the reign of Darius, the Greek cities of Ionia revolted from the Persian Empire. The revolt was crushed after five years; the city of Miletus, which had led the uprising, was punished especially harshly. In the course of the revolt the Ionians had sacked and burnt Sardis, the capital of the satrapy of Lydia. In this, the city of Athens had played a small part—they had sent a few ships to Ionia in support of the revolt.

Later, the Greeks believed that when Darius invaded Attica in 490 B.C., he was seeking revenge for the destruction of Sardis. When his force landed at Marathon in northern Attica, it was met and routed by an Athenian hoplite army. Herodotus writes that while all ten Athenian generals were present at Marathon, one of them—Militades—provided the strategy and the leadership that won the battle.

At Marathon, the Athenians opposed the Persians alone, aided only by the tiny city of Plataea. They asked the Spartans for support, but the Spartans were observing a religious holiday and refused to send help. As yet it seemed impossible for the Greeks to combine in a military effort under a single leader, but the response to the next Persian attack was somewhat different.

In 480 B.C., Darius' successor, Xerxes, launched an invasion of Greece by land and sea. He bridged the strait of the Hellespont and marched his army through Thrace to the Greek peninsula; the navy accompanied the army, sailing along the coast. The size of the invading force awed the Greeks— Herodotus writes that it numbered over 2 million, an impossibly high figure. Many Greek cities, especially those in the north that could not be defended, surrendered without a struggle. But this time, a coalition of some Greek cities formed to oppose the Persians. The Spartans, because of their military reputation, commanded this unified army—but not without dissent and bickering from other cities. Even now, it was not easy for the Greeks to unite in a Panhellenic effort. Not all Greeks joined the resistance to Persia, and the alliance that did arise was an uneasy one.

The Greeks first attempted to stop the Persians at Thermopylae, a narrow pass between the mountains and the sea. They were unsuccessful; legend later told of the band of three hundred Spartans who remained to fight and die even after all was lost, a story that greatly contributed to Sparta's military mystique.

The city of Athens played the starring role in the final act of the Persian wars. After Thermopylae, central Greece could no longer be defended; rather than surrender, the Athenians evacuated their city and left it for the Persians to destroy. The Greek navy—to which the Athenians contributed more ships than any other city—inflicted a crushing defeat on the Persians in the Strait of Salamis, near Athens. Herodotus writes that it was an Athenian general, Themistocles, who devised the winning strategy of fighting in the narrow waters and who lured the Persians into the trap.

Herodotus: The First History

Herodotus finished his book about fifty years after the end of the war. In his first sentence, he uses the word *historiae* to describe its contents; in Greek, this word means "inquiries," and it is the origin of our word "history." Herodotus traveled far and wide gathering information; in the process of tracing the origins of the war, he recounts over two hundred years of Greek and Persian history and describes the geography and peoples of the entire known world.

Herodotus wrote decades after the last events he describes, in a world where oral tradition was by far the most usual way of preserving information. As a result, his stories sound like folktales to the modern reader. Most of them have characteristics that are typical of folktales: For example, the history is imbued with a mysterious and tragic fatalism, in which disastrous events balance ancient transgressions and ambiguous oracles come true in unexpected ways. Herodotus himself accepted this way of understanding history, and thus may strike modern readers as naive.

On the other hand, he did not simply repeat the stories he heard. He sometimes offers multiple versions of a story from different sources, implying that one should consider their biases when deciding what to believe. Sometimes he rejects a story as incredible or untrustworthy. He also gives thought to the limits of knowledge: For example, although he begins his work by reviewing mythical conflicts (such as the Trojan war) between Greeks and Asians, he suggests that this period is not truly knowable in the same way that more recent events are. Herodotus was the first to apply a method to the writing of history—diligent research, combined with a critical attitude toward the information he gathered.

Greeks and Barbarians

Herodotus looked to Homer's *Iliad* as one of his models: Homer, too, had written about a great war between a Greek force and an Eastern enemy. Although Homer had not emphasized the differences between the Greek and Trojan heroes in his poem (he portrays them worshipping the same gods and speaking the same language), the *Iliad* had always been one of the works that defined Greek identity. This is also one of the functions of Herodotus' work.

Its fascinating accounts of foreign peoples (including Egyptians, Persians, and Scythians) reflect new ideas about the foreigner or barbarian and about Hellenic identity.

The barbarian appears not only in Herodotus' history, but in other Greek literature of the Classical period: in the tragedies and comedies of fifth-century Athens and in philosophical and medical treatises. In describing barbarians, the Greeks indirectly described themselves—their image of foreign political institutions, religious practices, gender roles, even diet and clothing, reflects their ideas about the defining features of Greek culture. When describing the Persians, the Greeks emphasized their subjection to a single ruler—the despotic king Xerxes—and contrasted this with the "freedom" of the Greek *polis*. They portrayed the Persians as cowardly and weakened by an effeminate, luxurious lifestyle, while they thought of themselves as warlike, brave, and fortified by simple living. Greek ideas of "East" and "West," first formulated in the fifth century B.C., are still influential today.

Democracy and Empire: Athens at Its Height

The naval victory at Salamis demonstrated the power of a new kind of city-state: not the city of hoplite warriors and farmers, but a city that built and maintained a navy from a central fund of resources and manned it with its poorest citizens.

In the interval between the two Persian wars, the Athenians had made a historic decision: They used the income from silver mines in Attica to build a fleet of warships. By the time of the battle of Salamis, their fleet was larger than that of any other Greek city.

The Greek warship of Salamis and of the Classical period was the **trireme**. These were long, fast ships with bronze rams fitted to their prows; each was rowed by 170 oarsmen, arranged in three banks, and carried a small number of marines, archers, and sailors for a total crew of two hundred. Triremes fought by ramming one another at high speeds.

Naval warfare required large numbers of citizen-rowers. A fleet of one hundred ships needed a crew of twenty thousand to be fully manned. This is why democracy, with its broader definition of citizenship, was associated with naval warfare and vice-versa. Athenian oarsmen were drawn from the lowest property class, the *thetes*—those who were too poor to be ranked as hoplites.

The navy required money. Triremes were expensive to build, and their large crews had to be paid. Until the dissolution of their empire at the end of the Peloponnesian war, the Athenian fleet was financed mainly by the tribute that Athens collected from its allies and subjects. After that, the Athenians maintained a smaller fleet by means of taxes levied on the richest classes.

As the Athenians achieved dominance over the Aegean Sea with their navy, their *politeia* became more democratic. We do not know when some of the reforms took place, but by 400 B.C. Athens was a radical democracy. Any citizen, regardless of class, could speak at the assembly. Most offices were

The trireme Olympias *is a modern reconstruction designed by naval architect John Coates and built by the Greek navy in 1987. Triremes carried sails and used them to travel long distances, but in battle they were rowed by a large crew, as here.*   (Photo by Alexandra Guest, courtesy of the Trireme Trust)

probably open to all citizens. The city's nine chief magistrates—the archons— were appointed annually by lot; so were the members of the Council of 500 and the jurors who decided each year's innumerable court cases. Of the city's important officials, only the ten *strategoi* were elected; the Athenians considered election an undemocratic process because the rich tended to win more often than the poor. Citizens were paid for attending the assembly, for serving on the council, and for sitting on juries—measures designed to increase the participation of the poorest classes. The city's most important decisions were made in the assembly, by majority vote; the assembly met forty times a year, and at least six thousand citizens attended each meeting.

But as the *politeia* became more egalitarian, it also became more exclusive. In 451 B.C., the assembly passed a proposal that restricted citizenship to those with two Athenian parents. The class of citizens was effectively closed, and non-Athenians could only gain citizenship by special decree of the assembly.

From League to Empire.   When the Persians retreated from Greece in 479 B.C., the Greeks pursued the war on Persian territory. At first the Spartans continued to lead the Greek forces, but in 478 the Athenians took over. In the alliance they founded, each city was required to contribute either a quota of ships or a sum of money. The headquarters of the alliance and its treasury were located on the sacred island of Delos; for this reason modern scholars call it the "Delian League." Its members were mainly the Greek cities of the Aegean Islands and Ionia.

Gradually, the Athenians exercised more control over their allies. Some cities tried to leave the alliance and were subdued, sometimes brutally. Stripped of their navies, they were forced to contribute money (**tribute**) instead of ships. In 454 B.C., the alliance's treasury was moved to Athens. The Athenians came to think of the allies as their subjects, and the league as their empire.

In the early fifth century B.C., the Athenians ambitiously expanded their military power. They built a fortification wall around their city, and "Long Walls" that connected it to their port, Piraeus, four miles away. They won a stunning victory over the Persians at Eurymedon in Asia Minor, sent a large force to Egypt, and campaigned in Cyprus. In a conflict with Sparta and its allies, they conquered the territory of Boeotia on the Greek mainland. But they suffered setbacks too: The naval expedition to Egypt was destroyed in 453 B.C., and in 446 several allies revolted and the Spartans invaded at the same time. The Athenians were forced to abandon their control of Boeotia and sign a thirty-year truce with the Spartans.

One of the most prominent politicians in Athens at this time was Pericles. From about 443 to 431, he was elected *strategos* every year. He led democratic reforms to the Athenian *politeia* and socialized with some of Athens' leading intellectuals. The Parthenon and other monuments that stand on the Athenian acropolis were constructed on his proposal.

Culture in Imperial Athens

In the early Classical period, as Athens became Greece's largest, most powerful *polis*, the idea of the city suffused its culture. Pericles' building program celebrated the greatness of Athens, and the historian Thucydides cast the city as the hero of his tragic story of the Peloponnesian war. The city was a central theme in comedies and tragedies, which were produced at great civic festivals. Philosophers speculated about the origins of the city and its laws and taught their students the skills they needed to be political leaders.

The Acropolis and the Image of Athens. In antiquity as today, the most famous monuments of classical Greece were the temples constructed on the acropolis of Athens. All of these were dedicated to Athena, the city's patron goddess. The first to be built (447–432 B.C.) was also the largest and most famous: the Parthenon, or temple to Athena *Parthenos* (meaning "unmarried maiden"; see p. 68). While the Parthenon was still under construction, a monumental entryway called the Propylaea (meaning "gateway") was begun, but never finished. A small Ionic temple to Athena Nike (meaning "victory")

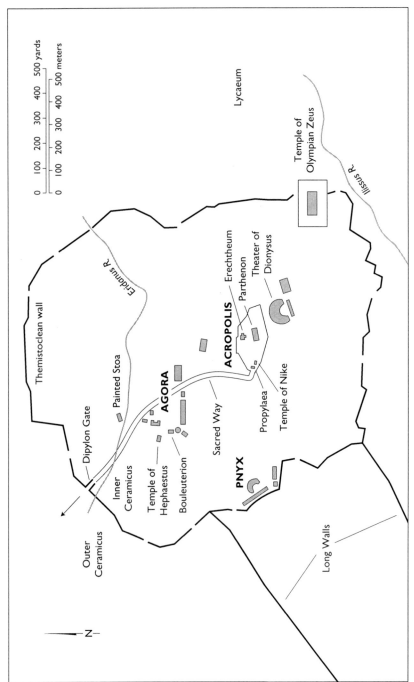

Classical Athens

The Parthenon dominates this view of the Athenian acropolis. In front of it are the remains of the Propylaea—the monumental gateway to the acropolis—with the small Ionic temple to Nike on the far right. On the far left, part of the Erechtheum is visible. (Scala/Art Resource, NY)

projects from its foundation; relief sculpture on the temple depicts a battle between Greeks (portrayed nude) and an enemy clad in the baggy trousers Greeks associated with Eastern peoples. The subject is probably either the Trojan war or the battle of Marathon. Finally, a temple called the Erechtheum (after the legendary king Erechtheus) replaced the temple of Athena Polias that had been destroyed by the Persians and housed some of the city's oldest and most important cults, including the statue of Athena Polias. Pericles is supposed to have proposed the program that planned and paid for all of these buildings. Constructed in a relatively short time—they were all complete before 407 B.C.—they seemed to later generations to represent the ephemeral greatness of the Athenian Empire.

The Parthenon is a Doric temple, but it also has some Ionic elements, including a sculpted frieze around the walls. The sculpture that decorated it was supervised by Phidias, one of classical antiquity's most famous artists. His colossal cult-statue of gold and ivory for the interior depicted Athena in her helmet and shield, holding a winged Victory in the palm of her hand.

The Parthenon and the whole of Pericles' building program are difficult to interpret. It is possible to relate them to the military imperialism that preoccupied Athens at the time that they were constructed. Tradition held that Pericles proposed to pay for the buildings with the tribute that Athens collected from its allies (but it is not clear that this is true). In fact, the acropolis complex is the only example of a planned, state-funded building program in classical Greece, and it reflects the uniqueness of Athens' achievement.

Military themes are prominent in the sculpture of the acropolis buildings: They appear in the cult-statue of Athena in full battle dress and in the temple to Victory with its battle frieze. Sculpture on the Parthenon's metopes also portrayed mythic conflicts, such as the Trojan war and a battle between centaurs (a monstrous race that was half horse, half man) and Lapiths (Greeks of Thessaly). The blending of Ionic and Doric forms on the Parthenon may reflect Athens' solidarity with the Ionian subjects of its empire.

But in general the building program, like classical Greek architecture and sculpture generally, lacks any obvious reference to its historical context. Mythical battles are typical themes on all classical Greek temples; they may reflect a growing sense of Greek identity (contrasting civilized heroes with the barbarous or monstrous opponents they face), or they may reflect the struggle between man and nature that is a fundamental theme of many religions. With the dubious exception of the frieze on the Temple of Nike, historical events are not depicted in classical sculpture at all. The close connection between art, history, and the needs of the state that characterizes much of Hellenistic and Roman sculpture is absent.

Drama.   Drama—both comedy and tragedy—developed and flourished in the era of imperial conquest. All of the examples of classical drama that survive were produced in Athens by a small number of playwrights. The surviving tragedians, in chronological order (although their lives and works overlapped), are Aeschylus, Sophocles, and Euripides. The only classical comic writer whose works are preserved intact is Aristophanes.

Nearly all surviving comic and tragic dramas were produced in the fifth century B.C. Aeschylus' earliest extant play (*The Persians*) dates to 472 B.C. and the last play of Euripides dates to 406; Aristophanes' surviving plays all date between 425 and 388 B.C. But both types of drama arose much earlier, probably in the 500s B.C. Legend told how tragic drama was invented in the reign of Pisistratus, when a poet named Thespis added speeches and an actor to the tragic chorus. Comedy may be as old as tragedy, or older; comic choruses (identifiable by their funny animal costumes) appear on vases from Attica as early as the mid-500s B.C.

Drama had a central place in Athenian political life. Comedies and tragedies were both performed in competition at Athens' great civic festivals in honor of the god Dionysus; the contests were judged by citizens selected by lot. To prepare for the competition, the city provided each playwright with funding; the financing of comedies and tragedies was one of the duties undertaken by rich citizens. Each play needed a **chorus** to sing and dance the odes that were the foundation of the performance, as well as a few actors (two or three for tragedies, as many as four for comedies) to recite the dialogue. The actors were professionals, paid directly by the city. The chorus was composed of ordinary citizens (metics and slaves were not allowed to participate); one of the main jobs of the playwright, who also directed the play, was

The Theater of Dionysus in Athens, where comedies and tragedies were performed. Its stone seats, orchestra, and stage date to the mid-300s B.C. or later. Before that, the theater was constructed of wood or simply carved into the hillside. (Photo by Susan P. Mattern-Parkes)

to train this amateur chorus in rehearsals. The city is often a key theme in both comedies and tragedies; tragic choruses sometimes seem to speak for the (citizen) audience and articulate its reactions, while comedies often ridicule prominent statesmen and comment on political events.

Our understanding of classical theaters is imperfect, since surviving theaters generally date to the Hellenistic period. The stone seats and elaborate stone set of the Theater of Dionysus, on the south slope of the Athenian Acropolis, were constructed in the mid-fourth century or later. Like most theaters, it was originally just a hillside overlooking a flat area (called the *orchestra*, or "dancing-place") where the chorus performed; eventually the hill was hollowed into a semicircle and provided with wooden seating and a wooden backdrop.

The arrangement of the spectators in the theater reflected Athens' civic structure. Special seats were reserved for priests and magistrates, the sons of veterans killed in battle, and ambassadors from other cities. The Council of 500 sat together; the ephebes (youths undergoing military training) also sat together; and metics had their own section. The rest of the audience was perhaps organized by tribe.

According to tradition, dramatic performances were free at first, but because the crowds became unruly, the city began to issue tickets (some of these small lead tablets survive). By the end of the Classical period, however, a special fund called the *theoric fund* had been established to purchase tickets for poor citizens who otherwise could not afford them. This became a large, widely used, and very popular fund, maintained even in times of war—so integral did the Athenians consider the theater to civic life.

Sophists and Scientists.   In Athens, skill at public speaking brought great rewards. An eloquent speaker could win his case against an enemy in court or persuade the assembly to vote for his proposal. Athenian democratic values allowed anyone, regardless of class, to seek honor in the assembly or in the law-court, but the most successful men would be the best speakers.

A traditional education focused on gymnastics and music—students would learn to sing and dance the poetry that was the foundation of Greek culture. But beginning in the mid-fifth century B.C., it was possible to pay for a more advanced education in persuasive speaking, a skill the Greeks called **rhetoric**. Rhetoric was taught by experts known as **sophists** (from the Greek word *sophos*, meaning "wise"). The sophists were usually not citizens; they came to Athens from all over the Greek world, perhaps attracted by the demand for training in rhetoric that the democracy created. The sophists were philosophers as well as teachers. They reasoned and speculated about a range of subjects that included language, mathematics, music, and sociology. They were notorious for their intellectual and moral relativism—the idea that absolute truth does not exist and that reality depends on the viewer's perspective. Thus the most famous sophist, Protagoras, is credited with the saying "man is the measure of all things." His ability to produce an argument for any situation made many suspicious of him and other sophists; Protagoras was accused of boasting that he could "make the weaker argument stronger."

The sophists were not the imperial period's only philosophers—philosophy flourished in the fifth century, and not just at Athens. In fact, most of the era's most important thinkers were from other cities, such as Parmenides of Elea, in Italy; his long poem *On Being* broke new ground by rejecting the evidence of the physical senses and arguing that true reality was single, unchangeable, and eternal. Two influential theories of physics developed in the Classical period: Empedocles of Acragas argued that everything in the universe was made of four elements (earth, fire, air, and water), and this became the dominant theory later; Democritus of Abdera proposed a theory of atoms or tiny, indivisible particles from which all matter is composed. Mathematicians tackled problems of geometry and number theory, and in the early fifth century B.C. Zeno of Elea proposed the famous paradoxes that remain problematic today (for example, he demonstrated if the "swift-footed" hero Achilles were to race a tortoise, he could not possibly win as long as the tortoise had a modest head start).

As far as their ideas can be reconstructed from fragmentary evidence, most early classical philosophers argued in abstract and theoretical terms, even when their subject was the natural world. In the later Classical period and especially in the Hellenistic period, observation and experience played more of a role, but theory and logical demonstration continued to dominate the language of philosophy, and philosophers continued to argue about the

Art and Society

SCULPTING THE BODY IN CLASSICAL GREECE

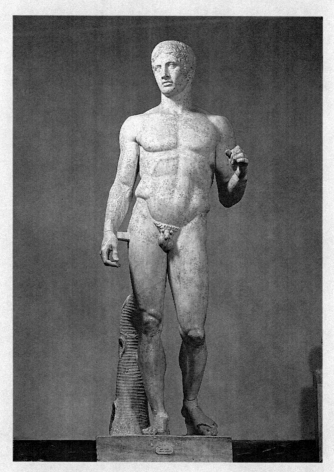

Polyclitus's Doryphoros. (Roman copy) (Scala/Art Resource, NY)

In the Classical period Greek sculptors abandoned the *kouros* and depicted male subjects in poses that created graceful curves, explored how the body's weight was distributed, and made the subjects seem more natural and involved in their surroundings. At the same time, it is not quite accurate to say that the Greeks arrived at a realistic image of the body. The men of classical sculpture are still idealized; with few exceptions, they are young, beardless, and beautiful. Greeks continued to theorize about the body and to depict it in ways that conformed to these theories. For example, in the mid-fifth century B.C. Polyclitus published a work called *Canon* in which he described the best way to portray the

male body—this was probably (at least in part) a theory of symmetry and proportion. His statue of the *Doryphoros*, or "club-bearer," may illustrate the canon
he invented.

Sculptors continued to portray women clothed, and drapery was depicted
with increasing virtuosity and naturalism. On the other hand, the female body
emerges in more detail from beneath increasingly diaphanous drapery. The
"Victory of Paeonius," dating to the 424 B.C., illustrates both of these trends.
Later, around 380 B.C., the sculptor Praxiteles shocked the Greek world by
depicting the goddess Aphrodite naked in a cult-statue for a temple at Cnidus.
Interrrupted during a bath, she shields herself shyly with her hand. Her coy
response to the viewer, as well as the erotic response she provoked in those who

The Nike of Paeonius.   (Scala/Art Resource, NY)

saw her (stories in ancient sources describe this), show that she was imagined as the object of the observer's gaze and desire in a way that male nudes were not.

Praxiteles' Aphrodite of Cnidus. (Roman copy)
(Scala / Art Resource, NY)

reliability of the senses and the validity of **phainomena** (literally, "the things that are apparent") as evidence.

The Peloponnesian War

From 431 to 404 B.C., the Athenians and the Spartans fought a war that devastated the population of both cities and involved much of the Greek world. Scholars call this war the "Peloponnesian war" because most of Sparta's

allies were located on the Peloponnese, the southern part of the Greek peninsula. This reflects the fact that the Athenian point of view is the only one that
survives (the Spartans would not have called the war "Peloponnesian").

Thucydides.   The Peloponnesian war inspired the next great history in
Greek, the work of Thucydides. He was an Athenian who took part in the war
as a general, but was exiled in 424 B.C. when the mission he led was unsuccessful. One important way in which Thucydides' history differed from
Herodotus' is that he did not describe a war between Greeks and foreigners,
but one that that engulfed much of the Greek world. One of his themes is the
idea of Athens and especially the qualities and values that distinguished it
from Sparta. Thucydides' image of Athens emerges especially clearly in a
funeral oration that Pericles gave for those killed in the first year of the war
(book 2, chapters 34–46). This is the most famous passage from his work, but
modern readers should note that Thucydides had no written text of any of
the speeches he records and was working from memory (his or someone
else's); he writes that his speeches do not necessarily represent what was
actually said but what he thought the occasion called for (1.22). Pericles' real
funeral speech may have been very different from the one Thucydides
relates, and Thucydides' speech may represent the Athenians' views of themselves only imperfectly.

   Thucydides is much more critical than Herodotus of certain themes that he
identifies with poetry and oral tradition. He states that he has relied on eye-
witness testimony whenever possible (this was much easier for him than for
Herodotus, since he wrote of events that occurred in his lifetime and he
observed some of them himself). He used a dry writing style that he viewed
as practical rather than entertaining. He eliminated from his history all references to divine intervention as well as other material that he found suspicious (for example, his history—in sharp contrast to Herodotus'—contains
no substantive references to women). As a result, Thucydides' work seems
more scientific and objective than Herodotus'. However, a careful reading
reveals that it is just as full of ingenious symmetry, foreshadowing, and certain tragic themes as Herodotus' is. Although Thucydides viewed human
nature as the driving force behind history, rather than mysterious divine
forces or individual personalities, his work is no less artfully intricate and
compelling than his predecessor's.

Athens and Sparta at War.   To Thucydides, in hindsight, it seemed inevitable
that Athenian imperial ambitions would eventually cause a reaction from the
conservative and anxious Spartans. But he also describes a series of specific
incidents that led the Spartans to declare war; one of these immediate causes
was the defection of Corcyra, a colony of Corinth with a strong navy, to the
Athenian alliance.

   Part of the Athenian strategy in the first years of the war was to withdraw
Attica's population behind the city's walls. In the overcrowded conditions
that resulted, a devastating epidemic disease broke out; its victims included

Pericles. Nevertheless, the Athenians were successful in the first part of the war; they fortified Pylos in the southern Peloponnese and captured over four hundred Spartan citizens alive. The Spartans offered peace, and a treaty was concluded in 421 B.C. But in 415, the Athenians decided to invade Sicily with a large force of one hundred ships. Thucydides writes that they hoped to add the entire island to their empire. The Spartans supported the city of Syracuse against the Athenians, and in a disastrous series of setbacks the entire Athenian force was lost.

The Athenians and Spartans were now at war again. In this second phase of the conflict, the Athenians contended with internal political strife and the revolt of its most important allies. The Spartans fortified Decelea in Attica, which allowed them to pillage the Athenian countryside at will and became a refuge for thousands of runaway slaves. Nevertheless, the Athenians persisted in the war and even achieved some successes until 405 B.C., when the Spartans defeated them in the naval battle of Aegospotami. The Athenians were forced to surrender unconditionally. For a time it was uncertain whether the Spartans would allow the city to survive or would execute the male citizens and enslave the rest of the population, as Athens had done to some of its own enemies; but the Spartans spared Athens. They forced the Athenians to tear down their walls and join the Spartan alliance; they also dissolved the democracy and installed a narrow oligarchy, called the "Thirty Tyrants" in Athenian sources.

Stasis. After the Sicilian disaster, in the difficult second phase of the Peloponnesian war, civil conflict (called *stasis* in Greek) broke out in Athens—a group of revolutionaries who hoped to win the military support of the Persians proposed replacing the democracy with an oligarchy of five thousand. They persuaded or bullied the assembly into passing the proposal. At first a small, extremist group of four hundred seized power for itself; in 410 B.C. the oligarchy of five thousand was instituted, but it did not last long, and the full democracy was restored after a brief interval.

Thucydides and other sources refer to many episodes of *stasis* in Greek cities, and they tend to identify the same cause: conflict between the rich and the poor (or "the few" and "the many") over issues of political power, oligarchy, and democracy. Whether class conflict of this kind was the real cause of *stasis* in classical Greek cities, or whether this is simply the way that observers chose to describe it, is not clear. But it is interesting that ancient sources perceive economic class as an issue of major significance in Greek politics.

Athens after the War

Athens suffered devastating loss of life in the years of the Peloponnesian war, especially from disease and the Sicilian expedition. But in many ways it recovered from the effects of the war quickly. The rule of the Thirty Tyrants was brief; by 403 B.C., the democracy had been restored. In the first half of the fourth century B.C., the Athenians even attempted to revive their empire and confronted Sparta and other cities in a series of conflicts. In 371 their ally, the city of Thebes, defeated the Spartans in battle and became a major military power in Greece.

Some of Athens' most famous writers and citizens—such as Plato the philosopher and Demosthenes the statesman and orator—lived in this period. But the literature that survives from the fourth century is mainly in prose: Dramatic poetry was still produced, but in general it does not survive.

Philosophy. In 399 B.C. an Athenian jury found a fellow citizen named Socrates guilty of impiety and corrupting the youth and condemned him to death. Although he was one of the most influential thinkers of classical Athens, he wrote no works of his own and we only know about him through the writings of his students, especially Plato. It is hard to tell how accurately Plato portrays his teacher, especially because his dialogues do not present a consistent picture. Perhaps the most useful text for reconstructing the historical Socrates is the *Apology*, Plato's version of the speech Socrates gave at his trial; but although Plato was present at the trial, the speech is his own creation and its relationship to Socrates' actual words is tenuous.

In the *Apology* Socrates describes his way of life and his role in Athenian society. One activity he mentions here—and also demonstrates—is his habit of exposing the ignorance of others who claim wisdom or expertise by subjecting them to probing questions; the Greek word **dialectic** sometimes refers to his method of questioning and arguing toward truth. Socrates' favorite targets were sophists, but they also included craftsmen, poets, and politicians.

While Socrates insisted that he did not, like the sophists, teach for money, he attracted an entourage of young men who admired his ideas and accompanied him in public. Most of them came from wealthy families, and some were among the "Thirty Tyrants" who ruled Athens briefly after the Peloponnesian war. For this and other reasons, Socrates' politics seemed antidemocratic and one of his arguments in the *Apology* ridicules the idea that an ordinary Athenian could be a good model and instructor for young men. Suspicions of elitism partly lay behind his indictment and prosecution.

Plato was Socrates' most famous student. He founded the West's first university—the Academy, which offered instruction in many subjects from rhetoric and dialectic to music and mathematics—and became one of its most influential thinkers. Almost all of his known works survive, and all of them except the *Apology* are written as dialogues, like plays—they are not expositions of a single view, but examples of dialectic reasoning. Although many readers have assumed that the words of Socrates, who usually plays a leading role, reflect Plato's own views, this interpretation does not explain why Plato wrote in dialogue form in the first place. The problem is even more complicated because, while Plato's dialogues involve real historical figures, he never portrays himself as one of the speakers or (except in the *Apology*) as a witness. The dialogues often begin with prologues suggesting that the reader is hearing the story second- or third-hand, many years after the event.

The result is to create doubt in the reader about what to believe—is Plato endorsing the views he expresses, or not? Which views are Plato's, anyway?

One of Plato's most influential works is the *Republic* (in Greek, *Politeia*); here, Socrates and his interlocutors attempt to describe an imaginary, ideal city. The *Republic* explores many problems that recur throughout Plato's corpus, such as epistemology (the theory of knowledge), the city and government, and the soul. This work also contains a famous discussion of the social role of poetry.

Plato's *politeia* is governed by an elite class of "Guardians," qualified by their merits and virtues and including both men and women. This class seems to be closed and hereditary. The rest of the citizens are also divided into classes—for example, soldiers and artisans—according to their abilities. Plato's view of a rigid hierarchy where all power is wielded by a narrow elite seems oligarchic and even, to some readers, totalitarian.

The *Republic* contains some of Plato's best-known speculation about the human soul, a subject explored in many of his dialogues. The sharp, dualistic contrast he often draws between the immortal, divine soul and the mortal, corrupt body is one of his most influential legacies. However, his thinking on this issue should not be oversimplified; some dialogues (such as *Timaeus*, which explains the origin and function of the human body) suggest a complicated interrelationship between soul and body. In the *Republic*, Plato describes the ideal city as a mirror of the soul, which is divided into three parts: the rational part (analogous to the Guardians); the emotional part (analogous to the soldiers); and the appetites, associated with the lower classes. In a well-governed individual the emotions and appetites are subjected to reason. At the end of the *Republic*, Plato relates a story about the afterlife, the "myth of Er," which is designed to teach people the importance of living virtuously. Here, souls are reincarnated in the bodies of animals and people, and are thus rewarded or punished for their behavior in their previous life.

Like many philosophers before him, Plato was interested in problems of reality and perception. He is skeptical about the idea that truth can be understood with the physical senses and sometimes suggests that observable objects are not truly real, nor can true knowledge be achieved through the senses. In the *Republic*, Plato argues that only ideal objects called "forms" are truly real, and that they can only be perceived through abstract reasoning.

Plato was also critical of poetry and prophecy as ways of perceiving truth—a theme that is especially important because of the foundational role that poetry, mostly performed as songs and chants, played in Greek culture. While he assumes that poetry is divinely inspired, he argues that it lacks social value, for example, when it portrays the gods committing sins and crimes. He criticizes the way in which poets imitate the voices, mannerisms, and emotions of the characters they portray. All poetry is banned from his ideal city.

Another prominent theme in Plato's dialogues is love; this is the subject of one of his most renowned and entertaining treatises, the *Symposium*. A **sym-**

posium was a drinking-party, a type of entertainment well attested in ancient Greek sources for men of the leisure class. No respectable women were allowed; prostitutes and flute-girls of slave status entertained the guests with music and sex. Larger houses had an *andron*, or "men's room," that could accommodate the couches on which the male guests reclined to eat, drink, and have sex with the women or with one another. Plato's speakers decide to dismiss the flute-girl and to drink moderately at this particular party, amusing themselves instead with speeches in praise of Eros, or sexual love—an appropriate topic for a symposium.

For the most part the speakers assume that *eros* refers to homosexual love between men. One speech, that of Pausanias, seeks to make sense of the value system behind these relationships. Why is the lover encouraged to pursue his beloved and applauded for his conquests, while the beloved is covered in shame if he submits? This speech suggests that while Athenians did not stigmatize homosexual love as such (many, like Plato, valorized it), they did condemn and ridicule those who played a passive sexual role. Pausanias' speech describes how parents guarded their sons as well as their daughters against sexual predators; those who could afford it had slaves called "pedagogues" (*paidagogoi*) to chaperon their sons in public.

Plato's speakers condemn love based mainly on sexual desire (although it is less clear whether they condemn sex as such) and praise its moral, intellectual, and spiritual aspects. For example, it inspires courage; lovers are brave soldiers, as they seek to prove themselves before each other or to rescue each other from danger. Several speakers portray the ideal lover as an educator—a mentor providing moral instruction for the beloved. Socrates himself expounds a mystical view of love that he attributes to a prophetess named Diotima: Eros is not a god but a *daimon*, a creature intermediate between gods and mortals; the desire that the beloved's beauty inspires is really a longing for divine beauty and goodness. Through love, humans can arrive at a vision and understanding of divinity.

Science and Medicine. The first Greek medical writing dates to the later Classical period. Gradually, in the late fifth and fourth centuries B.C., a canon of treatises evolved that was attributed to a great physician named Hippocrates, who lived on the island of Cos. Even in antiquity, commentators argued that some of the treatises in the collection were not by Hippocrates, and today scholars are not sure which, if any, are authentic. But the Hippocratic Corpus* remained one of the West's most influential medical texts through the eighteenth century.

Some of the treatises speculate about the nature of the human body, proposing that it is composed of as many as four types of liquid or "humors" (the theory of four humors eventually became widespread, but not all Hippocratic treatises recognize four humors). They also speculate about anatomy, describing, for example, the body's network of blood vessels. But dissection

---

Corpus means "body" in Latin; here, it refers to a body of work.

Doing History

LITERATURE AND LITERACY

Written texts—literature, documents, and inscriptions on stone, for example—are some of the most important sources of evidence for the ancient historian. But a tendency to rely on texts can skew our understanding of ancient societies in which writing was not as important as it is today. While it is tempting for the historian to attribute great significance to the distinction between literate and preliterate or "oral" societies, not all cultures with writing use it in the same way or to the same extent. Studying literacy in the ancient world means not just tracing the introduction of the alphabet or determining how many people could read or write (a question we cannot answer accurately anyway), but trying to define the role of writing in society.

Literary texts of many kinds survive from classical Greece—but what was their purpose? Most were intended to be performed before an audience as songs, plays, and speeches. In fact, only a restricted group of texts were written to be read privately—these include Thucydides' history and many medical and philosophical works (although some of the latter were probably written as lectures). Poetry was sung or chanted; comedies and tragedies were staged in theaters, where a chorus danced out the main musical themes. Some evidence suggests that Herodotus' histories were mostly experienced in public readings.

Careful readers of classical Athenian literature will find it full of surprising evidence that culture was primarily oral. When Plato criticized the poetry that was still the foundation of education in his time, he focused not on how it was read, but on how it was performed. When Thucydides explained his new, more critical and scientific approach to history, he emphasized that he relied on the evidence of eyewitnesses—not documents—and he refers to few documents in his work. The overwhelming bulk of Greek culture—its traditions about the past, its songs and speeches—was never written down at all.

---

is not well attested in the Hippocratic corpus; Aristotle, who performed animal dissections himself, is responsible for many advances in anatomy in the late Classical period.

Aristotle was a citizen of Stagira, in northern Greece. He studied with Plato at the Academy but left Athens when Plato died in 348 B.C. A few years later he moved to the Macedonian court as tutor to the young Alexander the Great; he returned to Athens in 335 and founded a new school there, called the Lycaeum.

Aristotle did not write with the same level of stylistic artistry as Plato; he used plain expository prose, and his surviving works make no use of drama or dialogue. Many of his writings read like lecture notes, and that may be their origin. An enormous corpus of his work survives; his ideas on government (in the *Politics*) and on dramatic poetry (in *Poetics*) are especially well known and influential today. His treatises on logic developed new, rigorous standards for demonstrative proof. But Aristotle's contributions to natural science are perhaps his most important legacy.

Aristotle's ideas on physics—the first principles of nature—are complex and highly abstract. He identifies four basic aspects of existence (form, substance, origin or cause, and purpose) and investigates questions of motion, weight, and the fundamental constituents of matter. But his favorite subject was biology, especially the study of animals—their classification, anatomy, physiology, origins, development, and behavior. He describes an enormous variety of animals from insects to mollusks to large mammals; his discussions of marine animals are especially impressive. Aristotle's view of nature was profoundly teleological—he believed that nature created every part of an animal for a purpose, to help the creature or its species survive. While many of his conclusions are based on logical deduction, literary tradition, or second-hand accounts (from beekeepers and the like), he also used deliberate observation and dissection much more than other classical writers.

Society in Classical Athens

Compared to many other civilizations, classical Greece was less stratified economically—that is, the rich were not that rich compared to ordinary people. But while egalitarian and democratic ideas were important, powerful and complex class distinctions—between citizens and aliens, aristocrats and commoners, men and women—still pervaded Athenian culture. The courtroom orations of the fourth century offer some of the best information on social issues in classical Athens; other sources, especially the comedies of Aristophanes, also help us understand how Athenian society was organized.

Oratory and Honor. Rhetoric was important at Athens in the imperial period, but most surviving speeches date to the fourth century B.C. Like dramatic performances, the orations were delivered in public settings before an audience of ordinary citizens—either the citizens of the assembly or the jurors in a courtroom. Either way, the citizens passed judgment on the speech by voting, but they also voiced their opinions by cheering and heckling. The speaker risked his image and reputation—his honor—with every performance.

Oratory is a good source for the social values of classical Athens. This is especially true of forensic (that is, legal) speeches because they describe conflicts among relatively ordinary people and because they were designed to appeal to a citizen jury. Every year, a panel of six thousand jurors was chosen by lot from among citizens who volunteered to serve for pay. Juries were large, usually in the hundreds, and decisions were made by majority vote. A large number of forensic orations survive, many written by professional speechwriters but not delivered by them—the parties to a lawsuit in Athens were required to speak for themselves.

The speeches reveal that Athenian society was intensely competitive. Men tended to become involved in long-standing feuds with other men, along with their friends and families. Thus many speeches begin by describing a complicated history of hostility between the two parties. For example, when Demosthenes prosecutes Meidias for punching him at a festival, he tells a story about his past relationship with the defendant that includes among other events a slander suit, an allegation of murder, and an insult to Demosthenes' mother. Women are usually passive in these stories: Abusing a female family member is construed as an insult to its men. Athenian orators tell the stories as though they expect the jurors to agree that the courts are an appropriate forum for personal revenge.

The Greek word for "insult" or "outrage" was **hybris.** An act of *hybris* embarrassed and humiliated its victim, who could only regain his image and self-respect by retaliation. The courts provided one way of playing out this type of drama and, especially, offered a non-violent way for Athenians to insult one another and avenge themselves. The audience of jurors, representing public opinion, would determine which man was winning this perpetual contest for honor—at least until the next round.

Citizens. The Athenian citizen body was divided into four official property classes; but citizenship was itself a social class. It was defined by birth: After 451 B.C., two citizen parents were required for citizenship. This meant that all Athenian citizens were conscious of inherited privilege. The right to hold political office, to participate in the assembly, to serve as jurors in the law-courts, and even to own land in Athens was exclusively theirs by birth. Thus Athenian citizens proudly distinguished themselves from the slaves and resident aliens who lived among them.

Nevertheless, there were inequalities within the citizen class between rich and poor, educated and uneducated, well-born and common. The speakers who made proposals in the assembly tended to be rich and aristocratic, although every citizen had the right to speak. Education in rhetoric, which was important for success in the assembly and in the law-courts, was available to the leisure classes but not to the ordinary Athenian. Aristocrats considered themselves better than their social inferiors and called themselves the *kaloi k'agathoi*, the "handsome and noble." Athenian values granted the highest social status to men who did not have to work for money and whose wives and daughters stayed within the confines of the house. Wealth made a statesman more credible and less corruptible in the eyes of the Athenian *demos*. Through a kind of tax called **liturgies,** the wealthy financed ships for the navy or the dramatic performances that all citizens enjoyed; the Athenians valued these contributions highly.

But while values privileging the rich and well-born emerge strongly from some classical texts, others—or sometimes the same ones—show that a democratic value system was also prominent. Orators often appeal to the jury's suspicions of educated, clever speakers and to their hostility to the arrogance and displays of luxury associated with the rich. Some speeches show that all citizens might think of themselves as well-born and "noble" compared to noncitizens.

A Closer Look

THE *AGORA*

The **agora,** the marketplace, was the heart of the ancient Greek city. Essentially, an agora was simply an open space for public use, and functions of all kinds took place there. People might visit the agora to shop; to watch a contest, a parade, or a lawsuit in progress; to hear the latest news; or to socialize. Vendors hawked products of every possible kind, and livestock mixed with the human crowds. Socrates met with his friends and followers and had some of his most important conversations in the *agora*. Ostracisms took place at the *agora*, and over a thousand ostraka inscribed with the names of politicians (including Pericles, Themistocles, and many others) have been found there.

Gradually the *agora* became the site of some of the city's most important monumental buildings, including a permanent courthouse, a meeting-house for the Council of 500 and an office for the ten generals, a number of altars dedicated to gods, the Temple of Hephaestus (which is well-preserved today), and

Ostraka from the agora at Athens inscribed with the names of prominent statesmen. The round ostraka (made from the bottoms of cups) read "Themistocles son of Neocles," referring to the famous strategist of the battle of Salamis, and were apparently mass-produced by a few individuals. (Scala/Art Resource, NY)

(possibly) a prison, as well as some private houses and a host of temporary shops that do not survive. Several **stoas**—long, colonnaded buildings—provided shade and shelter for socializing or for vendors offering their wares.

Boundary stones like this one marked the entrances to the *agora*. The inscription reads, "I am the boundary of the *agora*." The stone dates to about 500 B.C. (American School of Classical Studies at Athens: Agora Excavations)

Slaves and Metics. Nobody knows exactly how many slaves there were in classical Athens, or what percentage of the population they formed—only that there were many, and the percentage was large. Even modest households might own one or more slaves, but slaves played a much larger role in classical Athens than just domestic service. They were a fundamental part of the Athenian economy and society.

The role of slaves in Athens' economy was very diverse. Some were owned by the state, including the corps of three hundred "Scythian archers" who enforced order in the city. Private individuals often bought slaves as an investment—some of these slaves lived and worked independently as craftsmen; others were hired out as agricultural laborers, workers in the state mines (an especially miserable fate), or prostitutes. Other slaves worked directly for their masters as domestic servants or field hands. Domestic slaves were sometimes freed, and wage-earning slaves might buy their freedom. But the boundary between slave and citizen was difficult to cross. Citizens could not be enslaved for debt or as punishment for a crime, and freed slaves became metics, not citizens.

Athens' population of metics, who could be "barbarians" or Greeks from other cities, was very substantial. They were not allowed to own land, with the result that they dominated other areas of the Athenian economy, such as banking and craftsmanship. Some metics, including the logographer Lysias (see later) and most of the sophists, made a living teaching rhetoric or selling speeches. While citizens looked down on metics socially, they perceived their economic contributions as necessary. Metics were excluded from all political participation and had limited legal rights; they were required to have the support of a citizen patron, and they paid a special tax. It was difficult and rare for a metic to become a citizen; this could only be done by a special decree of the assembly.

Women and Family.   The status of women in classical Athens is one of the most controversial problems in the study of this period. Some scholars emphasize women's seclusion and lack of economic and political power, while others point out the ways in which they were empowered—ways that a modern Western audience, accustomed to a different role for women in society, might easily overlook.

Athenian legal orations and some other classical documents suggest that women's ability to own or control property was strictly limited in theory and also in fact. Every woman was under the power of a *kyrios*, or "guardian," usually either her husband or father, and could perform no public transactions in her own name. A man's property went to his legitimate sons on his death; if he had only a daughter, she could be claimed in marriage by her father's closest male relative, often his brother, who then controlled the property. On the other hand, some orations reveal that women could be knowledgeable about family accounts and sometimes made or influenced decisions about property.

Marriages were arranged between the bridegroom and the bride's male relatives and her consent was not legally required. Literary sources suggest that women in Athens were married in their early teens, to men who were about thirty. Marriages between first cousins and between uncle and niece were not unusual, probably for economic reasons—to keep property in the family.

In Athenian literature the ideal wife remains at home, appears in public only on well-defined occasions such as religious festivals and funerals, and is

Art and Society

THE FAMILY ON ATHENIAN FUNERARY MONUMENTS

This gravestone from Attica dates to about 350 B.C. It is inscribed with the individuals' names: The man is Phainippos and both women are named Mnesarete.
(Réunion des Musées Nationaux/Art Resource, NY)

The classical Greeks avoided portraiture—statues that represented the individual features of their subjects. Bodies and faces are idealized, and most subjects are in the prime of life. This is mainly true even of tombstone reliefs, which are supposed to depict the deceased and members of his or her family. But these reliefs are unique in several ways. Many depict people of different ages, including mature men, aged parents, and infants. Women are dressed soberly as matrons, in contrast to the coquettishly draped freestanding sculptures; strikingly, their names appear on their tombstones, making these the main source for women's names in classical Athens. Family scenes are common, as the dead say good-bye to their children and parents, spouses, slaves, and even pets.

never mentioned in public (this is why orators refer to respectable women as "the wife of X" or "the daughter of Y"). Some sources suggest that even within the house, women inhabited a separate *gynaikonitis*, or "women's quarters," where they were less accessible to visitors and passers-by. The honor of the family's men was deeply vested in the chastity of its women, and stereotypes portrayed women as deceptive and unable to control their passions. A feeling of anxiety about the control of women, and even of hostility toward women, thus pervades much of Athenian literature.

But the ideal of the secluded woman diverged from the reality. Even respectable women left their homes to visit female friends. Not all households could afford servants to answer the door, fetch water, and perform other chores that would otherwise bring the wife into contact with men or into public view; nor could all households afford a lifestyle in which women did no work outside the home. In the marketplace, women (often metics or slaves rather than respectable citizens) could be found selling a wide variety of goods; they also held jobs as bakers, innkeepers, nurses to the sick, midwives, wetnurses, dancers, and prostitutes. Woolworking was a trade that could be practiced at home, and some women sold their wares for profit. Rural women often worked in the fields, especially if their husbands were off at war.

Athenian values granted women power in the domestic and religious spheres. They supervised the household's servants, raised its children, and managed its budget; they took charge of family rituals, such as weddings and funerals, and participated in important civic festivals. Women traditionally produced their family's clothes, blankets, and other textiles at home. They could be powerful figures in the family and played a crucial role in the economy.

Athens' numerous prostitutes came mainly from its metic and slave population. Some prostitutes who formed lasting relationships with citizen men were called **hetairai**—"companions." Men could bring their *hetairai*, but not their wives, to the *symposia* that were central to male social life. In this way they might mingle with the city's poets and politicians and even become famous (or notorious). Pericles' *hetaira*, Aspasia, was renowned for her friendship with Socrates and other Athenian intellectuals and for her influence over Pericles. But we should not idealize the life of the *hetaira*. The story of a *hetaira* named Neaera, told in a legal oration, reveals some of the harsh realities of her background: She was sold to a madam as a small girl and practiced prostitution from childhood. When she tried to leave a lover who treated her abusively, he sued for her return with partial success. Although she counted famous cultural figures (a poet, an actor) among her lovers, she was in many ways at the mercy of the men who supported her.

Women Outside Athens.   The evidence for women outside of Athens is much scarcer, but it suggests that their status was not the same everywhere in Hellas. The Athenians themselves contrasted the secluded, sedentary lives of their women with the more active, public lives of Spartan women. Aristotle

The Written Record

AN ATHENIAN FAMILY

Lysias, a professional speechwriter, wrote this oration for a client named Euphiletus, who was charged with murder. Euphiletus' defense is that he caught the victim committing adultery with his wife and that the law allows him to kill the victim in these circumstances. This passage is full of fascinating details about Euphiletus' household.

In the early days [of my marriage], Athenians, she was the best of wives; for she was a clever and thrifty housekeeper, and she kept everything well-organized. But when my mother died, this became the cause of all my problems. For when my wife attended her funeral, she was seen by that man [Eratosthenes, the victim], and in time she was led astray. He kept watch for the female slave when she went to the market, and sent messages through her, and corrupted my wife. But first, gentlemen, it is necessary for me to explain that my house has two stories; the upper floor, the women's quarters, is equal [in size] to the men's quarters on the lower floor. But when our child was born, my wife breastfed him; and so that she did not have to risk going down the stairs whenever he needed to be washed, I lived above, and the women below. At this time it was quite usual for my wife to go off and sleep below, so that she could give the baby the breast and he would not cry. (Lysias 1.7–10)

writes that Spartan women owned two-fifths of the land there, contrasting this situation with the restricted economic rights of women at Athens. Evidence from Gortyn on Crete, where a long inscription recording some of the city's laws survives, indicates that women there also had more property rights than women in Athens.

The best evidence for classical Greek houses comes from Olynthus, in northern Greece; there, the distribution of artifacts throughout the houses suggests that women used most rooms and no separate women's section existed. Houses were built around a central courtyard, a plan that would have made it difficult to segregate members of the household from one another; however, this plan was well adapted for separating women from visitors and outsiders, since access to all of the rooms was controlled from the courtyard. Some wealthy families built houses with two courtyards—men used the larger, more accessible court for entertaining, while women used the other for domestic activities. These large, wealthier houses incorporated segregated women's quarters in a way that smaller houses did not.

The Hellenistic World

Alexander's conquest of Persia, which ultimately spread Greek culture throughout the Near East, is among the most significant events in Western history. For centuries the educated, elite classes in Asia Minor, Syria, and Egypt spoke Greek, and Greek traditions in art, architecture, and literature dominated urban culture. This remained true even after the Romans conquered the Greco-Macedonian kingdoms that succeeded Alexander's empire. Modern scholars use the word **Hellenistic** to describe Greek history and culture after Alexander's conquests.

The Macedonian Conquerors

The kingdom of Macedonia lay north of Thessaly, between the Balkan Mountains and the Greek peninsula. Beginning in 359 B.C. its new king, Philip II, reformed the army (equipping the infantry phalanx with a long pike called the *sarisa*) and embarked on a program of imperialist expansion, conquering neighboring peoples including some Athenian allies and colonies. While the Athenian orator Demosthenes encouraged his fellow citizens to take a stand against him, the Athenians were occupied with problems closer to home and unable to convince other Greek cities to join in an alliance against Philip; they mounted no resistance until 341 B.C. In 338, Philip defeated the allied armies of Athens and Thebes at Chaeronea and occupied Thebes and other important Greek cities. The next year, the Greek cities jointly agreed to an alliance with Macedonia and appointed Philip their leader. At the same time, Philip proclaimed his intention to lead them in a war of revenge against Persia. But Philip was assassinated in 336 B.C.

Were the Macedonians Greeks?   In Demosthenes' speeches encouraging the Athenians to go to war with Philip, he portrays the Macedonian king as an uncivilized barbarian. At the same time a rival Athenian statesman, Isocrates, argued that all Greeks should unite under Philip's leadership and campaign against a barbarian enemy—the Persians—instead of fighting one another. Whether one viewed the Macedonians as invaders threatening the liberty of Greek cities or as leaders of a great Panhellenic cause depended partly on whether they and their kings seemed Greek or not.

Macedonian rulers had admired Greek culture and tried to present themselves as Greeks since the early fifth century B.C., when King Alexander I persuaded the Greeks to allow the Macedonian royal dynasty to compete in the Olympic games by tracing his descent to the Greek hero Heracles. Philip II was especially anxious to appear Greek, publicizing his victory in the Olympic chariot race of 356 B.C. and leading the Greek league that managed the sanctuary at Delphi in a "Sacred War." He even hired an Athenian philosopher, Aristotle, to tutor his son Alexander.

Not much is known about Macedonian culture before Greek influence. We are not sure whether the Macedonian language was a form of Greek. The Macedonians worshipped Greek gods (such as Zeus), but it is hard to tell whether these cults were native to them or imported from the Greek world. But regardless of whether the Macedonians were truly "Greek" or not, the culture that Philip's son Alexander and his successors spread around the

Near East was Hellenic: in its art and architecture, its literature and language, its cults and festivals.

Alexander the Great.   Alexander III ("The Great") was just twenty years old when he became king. He began his reign by crushing a revolt of the city of Thebes and enslaving its population. In 334 B.C. he began the Eastern campaign that his father had planned, crossing the Hellespont with an army of about fifty thousand troops. Like his father, Alexander portrayed himself as Greek: as a new Achilles leading a second Trojan war (he even slept with the *Iliad* under his pillow) and as an avenger of Xerxes' invasion. He defeated the Persian army at the Granicus river and again at Issus, in southern Asia Minor, a year later. In 332 he marched to Egypt, which surrendered without resistance. There he founded a city on the Nile Delta, which he named Alexandria after himself. In the centuries that followed, it would become one of the Mediterranean world's most populous cities and one of the main centers of Greek culture (and Hellenized Jewish culture).

Later that year Alexander marched again against the Persians and defeated them at Gaugamela in Mesopotamia. The Persian king escaped from the battle, but was murdered a year later. Alexander occupied the great cities of Babylon and Susa and plundered and burnt Persepolis, the capital.

His conquests were still unstable and revolts continued until 327 B.C. In the meantime, Alexander kept marching east, through what is now Afghanistan, to the frontier between Persia and India; he crossed the Indus river, defeated the Indian king Porus, and was approaching the Ganges river when his troops refused to march further. Reluctantly, Alexander turned back, retreating along the coast of the Indian Ocean. Ancient sources record that the journey westward was disastrous, as the army suffered heavy casualties from heat, thirst, and hunger. But Alexander was planning more conquests when he died at Babylon in 323 B.C.; he was thirty-three years old.

Alexander's military achievement was extraordinary; with a relatively small army he had conquered the world's largest empire and had marched through lands virtually unknown to the Greeks. The ultimate aim of his Indian campaign was probably to reach the limits of the world. He became the subject of numerous histories and biographies, of romantic adventure-stories in two dozen languages, and of a vast body of oral legend. But ancient writers (as well as modern ones) found Alexander an ambiguous subject— his military achievements were astonishing, but his character problematic. They criticized his violent temper, his overpowering drive to conquer, and his occasional arbitrary acts of despotism.

The Hellenistic Kingdoms.   Alexander's empire did not survive his death; his generals divided it among themselves. After much initial conflict and negotiation, three large kingdoms emerged that comprised most of the Greek world in the Hellenistic period. Seleucus and his descendants ruled over Asia Minor, Syria, and the eastern part of the empire (this kingdom of "Syria" was at first by far the largest of the Hellenistic kingdoms). The descendants of

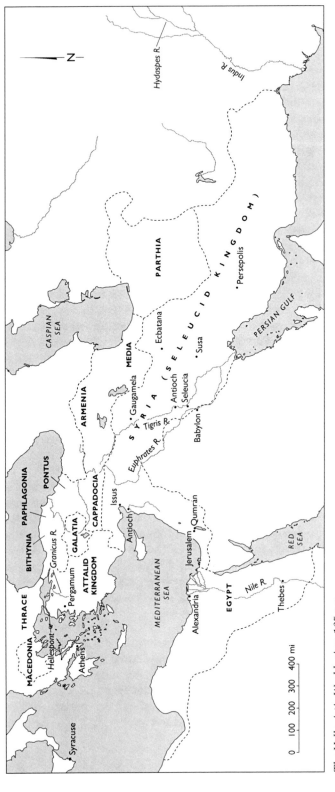

The Hellenistic World, circa 185 B.C.

Antigonus ruled over Macedonia and northern Greece and dominated southern Greece (which they left nominally independent) with a combination of military occupation and political manipulation; and Ptolemy and his descendants ruled over Egypt. Throughout the Hellenistic period, boundaries shifted as the kings fought one another, and two important new powers emerged. In the mid-200s B.C., under its leaders Eumenes and Attalus, the city of Pergamum expanded its power until it controlled most of Asia Minor. And in the later third century B.C. the Parthians, whose homeland was in the north of modern Iran, began a long campaign of expansion that eventually wrested much of its eastern territory from the Seleucid kingdom of Syria. By 100 B.C. Parthia ruled most of the former territory of the Persians and Seleucids as far as the Euphrates river.

One by one, in a long process that will be discussed in the next chapter, the Roman Empire absorbed all of the Macedonian kingdoms. The last of the Hellenistic monarchs was the famous Cleopatra VII of Egypt, who committed suicide after her defeat by the future emperor Augustus in 30 B.C.

Greeks and Natives

Alexander and his successors founded a large number of cities throughout the former Persian Empire (Alexander was said to have founded seventy cities himself). Some of the most important of these cities were Alexandria on the Nile Delta, Seleucia on the Tigris river, and Antioch on the Orontes river in Syria (now part of Turkey). Many of the earliest foundations were military colonies, settled by soldiers from Alexander's army, but in the centuries that followed the new cities attracted settlers from mainland Greece, Macedonia, and the Greek cities of Asia Minor. Like the classical Greek *poleis*, they had bodies of citizens organized into demes and tribes; they even had councils and assemblies, although they did not have the same political independence as classical cities but were subject to the Hellenistic monarchs. They were equipped with the public buildings that defined the Greek way of life: theaters, Greek-style temples, and especially **gymnasia**. The gymnasia were partly athletic facilities for the nude exercises and sports that were the favorite pastime of the Greek leisure class, but they were also schools and cultural centers.

Greeks also settled in older cities, such as Babylon, which acquired a theater, a gymnasium, and an *agora* in this period. The Hellenistic kings funded large-scale buildings, such as the Stoa of Attalus in the Athenian marketplace, or whole projects, such as the complex of buildings on the acropolis at Pergamum—with its library, theater, temples, and enormous, elaborately decorated altar of Zeus. The result is that many of the Greek world's most impressive architectural remains date to the Hellenistic period.

Today, scholars debate the effects of "Hellenization"—Greek influence—on the native populations of the Greco-Macedonian kingdoms. Some argue that Greek and native populations were segregated from one another, with little social or cultural mixing. In this view, the ruling class was composed almost exclusively of Greco-Macedonians, and Greek cultural institutions (like the gymnasia or Hellenic religious festivals) appealed only to Greeks, while indigenous traditions continued undisturbed among natives. Others point out the substantial evidence for intermarriage between Greeks and natives and argue that the participation of natives in government is well attested at some levels. It is likely that the reality is complex and that the picture of a neat division between Greek and native cultures is too simplistic.

For example, it is often impossible to determine the biological or racial background of individuals mentioned in Hellenistic documents. To obtain positions in the administration, natives might acquire a Greek education and take Greek names. Intermarriage between Greeks and natives is well attested, and people with Greek and native names might belong to the same family. Many people used two different names.

The problem of language in the Hellenistic world is equally complicated. On the one hand, Greek became the dominant literary and administrative language. In this period a standard form of Greek called **koine** (meaning "common") gradually replaced the different dialects. However, the native languages of the Near East continued in use, not only as spoken languages; documents and some literary works were written in them. The two most important native languages were Aramaic (a Semitic language widely spoken in the territories ruled by the Seleucids) and Egyptian (written in hieroglyphic, hieratic, and demotic script).

While a small number of the highest administrative posts were reserved for Greeks and Macedonians, the lower-ranking officials who kept records and collected taxes in the kingdoms' towns and villages could be either Greeks or natives who had learned Greek. The administrative structures of the kingdoms also reflected local traditions. For example, in Egypt, the nome remained the basic division of the kingdom, as it had been under the pharaohs; the Seleucids used a system of satraps and city governors similar to the Persian system.

The Ptolemies were careful to portray themselves in ways that appealed to Greco-Macedonians and also to native Egyptians: While their coins featured Greek-style portraits and Greek legends, they also appear on the walls of Egyptian temples in sculpted images like those of the pharaohs, with inscriptions in hieroglyphs. Egyptian law continued in use side-by-side with Greek law. Both Ptolemies and Seleucids generously supported native cults and temples. Respect for old traditions of government and the use of native elites in administration helped maintain a stable and efficient rule.

Although it may not be easy to define who counted as Greek, there was nevertheless a strong sense of Greek identity, especially among urban elites, in the Hellenistic period. Overall, the Hellenic minority tended to be wealthier, more urban, and more educated than non-Greeks, and Greeks considered themselves superior to the non-Greek population. On the other hand, nationalist feelings among native peoples are also attested and sometimes found important expression—for example, in the revolts that centered on Thebes in Egypt in the late third century B.C. or in the Jewish revolt under the Hasmonaeans, discussed later.

This relief from the temple of Hathor at Dendera, in Egypt, depicts Cleopatra VII and her son Caesarion—her child with Julius Caesar—on the left. Cleopatra, who ruled until 30 B.C., was the last of the Ptolemaic rulers of Egypt. Here, she portrays herself in native Egyptian style, on a temple to an Egyptian goddess. (Middle East Documentation Center, University of Chicago)

Religion in the Hellenistic World. Throughout the Hellenistic world, Greek-style temples were constructed to traditional Hellenic gods (such as Zeus) and their priesthoods were prestigious civic offices. The great Hellenistic cities all had their own Greek religious festivals, complete with competitions in athletics, poetry, drama, and rhetoric, and inscriptions commemorating the winners show that they usually had Greek names.

The Hellenistic rulers also established a cult of themselves. Alexander believed he was divine, claiming to be the son of Zeus or of the Egyptian sun-god Amen. The Seleucids and the Ptolemies found this tradition convenient; they encouraged cities and towns to dedicate altars, shrines, priesthoods, cult-statues, and festivals to them (or at least did not discourage this). The ruler-cult was especially important in Egypt, where the pharaohs had also been worshipped as gods.

At the same time, the worship of native Near Eastern gods continued in much the same way as before. The Hellenistic kings paid for renovations to the temples of the most important native gods, and these temples and their priesthoods continued to function. On a different level, local deities such as the Egyptian household god Bes (see p. 33) remained popular.

But perhaps the most interesting feature of Hellenistic religion is the way in which strange combinations of Greek and native ideas are attested at all levels of society (this promiscuous mixing of religious practices, like the wide-ranging mixture of cults in early Egypt, is sometimes called **syncretism**). For example, in the second century A.D., the most important temple in the Egyptian village of Karanis was a shrine to the local crocodile-god Sobek, attached to a large cemetery full of mummified crocodiles. Another temple was devoted to the god Sarapis-Zeus-Amen-Helios: Here two ancient Egyptian gods, Sarapis and Amen, have been associated with Greek equivalents, Zeus and Helios ("Sun"). This god shared the temple with the Egyptian goddess Isis and also with the popular crocodile god. Inscriptions and art objects recovered from the village mention both Greek and native Egyptian gods.

Judaism in the Second Temple Period

Jewish history is organized around different events than Greek history. The period from the return of the Babylonian exiles to Judah, when Solomon's temple was rebuilt, to the temple's destruction by the Romans in A.D. 70 is called the **Second Temple Period** of Judaism. The first part of the Second Temple Period will be discussed here; the Jews' struggle with the Romans will be described in the next chapter.

The Jewish State. After Alexander conquered the Persian Empire, Judah was politically subject to either the Seleucids or the Ptolemies, depending on who ruled over the area at the time. In 166 B.C., the Seleucids were in control when Judah Maccabee and his brothers led a revolt. The story of the revolt is told in the Biblical books I and II Maccabees,* and also by Josephus, a Jewish historian of the Roman period. These sources identify the Seleucid king Antiochus IV's insults to Jewish religion as the cause of the revolt: He pillaged the Temple of Jerusalem, occupied the city with troops, and issued edicts that forbade the practice of Jewish law (including circumcision, the observation of the Sabbath, and dietary rules). His most outrageous act was to install images of the Greek gods in the Temple of Jerusalem.

Eventually, after many vicissitudes, the revolt of the Maccabees resulted in the establishment of an independent kingdom of Judah in 141 B.C. Jewish independence lasted until 63 B.C., when the Roman general Pompey conquered Judah. During this time, the descendants of the Maccabees, who called themselves the Hasmonaeans after one of their ancestors, ruled as a dynasty of kings and high priests. In 166 B.C., Judah was a small territory centered on Jerusalem; but during the revolt and afterward, the Hasmoneans conquered their neighbors until they ruled most of the peoples of the southwest Levant.

Judaism and Hellenism. The history of the Jewish people in the Second Temple period is not only the history of the Hasmonaean kingdom. Ever

---

*These books are not part of the Tanakh, but Catholic Bibles include them.

since the Babylonian exile, Jewish communities could be found in cities throughout the eastern Mediterranean, a phenomenon often called the **diaspora**, which means "dispersal." The city of Alexandria in Egypt had an especially large Jewish population, and it was here that the Hebrew Bible was translated into Greek. (Legend told that seventy-two Jewish scholars working in isolation produced an identical, divinely inspired translation; it was called the **Septuagint**, from the Greek word for "seventy".) Like the peoples of Egypt and Mesopotamia, the Jews had a well-developed cultural tradition of their own; they also had a strong sense of ethnic identity and retained this sense even as they encountered and absorbed many aspects of Greek culture.

The especially rich and diverse Jewish literature of the Second Temple Period reflects Jewish interactions with Greek culture. It was written in Hebrew and Aramaic but also in Greek; Jews of the diaspora mostly wrote in Greek, and the Septuagint was produced for an audience of Jews who could read Greek but not Hebrew. Hellenistic Jewish literature includes works of history and biblical commentary, romances, epics, and apocalypses about the end of the world; a few became part of the canonical Bible, but a large body of nonbiblical works also survives. These include the papyrus scrolls that were discovered, beginning in 1947, in caves at Qumran near the Dead Sea; often called the "Dead Sea Scrolls," they date from about 250 B.C. to A.D. 70. While the mythology of the Bible remained the basic subject matter for most Jewish literature (as Greek myth did for Greek literature), the stories were reinterpreted and embellished in a wide variety of ways; Babylonian and Greek influences often mingled with Jewish traditions.

Jewish Sects. Judaism was a diverse religion in the Second Temple Period. As a result of the Babylonian exile, the diaspora, and the Maccabaean conquests, it was practiced in widely scattered communities with different histories, different geographic and cultural settings, and even different ethnic backgrounds (the Maccabees had converted some of the peoples they conquered). At the same time, the observance of Jewish law had become a crucial test of Jewish identity, and the interpretation of the Torah became an important intellectual discipline. Various sects arose that distinguished themselves largely by their different ways of interpreting and observing the law. One of these was the Samaritans, who trace their origins to the remnant of Israel's population that remained in Palestine after the kingdom's destruction in 722 B.C., and whose biblical canon includes only the Torah. Later sources describe another group called the Pharisees, who accepted an expanded version of Jewish law based on oral interpretations of the Torah. They were perceived as legal experts and, later, as early rabbis (see Chapter 3, p. 162). The Sadducees, a priestly and aristocratic class, rejected the Pharisees' tradition of interpreting the Torah and construed its laws more literally. Finally, the Jewish community at Qumran that produced the Dead Sea Scrolls believed that mainstream Judaism was corrupt and destined to be destroyed soon. They lived in the desert, in isolation and celibacy (no women were allowed in their community), according to a strict code that is described in one of the texts recovered from the site.

Greek Culture in the Hellenistic Period

Whereas Athens had been the geographic focus of Greek culture in the Classical period, the achievements of Hellenistic period are widely scattered. They come from great cities like Alexandria or Antioch, but also from other cities of the eastern and western Greek world.

Science and Technology. Greek science flourished, and even reached its height, in Hellenistic times. Astronomy, for example, became a sophisticated discipline in this period. In the third century B.C., Aristarchus of Samos developed a more accurate "heliocentric" (sun-centered) theory of the universe, although his ideas were unproveable at the time and most Hellenistic astronomers still accepted the geocentric ("earth-centered") theory that had been adopted by Plato and Aristotle. In the second century B.C., Hipparchus of Nicaea introduced mathematical calculation to the science of astronomy (in the process, he invented the techniques of trigonometry), which allowed him to predict celestial movements accurately. He also developed new instruments for making astronomical observations.

Geography was related to astronomy because it involved the idea of the world as a sphere, divided into climate zones that could be measured by astronomical observation. As early as the sixth century B.C., Ionian philosophers had speculated about the world's geography, and Herodotus had described the three known continents—Europe, Africa, and Asia—as well as he could in his history. When Alexander the Great set out to conquer the East, part of his mission was to advance Greek geographic knowledge. He measured the distances of his march and sent explorers along the coast of the Indian Ocean. Later, under the Seleucids, Greeks explored and wrote about India, the Caspian Sea, and even the North Sea. In the mid-third century B.C. Eratosthenes gathered together all of this information and published a geographic work that described the *oikoumene*—the "inhabited world," which he imagined as an oval-shaped land mass. Eratosthenes also invented the notion of longitude and latitude and calculated the circumference of the earth; although his method was inaccurate, his answer was close to the correct one.*

Hellenistic scientists investigated theoretical problems but were also interested in applied science—mechanics or engineering—and the same individuals often made contributions in both areas. In mathematics, Euclid (about whom little is known except the works that circulate under his name) published a sort of textbook called *Elements* that remained the basis for mathematical knowledge through the nineteenth century. The surviving works of

---

*Hipparchus disagreed with Eratosthenes' estimate and published his own calculation of the earth's circumference—about 20,500 miles, which is too small. In the second century A.D., Ptolemy used this estimate in his own work on geography, which was rediscovered in Europe in the late fourteenth century. It was this calculation that led Columbus to underestimate the westward distance from Europe to Asia and to believe that he had landed at islands off the coast of China (instead of in the Caribbean).

Archimedes of Syracuse, who lived in the third century B.C., are also theoretical in nature; they investigate problems in geometry, number theory, and hydrostatics. His most famous discovery was that the volume and density of a body could be calculated by the amount of liquid it displaced when immersed (an idea that occurred to him in the bath; he ran naked through the streets shouting "Eureka!"). But he was also remembered for his inventions, including the compound pulley and a screw used to lift water for irrigation or drainage that was named after him and widely used. His contemporary Ctesibius invented the forced-air pump, of which numerous examples have been found. Thus it is not correct to say that the aristocratic mentality of Hellenistic scientists prevented them from inventing machines of great practical utility. For example, in his treatise called *Pneumatics*, Hero of Alexandria's description of several amusing, elaborate toys (which were probably never built) reflects the leisured society in which he lived, but he also describes the screw-press, an important advance over the lever-press used to make olive oil. Military engineering also flourished in the Hellenistic period; especially, improved ballistic weapons were invented, including a sort of automatic catapult. Archimedes is supposed to have helped defend the city of Syracuse, besieged by the Romans, with weapons of his own design. It was the Hellenistic Greeks who invented some of the building techniques that were most widely influential in Roman architecture—such as the arch and vault and the underfloor heating system used in Roman baths.

The influence of Babylonian mathematics and astronomy on Greek thought is especially obvious in the Hellenistic era. Aristarchus, Euclid, and Hipparchus all developed ideas that seem to derive from a new familiarity with Babylonian science. Although Greeks had always (with brief interruptions) been in contact with other civilizations, a new level of cultural interaction was reached in the Hellenistic period.

Medicine. **Anatomy** means "cutting open" in Greek. One of the most important and influential developments in ancient Greek medicine was the use of dissection to find out about the body's internal structure. The authors of the Hippocratic Corpus had speculated about this, but they scarcely refer to dissection at all. Aristotle dissected animals and was able to make many accurate observations about their anatomy, although logical deduction is usually more prominent than direct observation in his reasoning.

Most of the Greeks' most important anatomical discoveries date to the Hellenistic period. In the early third century B.C., two physicians working at Alexandria—Herophilus and Erasistratus—dissected human beings and perhaps vivisected them as well (that is, cut them open while they were still alive). They described the organs of the female reproductive system, the ventricles of the brain, the nerves (especially the paired nerves in the cranium), the membranes of the eye, and the valves of the heart much more accurately than physicians of the Classical period.

While dissections and vivisections of animals were performed at other times and places, the only solid evidence for the dissection of humans comes from early Alexandria. The patronage of a new dynasty—the Ptolemies—willing to break long-standing taboos might be part of the explanation; the influence of Egyptian culture, with its tradition of mummifying dead bodies (and removing and preserving their internal organs), might also have played a role.

Philosophy.   The story of philosophy in the Hellenistic period illustrates a prominent trend in the intellectual history of this time: the development of traditions called "schools" or "sects" today. The Greeks sometimes called this type of intellectual allegience **hairesis,** which means "choosing"—in this case, the choice of a particular set of ideas. Later, Christians used the same word to label those theological beliefs that they disapproved of (this is the origin of our word "heresy").

Athens remained the most prestigious place to study philosophy, and its philosophical schools—such as Plato's Academy—continued to function. But adopting the ideas of a sect did not necessarily mean attending (or teaching at) a particular school. The sects were simply traditions about philosophical truth, passed down from teacher to student.

The **Epicurean** sect was named after its founder, Epicurus, who established a new school called "the garden" at Athens around 300 B.C. The Epicureans adopted the atomic theory of physics and believed that the universe was the result of a chance amalgamation of atoms rather than the work of a providential god. They believed that gods existed but took no interest in what happens on earth and that the human soul is mortal and dissipates at death. They considered the pursuit of pleasure the best way to a happy life (a doctrine that made them notorious when it was misunderstood by later philosophers and Christians), but that most pleasures are outweighed by the pain associated with them. Therefore they advocated withdrawal from politics, love, and the pursuit of wealth and advocated a simple, austere way of life. The works of Epicurus himself survive only in fragments; the only complete Epicurean text that has come down to us is a work in Latin, by Lucretius, dating to the first century B.C.

Zeno founded the **Stoic** sect at about the same time that Epicurus established his new school. His sect was named after the "Painted Stoa," a building in the Athenian *agora* where he lectured to anyone who wanted to listen. Stoics believed in fate—that everything happens according to strict rules governed by divine providence, upon which human effort can have little effect. They believed that living a virtuous life was the best way to achieve happiness. They associated the idea of virtue closely with reason; believing that human nature was essentially rational, they argued that people should suppress their emotions and accept what fate brings them with equanimity.

Perhaps the most interesting and mysterious of the philosophical sects was the **Cynic** sect, which took its name from the Greek word for "dog." The first Cynic was Diogenes, who lived in Athens in the mid-300s B.C. Extremely antisocial, he challenged and exposed the hypocrisy of virtually all civilized institutions (such as education, class distinctions, and marriage) with his acid wit, outrageous behavior, scruffy appearance, and voluntary poverty (he lived outdoors and begged for food). Subsequent generations of Cynic philosophers were distinguished not so much by their belief in certain doctrines as by their way of life—bearded, wandering, simply dressed, carrying only a pouch and a staff, they were easy to spot wherever they appeared and were prominent in Greek cities throughout the Hellenistic and Roman periods. An interesting feature of Cynicism was that some of its most extreme advocates were able to stand up to Hellenistic kings and Roman emperors as no one else could—criticizing them openly and surviving the experience. Many tales of such encounters between Cynic philosophers and figures such as Alexander the Great or the notorious emperor Caligula survive. They were cultural heroes of a kind, and they may have represented the obligation of a ruler to abide by the values that society imposed on him and that philosophy—with its emphasis on ethics—expressed.

Literature and Literary Scholarship.   Tragedy, philosophy, history, epic, and other literary genres invented in the Archaic and Classical periods continued in use in Hellenistic times. Hellenistic authors consciously strove to imitate previous writers—such as Homer—while at the same time adapting the models they used in distinctive ways. But some new and influential types of literature also arose in this period. One of these was "New Comedy," which in some ways resembled modern situation comedy (with its stock characters and silly plot devices). Another was a type of poetry about herdsmen called "pastoral" poetry, which idealized the rural life in ways still influential today. The Greek romance novel was probably invented in the Hellenistic period (but since all surviving examples date to Roman times, they will be discussed in the next chapter).

Biography became a common literary form in the Hellenistic period. This increasing interest in describing individual lives may be related to the new place of portraiture in Hellenistic art: Not only the ruler-portraits described later, but also portraits of past and contemporary intellectuals (such as Homer, Socrates, or various Hellenistic philosophers) were produced in large quantities. Like portraiture, biography's subjects were great statesmen and generals, or intellectual figures such as philosophers and poets.

Biographies played a number of important roles in Greco-Roman culture. They tended to focus on moral issues and questions of character; by praising and blaming good and bad behavior, they reinforced social values. They could also be a type of propaganda, defending a political or intellectual leader against the accusations of rival sects. The focus on intellectual heroes reflects the key role of culture in the Greeks' sense of their identity and superiority.

One of the most important intellectual developments in the Hellenistic period was literary and textual scholarship. Scholars at Alexandria edited classical texts, eliminated discrepancies to arrive at a single standard text (Homer's works were now standardized in this way), attempted to determine which texts (or passages) were authentically written by their supposed authors, added punctuation marks that made them easier to read, and inter-

---

Art and Society

SCULPTURE AND THE CITY IN THE HELLENISTIC WORLD

It is almost impossible to generalize about sculpture in the Hellenistic period because its features are very diverse. But one of the most interesting trends that distinguishes it from classical sculpture is its political relevance: Much Hellenistic sculpture directly reflects its historical context and has a political purpose.

Eutychides' Tyche of Antioch (Roman copy).   (Scala/Art Resource, NY)

This statue by Eutychides (ca. 300 B.C.) portrays the Tyche, or "Fortune," of Antioch. The city is personified as a woman wearing a crown like a city wall, grasping an ear of wheat to represent prosperity, with her foot resting on a swimming, naked man—the personification of the river Orontes. The Tyche

---

represented the city much more clearly and directly than classical statues of patron gods and goddesses. By the end of the Hellenistic period at least forty-four Greek cities had similar statues.

Portrait of Alexander from Pergamum, dating to the early second century B.C.   (Erich Lessing/Art Resource, NY)

Portraiture became important in the Hellenistic period—especially portraits of rulers. Ancient tradition traced the origins of the ruler portrait to Alexander, whose likeness was sculpted by the famous artist Lysippus. While few or no sculpted portraits of Alexander dating to his lifetime survive, his very numerous portraits from later periods show features that reflect individual characteristics rather than an ideal of beauty—for example, his distinctive hairstyle with a cowlick in the center of his forehead. Other aspects of this Alexander portrait—such as the way he turns his head dramatically and looks upward—may project a heroic image; thus the ruler portrait (or any portrait) combines features that distinguish the subject as an individual with features that reflect the message that the artist wants to convey. Hellenistic rulers published their portraits on statues and coins so that all their subjects would become familiar with them.

Hellenistic sculpture sometimes portrayed historical events, especially a ruler's glorious military victories. Perhaps the most spectacular example of this

The "Dying Gaul," from Pergamum (Roman copy). The Gaul's right arm has been restored.   (Scala/Art Resource, NY)

kind of sculpture was a group of statues that once stood on the acropolis of Pergamum. This monument commemorated King Attalus I's victory over the Galatians—Gauls (a Celtic people) who had migrated from Europe to Asia Minor—around 233 B.C. Roman copies of some of these statues survive and depict naked Gauls in the highly dramatic poses typical of some Hellenistic art. Here, the subject sinks to the ground as blood gushes from a wound; his shaggy hair and mustache identify him as a Celtic "barbarian." The sculpture celebrates and publicizes a real and recent (rather than a remote and mythical) victory.

preted them in commentaries. The Alexandrians' focus on literary works as texts—as items to be read—may reflect the growing importance of writing in the Hellenistic period. Their choice of texts for editing forever influenced the future of Western culture, as this partly determined what would survive. The canon they established reflected the prestige of classical Athens, already perceived as Greek civilization's "high water mark."

Summary

Around 1100 B.C., Greece sank into a "dark age" of poverty, isolation, and population decline. When it began to emerge slowly from this period beginning in the 800s B.C., a different type of civilization arose. Although it included slavery, it was in some ways more egalitarian than other ancient societies—it was organized around the *polis* (or "city"), whose citizens could claim a certain amount of equality in rights and status.

In 480 B.C. the Greeks, under the leadership of the Athenians and Spartans, defeated a massive invasion of the Persian army. Afterward, the city of Athens established a type of imperial rule over the Greek cities under its control. It became the cultural center of the Greek world—most surviving literature of the fifth and fourth centuries B.C. was produced at Athens. While its constitution became more democratic in this period, inequalities based on citizenship and gender became more prominent.

Athens and Sparta fought a long and enervating war, which Athens lost. In the later 300s B.C., the kingdom of Macedonia gradually gained political control of the Greek world. In an extraordinary series of campaigns, its king Alexander the Great conquered Persia; after his death, the territory he had acquired was divided among his companions. The Hellenistic kingdoms were ruled by descendants of these Macedonian generals until, one by one, they were absorbed by the Roman Empire. As a result, Greek culture (including its language) became an influential force throughout the Near East.

THREE

The Romans and Their Empire

Roman Origins

On the Palatine, a hill near the city's busy forum where its wealthiest and most powerful families built their houses, the Romans preserved a structure they called the "hut of Romulus." They believed that this one-room cottage with a thatched roof was once the home of their legendary founder and first king. Post-holes cut into bedrock survive today, confirming that a settlement on the Palatine dating back to the eighth century B.C. existed. It was similar to other Iron Age villages in northern Italy, belonging to the simple culture that scholars call "Villanovan." Latin, the language of Rome and of the peoples around it ("Latium"), was just one of about forty languages spoken on the Italian peninsula at the time. Two civilizations in particular—the Etruscans to the north and the Greek colonies of the south—were more advanced than the early Romans. The story of Rome, as the Romans themselves told it, was the story of a people that rose from these humble origins to conquer the Mediterranean world.

The Romans did not begin writing their own history until about 200 B.C. As a result, much of the tradition about early Rome is based on oral sources and sounds like myth or folktale to a modern reader. But unlike Greek mythical figures, the heroes of Rome's early past were not taller, stronger, wealthier, or better-looking than their remote descendants; they were exceptional only in virtue. Today, the best-preserved account of Rome's early history in Latin is that of Livy, who lived from 59 B.C. to A.D. 17. Livy tells stories of leaders who sacrificed their lives, their bodies, or their children for the state—to guarantee military victory, freedom from tyranny, or political stability. A small farmer named Cincinnatus assumed supreme command of the army in an emergency, only to return to his farm when the crisis was over. Generations of generals with the same name—Publius Decius Mus—charged suicidally into enemy lines to win the favor of the gods in battle. Other stories warned of the power of imperialism to corrupt; thus the conquest of the wealthy city of Veii (396 B.C.) touched off a social crisis. Poverty and simplicity—exemplified in

---

| Doing History |

A NOTE ON ROMAN NAMES

Romans might have three names or more. By the late Republic a typical name consisted of a *praenomen* ("first name"), a *nomen gentilicium* ("family name"), and a *cognomen* ("surname"), which often originated as a nickname given to an individual. The family name and surname were hereditary; the first name was given at birth. The Romans used only a few first names, and when written down they were usually abbreviated; M. stood for Marcus, L. for Lucius, P. for Publius, C. for Gaius (because no separate letter G had been invented yet), Cn. for Gnaeus, and so on.

Women usually had only one name, the feminine version of the family name. Thus M. Tullius Cicero's daughter was called Tullia. This led to the paradox that all of the daughters in the same family had the same name, although sometimes they were distinguished by nicknames ("the younger," "the third," etc.). They did not change their names when they married.

When someone became a Roman citizen (for example, upon being freed from slavery), he or she adopted a Roman-style name. It was common to choose the first and family names of one's former master or of the person who had sponsored one's citizenship or, later, of the emperors. Thus M. Tullius Cicero's slave Tiro, when freed, became M. Tullius Tiro.

An interesting feature of Roman names is that they were not, as in many Indo-European cultures, honorific. While Greeks might be called "Famous for Wisdom" (Sophocles) or "leader of the people" (Archidamus), Roman names tend to express mundane or even negative ideas; some famous family names and surnames meant "Flabby," "Puppy," or "Pig-like." P. Decius Mus' cognomen meant "Mouse."

---

the "hut of Romulus"—were important Roman values, and the Romans' ambivalence about the conquests that enriched them is one of the most interesting themes in their literature.

The Romans had a profound sense of their origins and destiny. While their stories of the early past reflect—and helped to establish—their identity as a nation, it is difficult for modern historians to use them if our aims are different. Archaeology is the most important source of direct, contemporary evidence about early Rome.

Some written sources dating to early times were available to ancient Roman writers, although most are lost today. The most intriguing of these were called the **Annales maximi.** Every year from an early date, the city's chief priest posted a record of that year's most important events—such as wars and treaties, new public buildings, laws and grants of citizenship, famines, omens, and disasters. Because the *Annales* are now lost, it is difficult for us to tell how much they were embellished by those who published or used them. But in antiquity they were the main source of documentary evi-

IMPORTANT DATES IN EARLY ROMAN HISTORY

*753 B.C.	Foundation of Rome
*510 B.C.	Expulsion of the kings
*494 B.C.	First Secession of the Plebs; creation of tribunes
*451–450 B.C.	Promulgation of the Twelve Tables
*390 B.C.	Rome sacked by Gauls
264–241 B.C.	First Punic War
218–201 B.C.	Second Punic War
197 B.C.	Defeat of Philip V at Cynoscephalae in Second Macedonian War
184 B.C.	Censorship of Cato the Elder
168 B.C.	Perseus defeated at Pydna in Third Macedonian War
146 B.C.	Sack of Carthage in Third Punic War and sack of Corinth
133 B.C.	Assassination of Tiberius Gracchus
63 B.C.	Cicero's consulship
49–45 B.C.	Civil war between Caesar and Pompey
44 B.C.	Assassination of Julius Caesar

An asterisk (*) indicates that the date is traditional.

dence about Rome's remote past, and some aspects of Latin historiography—such as a tendency to organize the narrative year-by-year—reflect the influence of the *Annales*.

Who Were the Romans?

The Romans' sense of themselves was especially complicated because the boundaries of "Romanness" were very fluid. One did not have to be born a Roman to become one—they extended citizenship to freed slaves and to certain allies and conquered peoples. Two of the stories the Romans told about their origins reflect this openness. In one, Rome's original settlers were fugitive debtors and criminals granted asylum by its founder, Romulus. Because there were no women among them, Romulus arranged for the kidnap of virgins from a nearby tribe, the Sabines. Another story told how Romulus was descended from Aeneas, a Trojan hero from Homer's *Iliad*; he escaped from the city when it fell, wandered to Italy, and married a Latin princess. Thus the Romans imagined their founders as outcasts and their ancestors as ethnically mixed. The Aeneas legend also shows how they adapted elements of foreign cultures—although influenced by the Greeks, they created their own interpretation of Homeric myth that served their national needs.*

From Village to City

The oldest traces of settlement at Rome date to about 1000 B.C. Archaeologists date the Palatine huts and a dirt wall on the Palatine to the eighth century B.C., and most scholars in antiquity placed Romulus' foundation of Rome in 753 B.C. Beginning around 650 B.C., Rome began to develop into a city. The **forum** was drained and paved—at first just an open, public space, it became the city's nerve-center, like the *agora* of Athens. A large and famous temple of Jupiter was built on the Capitoline hill and dedicated in 510 B.C. Large stone houses built on the Palatine in the late 500s reflect the rise of a wealthy elite, and inscriptions show that the Romans were using writing for some public purposes. At this time Rome was the leading power in Latium, had a population of perhaps thirty thousand, and controlled a territory of about nine hundred square miles.

The Etruscans

Legend told that in the 500s B.C. Rome was subject to foreign kings—a dynasty of Etruscans, who built the public works and monuments that transformed it into a city. Etruscan civilization is known mainly through the excavation of tombs. Although they used a version of the Greek alphabet, their language is not well understood since it is not related to any known ancient or modern language. While thousands of Etruscan inscriptions survive, most are short, and no Etruscan literary works are known.

Scholars in antiquity argued about whether the Etruscans were native to the Italian peninsula or had emigrated from the East. Today, most scholars agree that Etruscan civilization developed from native Villanovan culture. Its homeland was the part of Italy today called "Tuscany," where ancient sources name twelve great Etruscan cities, some of which have been partially excavated, but evidence of Etruscan settlement has been found as far south as Campania.

The main Etruscan archaeological sites are cemeteries, where aristocrats were buried in round, mounded chamber-tombs called *tumuli*. Some tombs contained fine pots from Attica, art objects from the Greek and Near Eastern world, and elaborately worked items in precious metal, attesting to the Etruscans' extensive trade contacts and to the wealth of their highest social classes. Aristocratic women's burials were similar to those of men, suggesting (along with some other evidence) a degree of equality between men and women of high rank.

---

*The greatest expression of the Aeneas legend is the *Aeneid* by Vergil, a poet of the first century B.C.

The Romans associated divination with the Etruscans and traced many of their religious practices to them. This Etruscan mirror shows the seer Calchas examining an animal's internal organs, a type of divination called haruspicia *in Latin. Calchas was a figure from Greek mythology, illustrating the influence of Hellenic culture in Etruria.* (Scala/Art Resource, NY)

By about 600 B.C., perhaps under the influence of the Greeks, the Etruscans had begun to portray their gods "anthropomorphically"—as looking like humans. It was also perhaps from the Greeks that they got the idea of constructing temples, but they developed their own distinctive architectural style. The earliest archaeological example is a temple at Veii dating to about 500 B.C.: It had a raised platform with steps and columns in the front and an overhanging, pitched roof that was lavishly decorated with terracotta statues representing a scene from Greek mythology. Roman sources tell us that the nearly contemporary temple of Jupiter at Rome was built in the same style, by Etruscan craftsmen. They describe the Etruscans as skilled at divination and especially at the art of *haruspicia*—reading omens in the entrails of a sacrificed animal.

Modern scholars sometimes see seventh- and sixth-century B.C. developments in Roman culture such as urbanization, permanent stone houses, public architecture, and anthropomorphic religion as results of an Etruscan conquest of Rome, relying partly on the Roman legend of a dynasty of Etruscan kings. But, it is also possible that Latin and Etruscan culture developed side by side, stimulated by their encounters with one another or with other peoples, such as the Greeks, who began to colonize the Italian peninsula in the eighth century B.C.

Government and Society in the Early Republic

One of the most important stories the Romans told about their early history was the legend of the expulsion of the kings. This was a sexual drama in which a woman named Lucretia was raped by the king's son and avenged by her male relatives (led by her uncle's friend, L. Junius Brutus); in some ways it is similar to the Athenian legend of the assassination of Pisistratus' son by two male lovers. The precise year of the kings' expulsion was disputed in antiquity, but one scholarly tradition dated it to 510 B.C.—the same year as the expulsion of the last tyrant from Athens. The story reflects the Romans' impulse to relate their own history to that of the Greeks, whose more advanced culture influenced them from a very early date. The Romans were proud that, like the Greeks, they were no longer ruled by kings. They called the system of government that evolved in the centuries that followed the *Res publica*—literally, "the public matter."

The Ruling Class

In some ways the Roman constitution resembled a Greek *politeia*. It had an assembly, in which all citizens voted; a council, called the senate, whose essential role was to advise magistrates; and magistrates who commanded the army, proposed legislation, and judged legal cases. But the Roman political system was much more aristocratic and hierarchical than, for example, the constitution of classical Athens. Senators and the chief magistrates—two **consuls,** elected every year—came only from the best families. Romans voted in units, not as individuals; and in the most important assembly (the **comitia centuriata** or "centuriate assembly"), the highest economic classes had more voting units than the lower ones.

The consuls wielded **imperium,** which signified the power to command the army, and also to condemn people to death; it had a civil, judicial aspect as well as a military one. At Rome, legal authority tended to center on individuals of high status. These might be magistrates such as consuls, or the **praetor,** a sort of public judge; or the father in an aristocratic family; or a landowner, who might resolve disputes among his tenants or slaves. Whereas at Athens, judicial power lay in the hands of the people, at Rome it was the privilege and responsibility of the highest ranking men in a hierarchical society.

Italy in the Republican Period

From the earliest times throughout Rome's history, social relations were dominated by the system that modern authors call **patronage** or **clientela,** using Latin terms that described, for example, a legal advocate (patron) and his client.* The Romans had no word for this system, because to them it was just the way things were done. People of unequal rank were bound by ties of loyalty and gratitude—the higher-ranking person ("patron") would lend his support to the lower-ranking one (the "client"; "dependent" is sometimes a

---

*The master of a freed slave was also called his or her "patron," and the words are used in some other contexts.

better word). Sometimes this took the form of representation in court, but it could be almost any kind of favor. The client, from gratitude, did what he could for his benefactor. Men of high status could acquire power over large numbers of dependents, who would vote for them in an election (for example), but also could be called upon for many other purposes. Thus legend told that one aristocratic family, the Fabii, raised a private army from its clients. The visible crowd of clients around an aristocrat, or the invisible but well-known web of his connections, increased the respect in which he was held and also gave him the power to coerce or intimidate.

Who were the "patrons" in this system? This depended on the context. Anyone who could do favors could be a patron; wealth, high office, social connections, eloquence (for successful pleading in court), and military success (which brought booty, fame, and the loyalty of the soldiers) all increased one's ability to act as patron. A few aristocratic families occupied the top ranks of the Roman hierarchy, but a relatively ordinary person could be a patron in his own social circle and, at the same time, the client of a more powerful aristocrat (his connection with this man would also increase his perceived ability to do favors). Patronage was a dynamic system—everyone's status was constantly being challenged, reasserted, augmented, or imperiled. It relied not so much on legal or official roles as on social relationships (such as friendship) and emotions (such as gratitude) to work. One's privileges and obligations were not sharply defined, but depended on the situation.

Social relationships among people of roughly equal rank were also important. Aristocrats traditionally took the advice of a council of friends before making important decisions—this applied to generals in the field, judges hearing cases, or fathers making decisions for the family. But aristocrats also competed with one another for power, especially for election to the consulship and military command. Many stories of the early Republic heroize those commanders who subordinated their own ambitions to the good of the community, suggesting that competitiveness was a problem.

Plebeians and Patricians

Ancient accounts of the Republic's first centuries are dominated by the story of the "conflict of the orders"—a class struggle between two groups called **patricians** and **plebeians.** Only a small number of families had patrician status, and the class was hereditary; there was no way to become a patrician except to be born one. Patricians dominated the consulship, although the names of a few early plebeian consuls are known. Wealthy or well-born plebeians wanted a fair chance to be consul because of the prestige of the office and especially because it involved a military command. But the problem went deeper than just resentment over the consulship. Partly by monopolizing high political offices, patricians could oppress plebeians with unfair legal decisions. Patricians tended to be wealthier than plebeians; many plebeians were indebted to them, and debt laws were harsh.

Gradually, the plebeians succeeded in their struggle for more equality. A new type of magistrate called the **tribune** was invented; tribunes could cancel the actions of any other magistrate (including the consuls) with a "veto," which means "I prohibit." No one was allowed to assault or kill them, so that patricians could not coerce them physically. Tradition dated this change to 494 B.C. The plebeians also forced the patricians to publish parts of the law so that it might be applied more consistently; this first Roman legal code was called the **Twelve Tables.** The plebeians won the right to hold the consulship, and a new assembly called the **comitia tributa** was created; it was organized into geographic units called **tribes,** not by property class. In 287 B.C. a new law made the decrees of this assembly binding on all Romans, including patricians. This put an end to class conflict for about 150 years.

Society in the Twelve Tables

Ancient sources tell us that the Twelve Tables were drawn up by a board of ten magistrates in 451 B.C. No text has survived, and our knowledge of their contents is based on references in later sources. The accuracy of the Romans' memory of the Twelve Tables has been disputed; moreover, reality does not always conform with legal theory. Nevertheless, the Twelve Tables are our best evidence for early Roman society.

They reflect an environment where writing was not widespread. Although the laws themselves are supposed to have been written down, they never mention writing. Their language has features that made them easy to memorize (and schoolboys in the late Republic learned them this way), and the legal procedures they describe are all oral. One passage prohibits slanderous songs, a problem that seems typical of an oral society.

The economy of the Twelve Tables is overwhelmingly agricultural. They mention no professions other than farming and address problems typical of agrarian societies, such as right-of-way through farmland and property rights on the border between farms. They prescribe harsh penalties for defaulting debtors; creditors could seize them and sell them into slavery or even kill them. The law also mentions a notorious institution called *nexum*, which was probably a type of debt-bondage or temporary enslavement until the debt was worked off.

The family in the Twelve Tables is patriarchal, dominated by its male head, the **paterfamilias.** He held a type of power called *patria potestas* over his sons and daughters (even if they were grown), which included the power to sell them into slavery.

Manus, the power of a husband over his wife, was less comprehensive than *patria potestas*. Even in the Twelve Tables it was fairly easy for a wife to avoid coming under the legal authority of her husband. Independent women whose fathers were dead could inherit property. They were required to have guardians (this may reflect Greek influence), but one clause in the code protects women's property rights against embezzlement by their guardians, thus recognizing women as the true owners of their property. These are some early indications that the status of women in the Roman world would be higher that their status in classical Athens.

Warfare and the Conquest of Italy

The army of the early Republic was organized into **legions** under the command of the consuls. Legions originally numbered three thousand heavy-armed infantry. At first the Roman army fought like Greek hoplites, but it gradually developed a more flexible formation, and light-armed troops were added to the legion. There was a property qualification for serving in the army; the poorest citizens were not drafted.

The Romans went to war almost every year. By the middle of the third century B.C. they had brought most of Italy south of the Po river under their control. This was a long process, full of setbacks. One of these occurred in 390 B.C., when Rome was sacked by a tribe of Gauls invading from the north. The mass of legend that arose around this event shows its long-ranging psychological impact. Rome would not be sacked again until A.D. 410.

The Romans' conquest of the Samnites is a good example of their military achievement in Italy. The Samnites were a confederacy of tribes that lived in the mountains of south-central Italy. Between 343 and 290 B.C. the Romans fought three wars with them. In 321 they suffered a devastating defeat at the Caudine Forks, but they continued the war (this was their second against the Samnites) for sixteen more years until they could declare victory.

Thus peoples conquered by the Romans might have to be defeated several times. The Samnites continued to oppose Rome by taking sides with its enemies in the war with Pyrrhus (280–275 B.C.), the war with Hannibal (218–201 B.C.), and the Social War (91–89 B.C.). The Romans succeeded in conquering Italy not because of some superior knack for warfare, but because they kept fighting the same enemies year after year, without giving up.

The Romans did not treat all the defeated peoples of Italy in the same way; rather, they adapted their rule to the specific situation. Some, including most of the towns of Latium, were eventually granted citizenship; others held "Latin rights" (which included the right to acquire citizenship by emigrating to Rome); others were granted a limited "citizenship without the vote." Some communities had no special status but were simply called "allies."

Sometimes the Romans founded colonies that were settled by Roman citizens (usually veterans), who each received an allotment of land. But the Romans also annexed land belonging to their subjects—called **ager publicus,** or public land—and gave or rented it to citizens without founding a colony.

From an early date the Romans counted their citizens and assessed their property; this was called a **census,** and its main purpose was to gather information for taxation and the draft. Roman citizens paid a tax called *tributum* (**tribute**), which mainly paid for the army. Both citizens and allies were required to furnish military recruits. In this way Rome's military strength grew, and its subjects had an economic interest in fighting and winning since some of the booty would be distributed to them.

Gradually, Italy became more unified and "Romanized." The network of roads that the Romans built for the army also made travel easy throughout Italy. After 167 B.C., Italians no longer paid tribute and Roman military ven-

The sacrophagus of Lucius Cornelius Scipio Barbatus, who was consul in 298 B.C. and died in the mid-200s, stood near the door to the tomb of the Scipio family on the Appian Way, just outside Rome's walls. It is an early illustration of cultural values that characterized the Roman aristocracy throughout the Republican period. The sculpted motifs recall features of Greek architecture: an Ionic column capital and a Doric frieze of metopes and triglyphs. The epitaph is in Saturnian meter, a type of native Latin verse, and records the offices he held and the places he captured in war.   (Scala/Art Resource, NY)

tures were financed by taxes on its overseas subjects; and after the Social War of 91–89 B.C., citizenship was extended to all Italians (although the Romans resisted this for a long time).

Conquests Overseas

The most interesting ancient account of Rome's expansion overseas was written by Polybius, who was one of one thousand Greeks from Achaea deported to Rome in the 160s B.C. because they were suspected of opposing Roman influence. He became friends with prominent Roman aristocrats; he traveled widely and witnessed a dramatic moment in Rome's history, the destruction of Carthage in 146 B.C.; and late in life, he returned to Greece to help confirm Roman rule there. Polybius wrote a history of Rome that began with its first war with Carthage and told the story of its subsequent conquests including that of his own people. Written in Greek and apparently addressed to a Greek audience, it seeks to explain what he perceived as the Roman domination of the world.

Polybius thought that from as early as the First Punic War (i.e., the first war with Carthage, 264–241 B.C.) the Romans had formed the intention of conquering the world, and he argues that they had actually accomplished this by 168 B.C.—the year that they defeated Perseus, the last king of Macedonia. He did not mean that they had occupied or annexed most of the world to their empire; the Romans did not always try to do this, and only a few territories were under direct Roman rule at this time. Polybius did not imagine the empire as a geographic territory, but as a sphere of influence in which the Romans could dictate or coerce the actions of foreign kings and peoples. In fact, it is often difficult to tell when a specific area became a "province" of the Roman Empire in the modern sense of the word. The term **provincia,** which originally meant a magistrate's assigned sphere of action (especially, the likely theater of operations for a consul in command of an army), seems to have developed its territorial meaning only gradually.

Scholars today often criticize Polybius' attribution to the Romans of a deliberate strategy of world-conquest, pointing out that the Romans tended to react to circumstances rather than to attack purely for the sake of conquest. The solution to this paradox—how did the Romans acquire a vast empire while appearing to behave defensively?—lies in the social or psychological dimension of Roman strategy: The Romans believed they were in danger unless everyone was terrified of them and obedient to them; so that if a tribe or kingdom offended them, they took aggressive action to prevent similar behavior in the future. Thus even though the Romans seem to react to problems rather than to seek out conquests, their way of thinking led to imperial expansion.

Some of Rome's overseas wars were very lucrative, both for the generals and for the common soldiers, who received a share of the booty. Also, the Roman aristocracy granted high prestige to military prowess and these values influenced the senate's foreign policy decisions (although senators could also be very cautious about allowing other senators to achieve too much glory). But perhaps the most important factors driving Roman imperialism lay deeper than simple self-interest: their image of themselves as a warlike people and their social system in which the ability to command respect through benefaction or intimidation was paramount. The Romans believed in the need to reassert their authority aggressively if it was challenged and frequently showed their willingness to commit all their resources and make any sacrifice to do so.

Carthage and the West.   Rome's first overseas enemy was Carthage, on the coast of modern Tunisia. It was founded by Phoenicians in the ninth or eighth century B.C.; the Romans called the Phoenicians *Punici* and referred to their wars with Carthage as the **Punic wars.** In the 200s B.C. Carthage was a thriving port with a large merchant fleet as well as a strong navy. It had colonies and armies in Sicily, Sardinia, Spain, and all along the northern coast of Africa.

The Romans fought three wars with Carthage between 264 and 146 B.C. The first two Punic wars (264–241 and 218–201) were long and difficult, and the Romans suffered heavy losses. In the Second Punic War, the Carthaginian general Hannibal invaded Italy from Spain. There he won three devastating battles against the Romans; many of Rome's Italian allies changed sides, thinking that Hannibal was going to win. But the Romans did not surrender; they continued to fight Hannibal and their disloyal allies in Italy and also fought the Carthaginians in Spain. In 203 B.C. they invaded Africa and Hannibal was recalled to defend, unsuccessfully, the Carthaginian homeland. The Romans remained wary of the Carthaginians, and in 149 B.C. they responded to a Carthaginian treaty violation with a major invasion. Three years later, they totally destroyed the city; the inhabitants were killed or sold into slavery, and the city itself was demolished.

As a result of the Punic wars, Rome asserted its influence in areas that had formerly belonged to Carthage. From some peoples, they collected taxes—for example, in Sicily, whose inhabitants had been accustomed to pay tax to the Greek ruler of Syracuse. Some areas—such as Spain—needed to be occupied permanently if their peoples refused to acquiesce to Roman demands. In fact, the Romans kept two armies in Spain under two separate magistrates, who gradually increased the areas subject to them in a series of difficult, often brutal campaigns. The permanent occupation of Spain and some other overseas territories eventually put extreme pressure on the army, which was not composed of professional mercenaries but of peasant farmers who resented being kept from their land for long periods.

To command the armies and supervise the collection of taxes in these overseas territories, the Romans appointed magistrates with *imperium.* Since some of the *provinciae* needed permanent commands, the Romans raised the number of praetors gradually to six. They also extended magistrates' terms of office by a device called prorogation, so that an aristocrat might serve one year as praetor or consul and two or more years as propraetor or proconsul in his *provincia.*

Rome and the Hellenistic Kingdoms.   Gradually, Rome was drawn into the world of the Hellenistic kingdoms of the East. Its first major confrontations were with Philip V of Macedonia and Antiochus III of Syria. The Romans' crushing defeat of Philip at Cynoscephalae in 197 B.C. was a brutal shock to the Greek world—the Hellenistic kings were used to fighting one another, but now they found that they could not ignore this new power to the west.

In a famous proclamation at the Isthmian games in 196 B.C., the the consul Titus Quinctius Flamininus, victor over Philip V, announced the freedom of

---

The Written Record

A Triumphal Parade

In 189 b.c., L. Cornelius Scipio celebrated a victory over King Antiochus III of Syria with a **triumph**, a spectacular parade. Livy's description illustrates not only the relish with which the Romans celebrated the defeat and humiliation of their enemies but also the fabulous wealth that they brought back, as booty, from some of their conquests. Livy probably draws his statistics from the official triumphal records that the Romans kept (the *Acta triumphorum*).

He triumphed in the intercalary month, on the day before the first of March. . . . In the triumph he carried [on "floats"] 224 [captured] military standards, 134 models of [captured] towns, 1,231 ivory tusks, 234 gold crowns, 137,420 pounds of silver, 224,000 Attic four-drachma coins, 321,700 *cistophori* [another type of coin], 140,000 gold Philippic coins, and 1,023 pounds of silver vases, all decorated in relief. And 32 royal generals, prefects, and nobles were led before the chariot. Twenty-five *denarii* were given to each of the soldiers, twice that to the centurions, and three times that to the cavalrymen. (Livy 37.59)

---

the Greeks. His audience, which had resented Macedonian meddling in Greek politics and occupation of Greek cities, was ecstatic. But while the Romans did not occupy Greece or collect taxes from it, they expected the Greek cities to obey their will. Similarly, the Romans were content to leave defeated Hellenistic monarchs in place as long as they were obedient and respectful; but both the Greeks and the Hellenistic kings soon discovered that they would retaliate severely if their demands were ignored or if they thought that their subjects were showing insufficient deference to them. When Philip's son Perseus sought to reassert Macedonian power, the Romans declared war, inflicted a severe military defeat at Pydna in 168, and abolished the kingship, dividing the Macedonian kingdom into four "republics." In this war the Romans devastated the kingdom of Epirus (roughly modern Albania), which had supported Perseus, reportedly enslaving 150,000 prisoners. Later, when a pretender called Philip Andriscus tried to assert himself as king of Macedonia, the Romans invaded again (in 148), crushed the opposition, and occupied Macedonia with an army. When a confederacy of "free" Greek cities called the Achaean League declined to obey Roman commands and insulted Roman ambassadors, the Romans responded with the total destruction of the famous city of Corinth. This occurred in 146 b.c., the same year as the destruction of Carthage.

Over time, the Hellenistic monarchies disappeared. Perseus was the last king of Macedonia, as mentioned earlier. In 133 b.c., the last king of Pergamum died and left his kingdom to the Roman people. The Seleucids and Ptolemies continued to rule until the first century b.c., but eventually these dynasties also fell and their kingdoms were absorbed by the Roman Empire.

Imperialism and Culture

Carthage was Rome's first rich enemy. After the First Punic War, the Romans imposed an indemnity of over 25 million *denarii*,* to be paid to the Roman treasury. Much larger indemnities were collected from Carthage and other enemies in subsequent wars. Besides indemnities, the Romans collected both direct taxes (which they called tribute) and indirect taxes (especially customs duties) from their subjects; beginning in 167 B.C., Roman citizens no longer had to pay tribute. Spain and Macedonia had gold and silver mines which the Romans exploited vigorously. Some wars produced fabulous quantities of booty. Hundreds of thousands of prisoners were enslaved, and slaves came to form a large portion of Italy's population and labor force. The result was the transformation of the Roman economy and also of Roman society; the crisis that this caused will be discussed later in this chapter.

The effects of imperialism on Roman culture were equally dramatic. It is true that the Romans had been influenced by Greek culture as far back in their history as we can trace. (For example, some Greek gods had been worshipped at Rome from an early date, and the Romans had long associated their own gods with Greek equivalents, such as the sky-god Jupiter with Zeus.) But it was only after the Punic wars, which intensified Roman contact with the Greeks of southern Italy and Sicily, that the Romans began to write comedies, tragedies, and histories. By the early second century B.C., many aristocrats knew Greek. The city of Rome itself was transformed as new buildings were constructed in Greek architectural style. Greek art came to Rome as booty; M. Claudius Marcellus' sack of Syracuse in 211 B.C., in which the mathematician Archimedes was killed, was especially famous for the art objects that the general captured there. The industry of copying Greek sculptures flourished, and most of the works of classical Greece's great sculptors survive only as Roman copies.

The Romans did not simply display Greek art or erudition without being deeply influenced by Greek ideas, nor did their Eastern conquests turn them into Greeks. Although the Romans admired Greek culture, they also were suspicious of the ways in which it threatened to transform their society. The example of M. Porcius Cato "the Elder" illustrates the complexity of the Roman response to Hellenism.

Cato was what the Romans called a **new man;** born in the small town of Tusculum near Rome, he was the first in his family to become a senator. Through his social connections, his skill at legal oratory, his war record, and his reputation for virtue he achieved enormous political success, and he held the consulship in 195 B.C. In 184 B.C. he was **censor.** The censors' job included revising the roll of senators, and only two were elected every four years; this office was even more prestigious than the consulship.

---

*For most of the Roman period the silver **denarius** was equivalent to the Greek drachma. Each was roughly a day's pay for a medium-level wage-earner.

Cato cultivated his image as an exemplar of Roman virtues. A biography by the Greek author Plutarch, written in the second century A.D., portrays him as a hard-working farmer, a diligent legal advocate, and a war hero. He was famous for the dignity of his character, the severity of his judicial decisions, the pithiness of his wit, and his frugality to the point of stinginess (or beyond it, in Plutarch's opinion). Just as he embodied all of these traditional Roman qualities, Cato also had a reputation for hostility to Greeks. He was suspicious of Greek doctors, claiming that they had all taken an oath to poison "barbarians," including Romans. He also criticized Greek rhetoric, philosophy, and education as decadent, subversive, or insincere. He ridiculed the Greek language and deliberately used Latin instead of Greek when he gave a speech at Athens, so that everyone would hear how much longer the translation was than the Latin original.

But Cato was not simply anti-Hellenic; his attitude was much more complicated. Cato could read and speak Greek; in fact, he did much to bring Greek literary forms and ideas to Rome. He wrote the first history of Rome in Latin, which he called "Origins"; he published dozens of legal orations and was even called the "Roman Demosthenes"; and the surviving fragments of his works are full of references to Greek literature, myth, and history. From southern Italy he brought the poet Ennius to Rome, who wrote tragedies in Latin using themes from Greek myth and a poem in epic hexameter about Rome's history (he called it *Annales*).

Cato did not reject Greek culture; he simply thought it was inferior to Roman culture. He thought that a good Roman aristocrat should be familiar with Greek literature but should save his real energy for politics, warfare, and the running of his household. Cato himself absorbed much from the Hellenic world, but always sought to subordinate it to what he perceived as Roman values and ideals. In fact, his encounter with Hellenism may have led him to develop and clarify his idea of what it meant to be "Roman"—the ideals that seemed long traditional to him and his contemporaries probably took shape partly in response to their encounter with the Greeks.

The Late Republic: Society in Crisis

In the first century B.C., the Republican constitution ceased to function and the Roman government succumbed to a rising tide of violence, class conflict, and civil war. Social and economic changes that resulted from Rome's overseas conquests were partly to blame.

The Aristocracy

At the top of the Roman social hierarchy was the class of senators. This group was small—throughout most of the Republic's history there were only three hundred senators at any time. But because Roman society was linked by a dense web of vertical connections between aristocrats and the lower classes, what they did affected everyone.

Senators were large landowners. They were forbidden by law from owning ships and engaging in commerce, although some found ways around this prohibition. Most senators were the sons of senators, but men from new families could enter the senate if they were rich and gathered enough support to be elected to office; these were sometimes called "new men," especially if they reached the consulship (which was unusual).

Only senators could hold Rome's highest offices. Most senators were first elected to the quaestorship (quaestors assisted praetors and consuls and had financial responsibilities, in Rome or in the provinces). After Sulla's reforms in the 80s B.C., which also raised the number of senators to six hundred, all ex-quaestors were automatically enrolled in the senate. Senators were required to hold a praetorship before the consulship; they might also serve as tribune of the plebs or as aedile (aediles supervised public works and games and the distribution of free grain). There were age requirements for the major offices, and no one was supposed to hold the consulship twice in ten years.

These laws evolved gradually, as an effort to regulate the intensifying competition for power within the Roman aristocracy. Rome's imperial ventures vastly enriched the senatorial class, for example because the army's general and officers took the lion's share of the booty it captured. Some individuals acquired enormous fortunes in this way, at the same time that they were enhancing their prestige with military victories, winning the loyalty of the armies under their command, and gathering clients overseas by making connections with foreign kings and nobles.

Senatorial families had a strong sense of identity and of their place in a tradition. For example, at an aristocrat's funeral procession, actors impersonated his ancestors. They wore not only the ancestors' wax masks (see box) but also their official insignia and symbols of the civic or military honors they had won. Funeral orations, which were sometimes written down and published, emphasized the deceased's political career and his military accomplishments; epitaphs, although much shorter, were similar in focus. (By 100 B.C., some aristocratic women received funeral processions and orations as well. Julius Caesar's first major public act was an oration for his aunt Julia in 69 B.C.)

Thus aristocratic families defined themselves largely by their tradition of public achievement—especially offices held and military victories. The history of Rome could be (and often was) represented as a string of ancestral accomplishments. Aristocratic families thus identified themselves with the Roman state to a profound degree; one might even say they *were* the Roman state. Ultimately the Roman aristocracy's inability to subordinate its personal power and prestige to the needs of the state (or even to distinguish successfully between the two) was a factor in the Republic's decline. But for a long time the senatorial aristocracy, guided by the values embodied in its image of its ancestors, ruled successfully. The close connection that aristocratic families felt with the public accomplishments of their ancestors helped cement the senatorial class into the narrow ruling oligarchy that it was.

Art and Society

ARISTOCRATIC PORTRAITS

This sculpture dating to the late first century B.C. depicts a
Roman aristocrat wearing a toga, the civic garment, and
carrying portrait busts of his ancestors. The man's face and
those of the two busts are sculpted in veristic style.
(Scala/Art Resource, NY)

From a very early date, aristocratic Romans preserved wax portrait busts of
their senatorial ancestors: These were lifelike images made while the subjects
were still alive, and senators displayed them in the entrance-halls of their
houses. This practice may account for the unusual style—sometimes called
verism—of some late Republican portraits; they represent individual characteristics in painstaking detail, including warts, wrinkles, and bald spots.
Although mostly sculpted by Greek artists, they reflect the traditions of the
Roman aristocracy.

| *Doing History* |

THE HOUSES OF POMPEII

Pompeii, map of region VI. Note that the third block from the upper right is almost entirely occupied by a single house, called the House of the Faun after a sculpture found in one of its atria.   (German Archaeological Institute)

Written sources are not the only type of evidence available to historians. Archaeology can shed light on aspects of the ancient world that no other source can illuminate.

The city of Pompeii on the Bay of Naples was buried when a nearby volcano, Vesuvius, erupted in A.D. 79. Its houses and public buildings, paintings and inscriptions, even the dead bodies of its residents were preserved under the ash and offer a wealth of information about life in Italy in the late Republic and early Empire.

In his innovative book *Houses and Society in Pompeii and Herculaneum* (Princeton: Princeton University Press, 1994), Andrew Wallace-Hadrill studies Pompeiian houses to learn about the population's social structure. The diagram here shows the plan of a residential district in the city. Try tracing the outlines of the houses—they fit together like a jigsaw puzzle inside the city blocks; small and large houses adjoin one another. The large houses have open-roofed entryways called *atria* (now recognizable by a rectangular hole in the floor, which caught rainwater), and some have peristyles—interior courtyards surrounded by colonnades. They often have several dining rooms and bedrooms, and some have private kitchens and baths; smaller houses lack these amenities.

The plan shows that Pompeii's aristocrats lived public lives among crowds of friends, dependents, and domestic slaves. Their houses, with their open spaces and numerous rooms, were built to accommodate throngs of daily visitors, dinner guests, and servants. The aristocracy did not isolate itself from the crowd—on the contrary, aristocrats and the lower classes were linked in a complicated web of interdependence.

Peasants: Gracchus' Land Reform

In 133 B.C. an event occurred that seemed, in retrospect, to mark the beginning of the Republican government's decline. A mob of senators and their dependents lynched Tiberius Sempronius Gracchus, a tribune of the plebs, amid a throng of his supporters in the forum.

Gracchus, descended from two prestigious senatorial families, had taken up the cause of the peasantry by proposing the redistribution of land. Ancient sources tell us that he was responding to an economic crisis: Too much land had accumulated in the hands of Rome's wealthiest families; farms were being worked by gangs of slaves owned by absentee landlords. As a result, there were not enough farmers who met the property requirement for service in the army; the ancient class of Roman peasant-soldiers was endangered.

The growing wealth of Rome's aristocracy and the huge influx of slaves to Italy are certainly real phenomena. Cato the Elder's treatise on agriculture, discussed later (p. 138), describes farms of the type criticized by Gracchus, and long periods of military service overseas, combined with these economic factors, might have led to widespread poverty among the peasantry. But archaeological surveys that have attempted confirm the spread of large estates and the disappearance of small farms in the second century B.C. have not been able to do so, and it is not clear that the problem of the vanishing peasantry was a real one as opposed to a perceived one. While it is true that the Romans drastically lowered the property requirement for military service in the second century B.C., they may have been responding to an increasing resistance to the draft as more and more soldiers were stationed overseas, sometimes for years. However, it is the perceived decline of the peasantry that Tiberius Gracchus tried to alleviate. His proposal was to enforce a law that already existed—a law of 367 B.C. that limited the amount of public land that an individual could cultivate to five hundred *iugera*, about 350 acres.

The ancient sources suggest that it was not actually Gracchus' land proposal that angered his senatorial colleagues; after his death, the reform went through. Rather, they felt threatened by the power that he was accumulating. Partly they were responding to the new and aggressive ways in which

Gracchus used the tribune's constitutional privileges. He was the first to use the tribune's veto power and his power to propose binding laws in the *comitia tributa* as a weapon against the senate. But his enemies may also have seen Gracchus' proposal as an attempt to act as "patron" to the potentially very large class of people who would benefit from his reforms. A new era of "mass patronage" was beginning.

Tribunes after Gracchus—including his own younger brother, Gaius—continued to propose reforms designed to fix the growing empire's real and perceived problems: They offered land and colonies for the rural poor and grain subsidies for Rome's urban poor, new curbs on corruption in provincial administration, and citizenship for the Italians (who demanded this with increasing vigor once the *tributum* paid by citizens was abolished). The latter was granted in 90 B.C. only after a bloody revolt, called the "Social War" after the Latin word for "allies" (*socii*). Again and again, tribunes were assassinated—evidence that increasing competitiveness among the aristocracy was now crippling the business of government.

Slaves

By the end of the Republic, perhaps one in four people in Italy was a slave. The wealthiest families might own hundreds; their households, which usually included a residence in Rome and one or more rural estates, might function like villages with their own micro-economies. Most slaves were of foreign origin; they or their ancestors had been captured in war, or kidnapped and sold by pirates, whose activities are well attested in the late Republic. They were found in every area of the Roman economy, including (but not limited to) agriculture and domestic service.

Cato the Elder's treatise on agriculture—his only work that survives intact—describes farms of moderate size worked by small gangs of slaves. Tenant farmers and wage workers provide additional labor; the owner visits only occasionally. The estate is run by a foreman (*vilicus*), also of slave status. Cato mentions using gangs of chained slaves for some tasks; he mentions runaway slaves as if they were not unusual and suggests posting guards to prevent this. He gives instructions for the provision of simple but apparently adequate rations for slaves and a rudimentary wardrobe (a tunic every other year and wooden shoes).

Urban domestic slaves might have very intimate ties with their owners—they often served as nannies, tutors, and wetnurses. In large households, slaves might have quite specialized jobs; a striking feature of the Roman economy is how frequently skilled workers (such as craftsmen, entertainers, hairdressers, doctors, and midwives) are of slave or freed status. Some slaves were highly educated and many served as literary secretaries, accountants, or stenographers. Some became scholars or poets of renown, after they were freed or even before.

It is difficult to tell how often slaves were freed, but emancipation is mentioned frequently in Roman law and literature as a normal occurrence, and inscriptions attest to large numbers of freedmen. Freed slaves often retained social and economic ties with their former masters (called "patrons"). Some continued to live with or work for their patrons; others set up their own businesses with the help of their patrons. Patrons counted their freedmen among the dependents who owed them gratitude and loyal service. While prejudice against freedmen is a prominent theme in Roman literature, they had more social mobility than ex-slaves in many other societies. Most became Roman citizens automatically; no law prevented the son of a freed slave from becoming a senator, and this sometimes happened.

Slaves rarely attempted organized revolt in the Roman period, although they had other ways of resisting their masters, such as running away. The main exception is the revolt of Spartacus, which began at a school for gladiators. By the time the rebellion was crushed in 71 B.C., his army had defeated three Roman legionary forces in battle and is supposed to have numbered more than 100,000.

The Knights: Provincial Government and Corruption

Some of the state's imperial riches made their way into private hands through contracts for public works, military supply, mining, and tax collection. The tax contract for the former kingdom of Pergamum, now the province of Asia, was especially lucrative; it was first auctioned in 123 B.C. Corporations of wealthy individuals (not including senators, who were officially banned from this practice) bid on the contracts and could reap big profits, if they were able to collect more tax from a province than they had bid to pay to the state. As these public contracts multiplied, the class of wealthy individuals who undertook them (they were called **publicani**) became more powerful. Most belonged to the order of "knights" (**equites**) for which the main qualification, at least by the first century B.C., was property in excess of 100,000 *denarii*.

Senators and *equites* had many interests in common and frequently intermarried; there was no sharp separation between the classes. Even after senators were banned from the official equestrian order (as part of a reform proposed by Gaius Gracchus), their sons remained *equites* until they were enrolled in the senate, and it was not unusual for knights who were not from senatorial families to join the senate. Nevertheless, some reforms of the late Republic pitted equestrians against senators. They focused on the composition of juries in the court, established in 149 B.C., that tried magistrates for extortion from Rome's provincial subjects (called **res repetundae,** "things to be recovered"). This type of corruption was a major source of wealth for the senatorial class; even a governor who did nothing illegal could come home from his province with a huge fortune. At first the juries were entirely composed of senators, but they proved unwilling to convict members of their own group. Gaius Gracchus replaced the jury of senators with a jury of knights—hoping to make the courts more effective, but also perhaps to win the gratitude of that class.

Knights also had a financial stake in imperial administration, especially in those provinces where they contracted to collect taxes. They might punish a senator who had tried to limit their predatory practices by convicting him of extortion, and at least one notorious case of this occurred. The composition of the extortion court's jury was changed and changed again, but it is not clear that it was ever very effective in curbing the rapacity of Roman governors.*

Soldiers: Marius' Military Reforms and Sulla's Dictatorship

From 104 to 100 B.C., despite long-standing legislation that expressly forbade this, the same man—C. Marius—was elected to the consulship for five consecutive years. At the time, the Romans faced terrifying invasions from migrating German tribes, who had defeated three consular armies and were approaching Italy. Marius' victories over them, and especially his annihilation of the Teutones at Aquae Sextiae in southern France in 102 B.C., won him immense popularity.

As consul he reformed the army in a way that fundamentally changed its character. His most daring step was to eliminate the property requirement for service. The results were, first, that many propertyless citizens became professional soldiers, serving as long as they could for pay; gradually the army changed from a force of citizen-farmers to one of professionals who served for a fixed term (this transformation was completed under Augustus). Also, soldiers came to expect grants of land when they were discharged; veterans were unwilling to resume an impoverished life as day-laborers or tenants. The state had no official policy of granting retirement bonuses; the army looked to its general for these rewards, and it was he who received their gratitude. Generals after Marius came increasingly to rely on the support of huge armies who were grateful and loyal to them personally.

The extraordinary events of the 80s B.C. illustrate many of the tensions that were undermining the Roman state, including the new and crucial role of the army. In 88 B.C. a crisis broke out in the east: King Mithradates VI of Pontus (in Asia Minor) invaded the Roman province of Asia and slaughtered all the Roman citizens there. The army that Rome sent against him was commanded by L. Cornelius Sulla, who had won distinction against the Italians in the Social War. But Marius, now nearly seventy, wanted the command for himself; he allied with one of the tribunes, who passed a law in the *comitia tributa* transferring Sulla's army to Marius. Sulla's response was stunning—he marched on Rome and occupied it with his army. Having killed and exiled his enemies, he then left for the east. In his absence, Marius raised an army from among his veterans, allied with one of the consuls (L. Cornelius Cinna), and occupied Rome himself. Sulla made a hasty and controversial peace with

---

*One of the best places to see the methods of extortion used by an imaginative governor is in Cicero's speeches *Against Verres* dating to 70 B.C., in which he prosecutes the corrupt propraetor of Sicily.

Mithradates, returned to Italy in 84, and recaptured Rome. He had the senate vote him **dictator:** This was traditionally an office held only for six months in a time of emergency, but Sulla held the dictatorship until he voluntarily retired in 78 B.C. In the meantime, he engaged in bloody purges of his enemies. Portraying himself as the ally of the senate against the radical tyrant Marius, he passed laws that strengthened its position against the tribunes and the *equites*. He also raised the senate's number to six hundred by enrolling *equites* who were loyal to him. The senatorial career (or *cursus honorum*, "course of honors") was more strictly regulated, the number of praetors was raised to eight, and all ex-quaestors were automatically enrolled in the senate.

Sulla emerges with a mixed reputation in Roman historiography—usually he is portrayed as a bloodthirsty tyrant, occasionally as a champion of the traditional oligarchy. But perhaps the most important lesson of the 80s B.C. was the way in which aristocrats used "client-armies" to wage their personal vendettas. While they might portray themselves as champions of the senate or the people, the real conflict between Sulla and Marius was the personal one over Sulla's military command—but because they were able to call on huge armies that were loyal to them, this private conflict affected a large number of people.

Cicero and Roman Society

We know more about the life and works of M. Tullius Cicero than about any other Roman of the late Republican period (or any period). In antiquity he was famous as an orator who rivaled the Greek Demosthenes. A "new man" from the town of Arpinum, he succeeded in entering the senate and even reached the consulship in 63 B.C., using his skill in oratory to prosecute and (more often) defend his fellow senators in the high criminal courts. But his political career was volatile—he suffered temporary exile from Rome for his hasty execution of some conspirators who revolted in his consulship, and eventually he was murdered by the followers of Marcus Antonius, whose rise to power he had vocally opposed.

Cicero's contribution to Latin culture was fundamental and was rooted in his thorough involvement in Greek literature. Like many others of his class, Cicero learned Greek in childhood and studied philosophy and rhetoric at Athens. He was one of the first to write philosophy in Latin. He published his speeches and wrote works on the theory of rhetoric, a subject that had not been addressed in Latin before.

Perhaps the most valuable of Cicero's works is the large collection of private letters that was published after his death. Since Cicero did not intend to publish them, their references to people and events can be hard to decipher, but for the same reason they are a unique source of information about social life in the late Republic.

The letters show that Cicero's friendships with his peers had a very public character. Friends praise one another in the senate, use their influence at elections, and show public support for one another in crises. They defend one another in court—purely for social reasons, as advocates were not allowed to accept fees. But friends supported one another financially as well, by lending money (Cicero himself was perpetually in arrears with his payments) and leaving legacies in their wills. Cicero counts women among his friends, and they sometimes play a part in the complicated network of alliances he describes.

Cicero has enemies as well as friends, who publicly denounce and humiliate him and threaten to prosecute him for treason. Violence often erupts in these conflicts, as enemies clash with their gangs of dependents; Cicero's house and that of his brother are burnt.

We also learn about the aristocracy's relationship with the crowd of common people at Rome. They applaud Cicero's entrance at the theater and the games; other senators may be greeted with heckling or, worse, with total silence. Crowds gather at Cicero's house to show support for his actions and throng to meet him at his return from exile; they can also be incited to violence against a political enemy. One of the best ways to curry favor with the crowd was to pay for lavish spectacles—dramas, athletic competitions, or bloody gladiatorial games and animal hunts.

Pompey and Caesar

The partnership and then the rivalry of C. Julius Caesar and Cn. Pompeius ("Pompey") dominated the politics of the dying Republic. Pompey especially had an extraordinary career. As a young man he rose to fame with a series of special military commands, celebrated two triumphs, and took the name "Magnus" ("the Great") in imitation of Alexander. He was still well below the legal age limit for the consulship when he held it in 70 B.C. In 66 B.C. he took over the war against Mithradates VI, whom he immediately defeated; he then campaigned in Armenia, the Caucasus Mountains, and Syria; he notoriously marched on Jerusalem and desecrated the Temple. He deposed the last Seleucid king and turned the kingdom of Syria into a Roman province. He rewarded those who had supported him with kingdoms and alliances with Rome, and it was to Pompey that the entire network of Near Eastern dynasts now owed their loyalty. No Roman general in history could claim greater military achievements. Pompey advertised his victories in ways that made him seem like a new Alexander who had conquered the entire Eastern world.

But Pompey's arrangements still had to be ratified by the senate, and he also needed land to settle his veterans. The senate, suspicious of his immense power and prestige, refused both. Pompey found a solution in his alliance with Julius Caesar. In 60 B.C. Caesar returned from Spain, where he had commanded an army as propraetor; motivated partly by the massive scale of his debts, he had aggressively expanded his province and enriched himself with booty. In return for Pompey's help in the upcoming consular election, Caesar agreed to support his petition in the senate. Caesar also won the support of M. Licinius Crassus, a long-standing rival of Pompey, by promising to reduce the amount due to the state from the *publicani* who had contracted to collect the tax from the province of Asia. Crassus perhaps had a secret interest in the corporation, which had overbid for the contract and was facing financial ruin. Modern scholars sometimes call this alliance the "First Triumvirate," but there was no sharp departure from the way politics was normally done—it was an exchange of favors between unusually powerful "friends."

As part of his province after his consulship, Caesar was granted Transalpine Gaul (that is, Gaul "across the Alps"), where he remained for ten years. In that time he waged a series of campaigns in which he reduced roughly all of what is now France to Roman rule, ransacked it for huge quantities of gold and silver, and reportedly enslaved a million prisoners. Caesar's own brilliant, subtly self-serving account of his Gallic campaigns survives and is an excellent source of information on the mentality behind Roman imperialism. His ethnographic descriptions of Gauls and Germans remained the basis for the Roman understanding of those peoples for centuries, although the distinctions he drew between them were largely misconceived.

By 53 b.c. the Roman constitution was in its death-throes. The atmosphere of violence and paranoia attested in Cicero's letters was all-pervasive. Rioting instigated by rival gangs of "clients" prevented consular elections from being held; the senate appointed Pompey sole consul for 52. Although he was supposed to leave for Spain, his allotted province, he remained in Italy with part of his army. The "triumvirate" was falling apart—Caesar's daughter Julia, whom Pompey had married, died and Pompey married the daughter of one of Caesar's enemies. Crassus was killed on campaign in Parthia, in the disastrous battle of Carrhae. Caesar was desperate to have his command prolonged in Gaul, afraid of prosecution if he became a private citizen; Pompey waffled on the issue. In 49 b.c., civil war broke out when Caesar marched into Italy with his army.

Like his account of the Gallic war, Caesar's commentaries on the civil war with Pompey were later published. The reasons he gives for his actions are revealing. Although he mentions a variety of constitutional issues and specific affronts, his language characterizes the conflict as a private contest for prestige between himself and Pompey. Caesar has been insulted and outraged; his honor and dignity have been challenged; his enemies are out to get him; he must avenge himself. The civil war that engulfed the entire Roman world between 49 and 45 b.c.— for it was fought in Italy, Greece, Macedonia, Spain, Asia, Egypt, and Africa—was an extension of the personal conflict between these men. Each had kings, cities, armies, and innumerable individuals loyal to him, bound by ties of gratitude, and through these they could bully and intimidate others. Thus they drafted enormous armies and flung at one another the combined manpower of the entire Roman Empire plus a score of peripheral kingdoms, in a war of unprecedented scale.

Pompey was murdered in Egypt in 48 b.c., and the last of his supporters were crushed at Munda in Spain in 45 b.c. In the end Pompey had portrayed himself as a champion of the traditional senatorial oligarchy against a populist usurper. His allies included M. Porcius Cato "the Younger," great-grandson of the Censor, who continued his family's reputation for conservative Roman values, combining them with Stoic philosophy in a way that was to remain influential. Cato committed suicide in 46 B.C. in the African city of Utica, an act that later came to symbolize the fall of the Republican government and the beginning of a new era.

The First Emperor

Julius Caesar was assassinated in March of 44 B.C. The leader of the conspiracy against him, M. Junius Brutus, traced his ancestry to the Brutus who had expelled the last of the Roman kings nearly five hundred years before. Like his remote ancestor, he claimed to have liberated Rome from a tyrant. But Brutus and his allies soon faced opposition from one of Caesar's generals, M. Antonius ("Mark Antony"), and from Caesar's grand-nephew, the eighteen-year-old C. Octavius. Caesar had adopted Octavius in his will and left him his property, and Octavius eagerly took up his political legacy as well. In accordance with tradition, he took the family names of his adopted father and became C. Julius Caesar Octavianus. Modern historians usually call him "Octavian" to avoid confusion, but none of his contemporaries called him that—they called him Caesar.

Octavian formed an alliance with Antony and a third senator, M. Aemilius Lepidus; the senate appointed them "triumvirs for the restoration of the state" (modern scholars often call this the "Second Triumvirate"). A bloody purge of their enemies followed in which Cicero, among others, was killed. After they had defeated Brutus and his allies, Antony took over the eastern half of the empire. He formed a political and sexual alliance with Cleopatra VII of Egypt, with whom he had three children; he also undertook an ambitious campaign against the Parthians, but it ended in disaster. Relations between him and Octavian became increasingly strained until they went to war in 31 B.C. Octavian's general Agrippa won a decisive naval victory at Actium in Greece; in the next year both Antony and Cleopatra committed suicide, and Egypt became a Roman province. Rome's long period of political violence and civil bloodshed was over; no one could compete in power or prestige with Octavian, who ruled until he died in A.D. 14.

Octavian was careful never to call himself a king; in fact, he claimed to be a champion of the Republican constitution. The offices and honors he held were mostly traditional ones or modifications of them; for example, in 23 B.C. the senate voted to give him all the powers of a tribune of the plebs for life. From then on he dated his reign by the year of his "tribunician power." But slowly new words and titles evolved that came to designate the unique position he held. In the Republic, the title **imperator** was a temporary honor voted to a victorious general by his army; Octavian used it as his first name, and our word "emperor" derives from it. In 27 B.C. he was voted the title **Augustus,** which simply meant "venerable" (modern historians usually refer to "Octavian" as Augustus after this date). Like *imperator*, this title was held by all subsequent emperors and was unique to them. Augustus also referred to himself as *princeps*, which simply meant "foremost," and in the Republic had designated those who held the most prestige in the senate. For this reason historians sometimes refer to the period that begins with Augustus' rule as the **Principate.**

In Augustus' reign the territory directly subject to the Roman Empire was roughly doubled. Armies led either by himself or, more often, by appointees acting under his *imperium*—called **legates**—campaigned in northern Spain, in the Alps, in the Danube region, and in Germany, Ethiopia, Armenia, and Arabia; some of these wars resulted in new provinces or in the expansion of old provinces. He even claimed victory over the Parthians, when their king agreed to return the military standards they had captured from Crassus in 53 B.C. and sent his children to live in Rome as diplomatic "hostages." Augustus also tried to occupy Germany between the Rhine and Elbe rivers, but a revolt in A.D. 9 wiped out the army there.

His reign was a time of enormous literary and artistic creativity; Augustus himself, or his friends, often sponsored cultural projects and the emperor is the subject of many of them. One theme is his ancestry—through Julius Caesar, Augustus claimed descent from Aeneas' son Iulus and thus from Aeneas himself and his divine mother, Venus. He secured a vote in the senate making Julius Caesar a god, and he took to calling himself *divi filius*, "son of a god." Recalling Aeneas, he portrayed himself as the new founder of Rome, leading it to its destiny of world-conquest and ushering in a golden age of peace and prosperity. Vergil's *Aeneid*, in a sense the Roman national epic, was composed in Augustus' reign (and, according to tradition, at his request). Among the many monuments built at Rome under Augustus was a new forum with a temple of the war-god Mars, here called "the Avenger"; Augustus thus commemorates his defeat of his adoptive father's assassins, which he portrayed as an act of filial piety. Here Venus and Julius Caesar were also worshipped, and statues of Aeneas, Romulus, and other Roman heroes and Julian ancestors were on display.

The Empire

The Emperors

After Augustus Rome was ruled by one man—his Latin-speaking subjects addressed him as *imperator*, Caesar, or Augustus, and Greek equivalents of all these titles existed. Most emperors chose their own successors; emperors with sons were succeeded by their sons, but most had no living male offspring at the time of their deaths. An emperor might designate his chosen successor by adopting him; thus Augustus adopted his stepson Tiberius. Occasionally two members of the same family shared the imperial title: from A.D. 161 to 169 Marcus Aurelius and his brother Verus shared the throne, and both Marcus Aurelius and Septimius Severus ruled together with their sons for a time. Imperial succession was not always a peaceful process; some

The Temple of Augustus and Rome at Ankara, in modern Turkey, was constructed in the 20s B.C. and was one of the earliest buildings dedicated to the worship of a Roman emperor. Its walls preserve a Latin copy, with Greek translation, of the epitaph that Augustus wrote for himself. It lists his military deeds as well as his other accomplishments (the honors and offices voted him by the senate, and the many public buildings, games, and handouts that he paid for). The epitaph was originally published on huge bronze doors in front of Augustus's mausoleum in Rome, but these do not survive.   (SEF/Art Resource, NY)

emperors were assassinated, and twice (in A.D. 69 and in A.D. 193) civil war broke out and would-be emperors led huge armies to battle in support of their claims.

The personal nature of the emperor's rule is very striking. Coins showed his likeness on the "heads" side; statues all around the empire bore his portrait and that of his predecessors. Emperors were routinely "deified" after their deaths (the process was called **apotheosis**) and also worshipped during their lifetimes; a cult of Augustus arose in Asia Minor as early as 29 B.C. Embassies representing cities, provinces, and foreign peoples appeared before them to beg favors or ask them to resolve disputes. Custom allowed Roman citizens to appeal the legal decisions of lesser magistrates to the emperor, either in person or in writing; a huge volume of imperial decisions from the second century onward survives.

It can be difficult to distinguish the emperor's personal relationships, household staff, and property from the apparatus of the state. The emperors, like the aristocrats of the Republic, made decisions with the help of a council of advisors whom they called "friends," or "companions," when they traveled together (for example, on campaign). They were people of high rank, senators or equestrians. At first, under Augustus and his successors, the freedmen of the emperor's own household handled the imperial records and bureaucracy, but later, equestrians occupied these posts. The emperors owned property all over the empire—much of it left to them by grateful or terrified individuals or confiscated from enemies—and the rents from these lands generated a vast income. From this they might fund roads, building projects in Rome or in provincial cities, and donations to the soldiers or the Roman plebs.

At first, the emperors mostly came from Italian families. However, over time the composition of the Roman ruling class changed. Veterans settled overseas and produced children and grandchildren (and freedmen) with Roman citizenship, and citizenship was granted to some prominent provincials. Finally, in A.D. 212, emperor Caracalla granted citizenship to all free inhabitants of the empire. Some of these non-Italian citizens became knights or senators, and even emperors. In A.D. 98, Trajan became the first emperor who was not born in Italy; he was from Baetica in Spain. From then on, emperors increasingly came from overseas provinces.

Most of what we know about individual emperors comes from histories and biographies written by members of Rome's ruling class, the senatorial and equestrian aristocracy. These sources include the *Annals* of Tacitus and a series of biographies by Suetonius, written in Latin in the early second century A.D., and Cassius Dio's history of Rome, written in Greek in the third century. The aristocracy judged emperors largely by how they treated members of their own class. Some emperors—such as Nero (r. 54–68) and Domitian (r. 81–96)—terrorized the senate with bloody purges, motivated by paranoid fears of conspiracy or by greed, as they confiscated the property of their victims. The historians excoriate these emperors, focusing on their cruelty but also accusing them of moral depravity and weakness in foreign policy. Besides a bad reputation in history, emperors who abused the senate also risked assassination; several emperors met violent ends at the hands of aristocratic conspirators. On the other hand, some emperors—such as Trajan—won a reputation for respectful treatment of the senate, generosity with the masses, and military victory. In these ways the senatorial aristocracy imposed its values on the emperor, who was after all one of them—a member of the same class, with the same education and background. When reading Roman works about the emperors, we should beware of their authors' limited perspective. For example, Nero emerges as one of the worst emperors in ancient historical sources, but he was so beloved by the Greek populace for his liberation of the province of Achaea (which included freedom from tribute) that revolts led by false "Neros" broke out sporadically for decades after his death.

The Roman Empire in the Second Century A.D.

ROMAN EMPERORS, 31 B.C. TO A.D. 238

Emperor	Years of reign
Augustus	31 B.C.–A.D. 14
Tiberius	A.D. 14–37
Gaius (Caligula)	37–41
Claudius	41–54
Nero	54–68
Galba	68–69
Otho	69
Vitellius	69
Vespasian	69–79
Titus	79–81
Domitian	81–96
Nerva	96–98
Trajan	98–117
Hadrian	117–138
Antoninus Pius	138–161
Marcus Aurelius	161–180
Lucius Verus	161–169
Commodus	176–192
Pertinax	193
Didius Julianus	193
Septimius Severus	193–211
Pescennius Niger	193–194
Clodius Albinus	193–197
Caracalla	198–217
Geta	209–211
Macrinus	217–218
Elagabalus	218–222
Severus Alexander	222–235
Maximinus Thrax	235–238

The Emperor and the City of Rome

Like the politicians of the late Republic, emperors cultivated their relationship with the Roman *plebs*—that is, the population of the city itself. They
appeared at the great public events to which the crowds flocked—such as

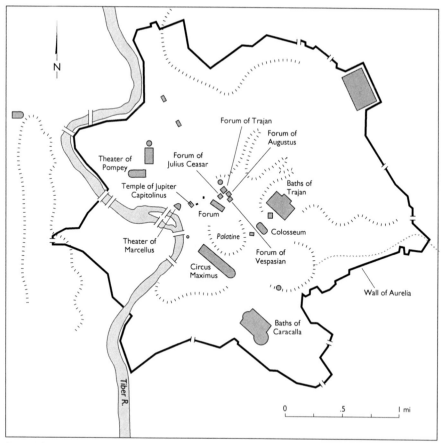

N

Forum of Trajan

Forum of
Augustus

Theater of
Pompey

Forum of
Julius Ceasar

Temple of Jupiter
Capitolinus

Baths of
Trajan

Forum

Theater of
Marcellus

Palatine

Colosseum

Circus
Maximus

Forum of
Vespasian

Wall of Aurelia

Baths of
Caracalla

Tiber R.

0   .5   1 mi

Imperial Rome

horse races, gladiatorial games, and dramatic performances. There the people might demonstrate, with rhythmic shouting, for lower grain prices; they might demand a cash distribution, or freedom for a slave actor, or even tax relief. The emperor addressed them himself, in speeches, or used a herald, or (like Claudius) had messages written on boards and carried around the amphitheater for all to read.

One way in which the emperor courted popularity with the masses of Rome was by paying for public buildings. When a fire destroyed much of Rome in A.D. 64, Nero rebuilt parts of the city at his own expense, according to a new code that improved fire safety and also beautified the city; historians otherwise hostile to the notorious emperor praised him for these measures. But Nero appropriated a huge tract of downtown Rome, including possibly all of the Palatine hill, as his private estate. There he constructed a palace, reportedly a mile long, surrounded by landscaped woods, fields, and a private lake. In the palace's enormous atrium he placed a statue of himself, 120 feet high (it was called "colossal" after the Colossus, a huge statue of the sun-god Helios at Rhodes).

The Colosseum at Rome, constructed by emperor Vespasian on the site of Nero's palace. (Photo by Susan P. Mattern-Parkes)

Senators may have resented being driven out of Rome's most prestigious locations, and this may lie behind some ancient authors' criticism of Nero's private building program; some even report accusations that Nero set the fire himself to make room for his palace. But this criticism also reflects the view, deeply held by the aristocracy and the common people alike, that the emperor was obliged to provide public facilities for the masses. Vespasian, who succeeded Nero after a civil war that followed his forced suicide, drained Nero's private lake and built an amphitheater on the site; this building was later called the Colosseum after Nero's statue, which still stood nearby. It was the largest amphitheater in the empire, holding a crowd of perhaps fifty thousand. There emperors staged lavish gladiatorial games, some involving thousands of pairs of combatants. The Colosseum's designers paid attention to crowd control, constructing an elaborate system of stairs and passages; numbers were posted over each of its seventy-six entrances, and spectators matched them with the numbers on their tickets when they arrived.

Later, Trajan would build a bath complex over part of Nero's palace. Like the Colosseum, Trajan's baths were larger than any other building of their type at the time. Besides the hot, warm, and cold baths, the complex contained a swimming pool, two colonnaded exercise-grounds, libraries, meeting-rooms, fountains, gardens, and a wealth of exquisite sculpture—like a Greek gymnasium, it housed a host of activities.

In the Imperial period, the buildings and monuments that the emperor paid for transformed the city of Rome. Some were for the amusement of the populace: We have mentioned the Colosseum and the Baths of Trajan. Augustus built a theater; Domitian built a stadium for athletic contests. Caracalla and Diocletian built baths even larger than Trajan's. The fora constructed by Augustus, Vespasian, and Trajan provided space for public meetings, socializing, and commerce, while they also advertised the emperors' military victories. These were all built near the Roman forum—that is, in the heart of the city—and were paved, open spaces surrounded by colonnades.

The Army

Under Augustus, the Roman army became a permanent, professional force. Augustus disbanded much of the huge army that had fought with him in the civil wars, and decided to keep only twenty-eight legions under arms. He had found it difficult to pay his troops, and also to pay the retirement bonuses of those he demobilized; Augustus kept the largest force he thought the empire could afford. Three legions were destroyed in A.D. 9, when Arminius, a tribal chief, rebelled and slaughtered the Roman army in Germany. They were not replaced; but gradually other emperors added new legions until they numbered thirty-three under the Severans.

In theory, a complete legion comprised about five thousand men, but soldiers died, deserted, or retired without being replaced, while others were posted away from the camp on a wide variety of duties. Legionary soldiers were generally Roman citizens. At first they mostly came from Italy, but as time went on the number of Italians dwindled and most of recruits came from citizen populations overseas. Noncitizen troops served as **auxiliaries**, who were organized into units of about five hundred or special, larger units of about eight hundred. Many of these were cavalry units; auxiliaries provided most of the cavalry for the Roman army. The total number of auxiliaries is not known accurately, but there were probably more auxiliaries than legionaries. In the third century when it was largest, the Roman army may have numbered about 450,000 altogether.

Soldiers were supposed to be discharged after twenty-five years, although many served longer. Legionary pay was modest, at 225 *denarii* per year, and was raised only once before Severus. Auxiliaries either received the same amount as legionaries or slightly less. Much of each soldier's pay—by some calculations, nearly all of it—was deducted for food and equipment; soldiers kept much of the remainder in the unit's treasury, which served as a sort of bank. On retirement, legionaries received a cash bonus; auxiliaries received Roman citizenship. Retired veterans usually settled in the provinces in which they had served. Although soldiers were not allowed to marry, many formed relationships with local women whom they married on retirement, and their children then became legitimate.

The army was unevenly distributed around the empire, concentrated in certain provinces. Some of these were frontier provinces where they might be needed to drive out an invading army or to invade enemy territory. Other provinces (sometimes, the same ones) had rebellious populations that had to

| Art and Society |

TRAJAN'S FORUM

Relief sculpture on the Column of Trajan, from the
Forum of Trajan at Rome, shows the Roman army on
campaign.   (Photo by Susan P. Mattern-Parkes)

The Forum of Trajan was by far the largest of Rome's imperial fora, and like the
others it was a vehicle to publicize the emperor's military achievements. It
incorporated a basilica, Greek and Latin libraries, and a temple to Trajan himself. A statue depicting Trajan in a chariot—an allusion to the triumphal
parade—adorned the triple arch of its entrance, and marble sculptures of tro-
phies, weapons, and barbarian prisoners decorated the colonnade. Between the
libraries was Trajan's own tomb—a hundred-foot column where his ashes were
kept. An extraordinary sculpted relief on the column depicts the events of the
wars in which Trajan had conquered Dacia. An inscription proclaimed that the
forum had been paid for "from the spoils of war."

These sculptures of Dacian prisoners probably come from Trajan's forum. They were reused in the fourth century on the Arch of Constantine in Rome, which celebrates that emperor's victory over his rival Maxentius in 312 A.D. (Photo by Susan P. Mattern-Parkes)

be controlled. Violent revolts were not uncommon, especially in newly conquered territory, but they could also break out in areas that had been subjected for centuries. In times of war units or detachments from units had to be moved, sometimes to a distant front. Troops usually marched overland and could travel about fifteen miles per day; a march from the Rhine to the Euphrates river would take about six months. When troops were transferred away from a province, the population sometimes took the opportunity to revolt, or enemies invaded. Many of the conquests that the Romans attempted in the Imperial period failed because troops could not be spared from provinces that needed them or because the army was not large enough to occupy the territory it conquered.

But the army's job was much broader than just invading or defending against invasion or suppressing revolt. It was also a sort of public labor force—the only large one available (although public slaves, often condemned criminals, were used for some tasks). The army policed roads and borders against bandits, guarded officials when they traveled, built roads and sewers, dug mines, gathered supplies, collected taxes—and did many other jobs that brought them into everyday contact with civilians. The army also manufactured much of its own equipment.

Documents from a fort at Vindolanda in Britain illustrate the variety of jobs that the army performed. A strength report for a cohort stationed there records that less than half of its men were at the fort when it was compiled; they were performing unknown duties at several different places. Workshops at Vindolanda produced weapons, vehicles, boots, and possibly leather and clothes. The fort had its own doctor and its own veterinarian, and military scribes kept a huge variety of records and accounts.

After Augustus the shape of the Roman Empire did not change nearly as drastically as it had in the centuries before. It came to have fixed boundaries, at least in the minds of ancient writers: These were the Rhine and Danube rivers in Europe, the Euphrates river in the east, and the desert in Egypt and Africa. (Archaeologists have shown, however, that it can be difficult to trace precise military or cultural boundaries between Rome and its neighbors, and in this sense it is better to imagine "frontier zones" than "frontier lines.") Three emperors added new provinces across these frontiers: Claudius conquered Britain, Trajan conquered Dacia (roughly, modern Romania), and Severus conquered northern Mesopotamia.

The Roman army's officers were drawn from the equestrian and senatorial classes. Legions were commanded by officers called "legates," senators in the early stages of their careers; each had a staff of six "tribunes," five equestrians and one senator, and one equestrian prefect, often a man of long military experience. Most auxiliary units were commanded by equestrian prefects. The highest rank open to an ordinary citizen was centurion—that is, commander of one of the eighty-man "centuries" into which legions were divided.

Each province's governor commanded its entire army. But in most provinces with large armies, the governor was a legate of the emperor appointed by him and subject to his *imperium* (this is not the same as the "legate" who commanded an individual legion). While in practice it was not always possible to communicate with the emperor about military decisions, and governors therefore took many actions on their own initiative, this was the way in which Augustus and his successors tried to prevent other senators from acquiring too much prestige from their military victories.

Taxes

The Roman government's main goal was to collect taxes. It used most of these revenues to pay or supply the army. The Romans collected a huge variety of taxes in cash, in kind, and in labor.

Every province paid tribute, but tribute was assessed differently in each; often tax systems were held over from previous regimes. In some places the tribute was a tax on land; in others it was a poll tax on one's "head"; some places paid both. Some provinces paid a percentage of the crop; others paid cash; one German tribe paid in ox-hides. All citizens paid an inheritance tax, slaves paid a tax when they were freed, and everyone paid a sales tax; customs taxes were collected at ports, at the boundaries between provinces, and at certain points of entry into the empire from abroad. All types of goods (but

---

The Written Record

THE ARMY IN PEACETIME

This inscription from Lambaesis in the Roman province of Africa describes the adventures of a military surveyor sent to supervise the digging of a tunnel for an aqueduct. The workers have made a funny mistake: Two teams starting from opposite sides of a mountain have missed each other and dug too far. Note the problem with bandits, and how the army supplies both the expertise and the labor for the project.

[To Marcus Valerius] Etruscus [legate of the legion III Augusta, stationed in Africa]: The most splendid town of Saldae, and I myself, together with the people of Saldae, ask you, my lord, to encourage Nonius Datus, veteran of the legion III Augusta, surveyor, to come to Saldae, so that he may complete what remains of his work.

[The "voice" of the inscription is now that of Nonius]: I set out and along the road I encountered bandits; I escaped, naked and wounded, with those who were with me; I arrived at Saldae; I met with the procurator Clemens. He led me to the mountain, where they were bewailing an underground channel of dubious work, which looked like it would have to be abandoned, as the tunnel had become longer than the width of the mountain [that they were digging through]. It seems that the tunnels had diverged from a straight line, so that the upper tunnel bent to the right toward the south, and the lower one similarly bent to the right [of those digging it] toward the north: the two sides therefore had strayed, abandoning the straight line. However, the straight line had been marked out on top of the mountain, from east to west. . . . When I distributed the work so that each man would know which part of the tunnel was his [responsibility], I made a competition of the work between the navy and the auxiliary soldiers; and thus they worked together in digging through the mountain. (*Inscriptiones Latinae Selectae* 5795)

---

especially food supplies and pack animals or horses) could be requisitioned by the army, especially in times of war; civilians might be reimbursed in cash at fixed rates, or sometimes not at all. (In the third century, the provincials' obligation to supply the army was formalized in a tax called the *annona militaris*.) Provincials were required to maintain the roads and provide transport to authorized persons who demanded it, a system that was often abused.

The tribute was not always paid on time. Arrears accumulated until they were canceled by a generous emperor, usually at the beginning of his reign. Provinces sometimes revolted when they were subjected to a census or when taxes were collected too vigorously. People sometimes fled from their land rather than pay taxes on it.

Over time the empire relied less on Italian *publicani* to collect taxes. Officials of equestrian rank called procurators supervised tax collection in each province, but the Romans relied mainly on locals to do the "dirty work." Each community's council of wealthy citizens (called **decurions**) was responsible for making sure that the tribute owed by their town was paid and for making up the difference if it was not.

The property qualification for membership in the local council was in some places not very high, and it could be difficult to find people willing to undertake the burden. The Romans imposed obligations on everyone who could reasonably be expected to spare some of his or her capital or labor. Exemption from **munera** (*munus* was the Latin word for "service" or "duty") was one of the empire's most coveted privileges, and the Romans bestowed it sparingly.

Roads and Cities

The network of roads that linked the Roman Empire, one of its most impressive achievements and probably the most labor-intensive one, has had a permanent effect on the landscape of most former Roman provinces. Roman roads were professionally surveyed and generally straight rather than winding, although they sometimes bent to skirt difficult territory. A "typical" road might have an excavated foundation, rammed hard or reinforced with timber, filled with rubble and sand, and surfaced with paving stones or gravel, but the Romans used a wide variety of construction techniques, depending on what materials were available locally. Along the roads, milestones marked the distance to the next city or to the provincial capital; thousands of these cylindrical stone columns survive.

Julius Caesar and Augustus each founded a large number of overseas colonies on land bought or seized from natives and distributed to their veterans, all over the Roman world. Surveyors planning a new colony first divided the land according to a grid pattern of perpendicular lines or roads, often covering large tracts of countryside. Like road building, this process (called **centuriation**) has left its mark on the landscape; traces can be found on the ground or seen from the air across parts of northern Italy, France, Tunisia, and other former Roman provinces.

The Roman administration depended on cities. All territory was subject to an urban center, which was responsible for collecting taxes from that territory. In some provinces this policy resulted in more urbanization of the countryside—native settlements grew and adopted Roman institutions, and towns developed in previously rural areas. In each city, the Romans recognized the wealthy class of decurions as the political leaders. They had the burdensome duty of collecting taxes, but also they benefited from Roman support for their political power. Many of the cultural transformations that occurred in the Roman provinces came about because urban aristocrats wanted to increase their prestige by emulating their Roman benefactors. For example, these aristocrats often paid for new, Roman-style buildings in their cities. Their social obligation to provide public buildings, games, and banquets, and to do favors for people of lesser rank and means, was the main way in which wealth was redistributed in the Roman Empire. (This type of

The Pont du Gard is part of a Roman aqueduct constructed in the first century A.D. *to bring water to the city of Nimes in France.* (Vanni/Art Resource, NY)

generosity is sometimes called **euergetism,** which means "good deed-doing" in Greek.)

Certain construction methods were typical of the Roman Empire's public buildings. In the third century B.C. the Romans had invented a very strong, waterproof cement that revolutionized architecture when it became widely used in concrete. Concrete, often with a cosmetic facing of brick, was the characteristic building material of the Roman Empire. Its characteristic architectural forms were the arch and the vault (essentially an elongated arch), both invented by the Greeks in the Hellenistic era but exploited on a large scale by the Romans. Arches supported aqueducts and bridges and turned massive walls into airy arcades; barrel-vaults were used for the tiered passageways of free-standing theaters and amphitheaters, and intersecting vaults could enclose spectacular interior spaces, notably in the gigantic Baths of Caracalla at Rome.

Aqueducts carried water to the towns and cities of the Roman world. Some cities had more than one; Rome itself had seven by the mid-first century A.D. Some aqueducts used a siphon system that allowed them to follow the contours of the ground, but most relied on gravity to move water. The latter had to be constructed on an even, continuous gradient; tunnels were dug through hills, and arcades were constructed over valleys, gorges, and flatlands. Water was piped from the aqueducts to fountains, baths, businesses, and sometimes private houses or farms in a continuous stream.

Although some Hellenistic Greek cities had baths, their central role in urban life is more characteristic of the Roman Empire. Even small towns might have several bath complexes. Besides baths of different temperatures, sweat-rooms, changing rooms, and latrines, many also incorporated swimming pools, exercise-grounds, and shady porticoes. Descriptions of the baths in literary sources mention activities like weightlifting, massage, wrestling, and playing ball; they frequently mention arguments and fights and encounters with beauticians, food-vendors, pimps, and thieves. The rich brought slaves with them to rub them down and guard their clothes. Even the largest complexes usually had only one bath of each type, and there is evidence that men and women continued to bathe together even after a law of Hadrian forbade this.

Perhaps no other architectural form is so readily associated with the Romans as the **amphitheater.** If present, it was usually the community's largest building, but because amphitheaters were expensive to construct, not all towns had one. The games that were viewed there—mainly gladiatorial games and bloody wild beast hunts—could also be presented in the forum, in any large open space, or in the theater of a Greek city (in fact, amphitheaters were rare in the East). Although the first gladiatorial games were offered in Rome in the third century B.C.—they were originally held at funerals—the oldest permanent amphitheater (the one at Pompeii) dates to the first century B.C.

Gladiators might be prisoners of war or condemned criminals, but most were trained professionals, either slaves bought as an investment or free men who chose this career. The danger of death was a major attraction of the games; professional gladiators who put on a good show were often spared, but the win, lose, and tie records that appear on their epitaphs show that the average gladiator survived only ten contests.

As the heart of a Greek city was its *agora*, the heart of a Roman city or town was the forum. This was generally a rectangular open space lined with colonnades that provided shade and shelter. Civic and commercial buildings clustered around; these might include shops, a senate-house, and a **basilica** (a long building with interior columns, used for a variety of purposes). Most fora featured at least one temple, often a smaller replica of the Capitolium at Rome, in the same architectural style and housing the same gods.

Law

Much of what we know about Roman imperial law comes from a codification called the *Corpus Juris Civilis*, or "Body of civil law," compiled in the sixth century A.D. under Emperor Justinian. Before the late Imperial period, the closest thing to a Roman legal code after the Twelve Tables was the "praetor's edict," a document that was published every year with slight modifications until it took its final form under Emperor Hadrian. It set out the principles and procedures by which the urban praetor, who was responsible for the administration of justice in Rome, would resolve the private disputes brought before him. We know most of the contents of the "praetor's edict"

The Written Record

A SENATOR'S GIFTS TO HIS HOMETOWN

This inscription honoring "Pliny the Younger," whose letters to his friends and to the emperor Trajan survive, was displayed over the baths at Comum, his hometown in northern Italy. The career it describes (Pliny's offices are listed in reverse order) was typical for a Roman senator who had begun political life as a knight; these aristocratic groups held all of the empire's highest civilian and military posts. The list of his very substantial donations to the town illustrates how the patronage of wealthy men (and sometimes women) shaped urban life.

Roman law allowed owners of more than five hundred slaves to free up to one hundred in their wills; this probably explains the one hundred freedmen of the inscription.

C. Plinius Caecilius Secundus, son of Lucius, member of the [voting] tribe of Oufentina: consul, augur, propraetorian legate with consular power of the provinces of Pontus and Bithynia; sent to that province, through a decree of the senate, by the Emperor Caesar Nerva Trajan Augustus Germanicus Dacicus, father of his country; curator of the channel and banks of the Tiber and of the sewers of the city [of Rome]; prefect of the treasury of Saturn; prefect of the military treasury; praetor; tribune of the people; quaestor of the emperor; sevir [one of six "presidents"] of the Roman knights; military tribune of the legion III Gallica; member of the Board of Ten for adjudicating lawsuits: gave as legacy in his will [these] public baths at the cost of . . . sesterces; and added for their equipment 300,000 sesterces; and beyond that for their maintenance, interest on 200,000 sesterces; and also, he left to the commonwealth 1,866,666 sesterces, for the support of one hundred of his freedmen, the interest on which is to be applied afterwards [i.e. ,after the freedmen have died?] to a banquet for the city's populace . . . and also while living he gave 500,000 sesterces for the support of boys and girls of the city's populace, and also a library, and 100,000 sesterces for the maintenance of the library. (*Inscriptiones Latinae Selectae* 2927)

---

through the comments on it that are published, along with interpretations of other types of Roman law, in the *Digest of Justinian*, part of the *Corpus Juris Civilis*. We also have numerous documents on papyrus that show how law was actually applied.

Roman law was not a fixed, rigid system. Emperor Justinian's codification was supposed to turn it into one—by resolving all contradictions, by superseding previous legal writings (which were banned), and by remaining free from commentary and interpretation, which was also banned. These aims were not achieved; not only do many contradictions remain in the code, but guides and summaries appeared immediately. For most of their history, the Romans understood that there was always a gap between legal theory and the realities of any specific situation, which must be bridged by the judgment of those who administer the law. Roman law was not mainly a theoretical system, but grew out of real-life situations. One of its basic principles was the idea of precedent—a ruling in a specific case by someone in authority, often the emperor, served as a guide for future rulings in similar cases. Another was flexibility; Roman law operated side-by-side with native custom and no sharp distinction between these systems is possible today.

Ultimately, the interpretation of the law was up to the governor, emperor, or other official who made the ruling in any specific case. He might base his decision on any previous legal decisions he was aware of, on the principles articulated in the "praetor's edict," on local custom in some situations, occasionally on old legislation by the Republican assemblies or by the senate (all of which were still considered valid), and finally on his own judgment. Governors (and also emperors) were generally aristocrats with no formal legal training, and their knowledge of the precedents that might apply was probably patchy. On the other hand, governors and emperors did not make their decisions alone; they consulted a council of friends. These might include one or more **jurists**—a group of senators and knights with recognized expertise in the law. Jurists sometimes published collections of their interpretations and opinions, which then also became authoritative sources of law. The "golden age" of jurisprudence was the early third century A.D.—the most famous jurists (Papinian, Ulpian, and Paul) all wrote under the Severan emperors.

Much of Roman law thus took shape as a system of responses: the emperor's responses to petitions or to cases referred to him, the jurists' responses to the problems they studied, or to the questions they were asked. This is an example of the reactive, rather than proactive, character of Roman rule. With few exceptions, the Romans did not invent sweeping ideas about how they would like their subjects to behave and then try to impose them through the law. Rather, the law developed as a complicated, sometimes contradictory, set of reactions to specific circumstances.

It is interesting to reflect on some of the similarities between Roman law and Jewish law of the same period. After the destruction of the Temple of Jerusalem in A.D. 70 (see p. 166), Jewish leadership devolved from the priestly class onto a class of scholars called **rabbis,** who saw themselves as the intellectual descendants of the Pharisees. They gave their opinions on questions of Jewish law, orally for people who asked them, but they also published written works. In the third century A.D. the opinions of some rabbis were organized and collected in a massive book called the Mishnah. The Mishnah itself then became a subject of scholarly study along with the Torah. In the fifth and sixth centuries some of this tradition was again codified in two great works, the Jerusalem Talmud and the Babylonian Talmud. Like the Roman jurists, the rabbis were experts who studied, interpreted, and sometimes published their opinions on the law. However, they were different socially. While jurists were aristocrats who mainly served as advisors to powerful magistrates, rabbis were usually middle-class landowners or tradesmen who judged and arbitrated disputes for ordinary people.

Women and Family in Roman Law.   Much of Roman law concerned property and inheritance in the family. While the relationship between law and life is complicated, nevertheless Roman law reflects a value system in which women had more status than in some other ancient societies.

Technically, the *paterfamilias*, or patriarch, of a family still owned all of its assets: The sons or daughters still in his power had limited economic rights. But the patriarch did not own his wife's property; the law carefully distinguished the property of spouses, even placing strict limits on the gifts they could give each other. All women were supposed to have a "tutor" to authorize legal transactions for them. However, by the Imperial period it was illegal for a tutor to refuse to carry out the wishes of his ward, and women were perceived as responsible for decisions about their property.

The dowry that a woman brought to her marriage might be donated by her father, her mother, her patron or patroness (if she was a freedwoman), relatives or friends, or even by the woman herself. Ownership of the dowry was a complicated question—although it was under the husband's control, there were restrictions on what he could do with it. Upon divorce it was normally returned to the woman herself.

Independent men and women with no male ascendants had the power to leave their property to whomever they wished in their wills. The wealthy left their property not only to their families but also to their friends, to their freedmen, to communities (for example, to pay for a new public building), or to the emperor. The laws that regulated succession when the deceased left no will recognized no superior right of inheritance for sons over daughters, although those who wrote wills generally favored sons.

Thus despite the power given to the *paterfamilias* of a family, women also had substantial economic power in Roman law. Life expectancy in the Roman world was low, and most adults did not have a living father or grandfather. It is perhaps for this reason that the laws about the *paterfamilias* remained intact—because they did not affect many people. Upon the patriarch's death, both sons and daughters became legally independent individuals.

Greek Culture in the Roman Empire

Throughout the Roman period the spoken language of educated elites in the eastern half of the empire, and the language most widely used for writing there, was Greek. Latin was the main written language in the western empire, and the language of the army. But well-educated aristocrats, even in the West, learned Greek in school or from their tutors. A large quantity of literature in Greek—including a vast body of early Christian writings, which will be discussed in the next chapter—survives from the first three centuries A.D.

The Second Sophistic.   Perhaps the most important cultural development in the Imperial period was the **Second Sophistic.** The biographer Philostratus, writing in the third century A.D., used this term to describe his subjects, the Roman world's new "sophists" or experts in public speaking. Like the sophists of classical Greece, they were professional educators, but they were also charismatic performers who could attract huge crowds. Some sophists were prominent benefactors of their cities who served as ambassadors to the emperor, some became the friends of emperors or of Roman aristocrats, and some worked directly for the emperor, taking charge of his Greek correspondence. The most famous celebrities of their time, they could wield great political influence.

Some features of the Second Sophistic have a broader significance because they pervade the Greek literature of the Roman period. The sophists imitated the language of classical Athens and used it in writing and speaking instead of *koine*—a movement called "Atticism." Their speeches often recalled the great moments of classical history, especially the history of Athens. The overall effect of their works and performances was to create a feeling of Hellenic identity—of being Greek—that drew its strength from Greece's classical heritage. But mastery of Atticism also defined people socially by confirming their membership in the Roman world's urban, educated class.

The Novel.   In the atmosphere of the Second Sophistic, a new literary genre became popular: the Greek novel. Five of these survive intact, all apparently dating to the first three centuries A.D. (although the dating of all Greek novels is problematic), and fragments of several others also survive. They are very formulaic in character; all tell the story of a young couple in their teens who are either in love or recently married, become separated, and find their way back to each other after a series of adventures. These typically include shipwreck, kindap by pirates or bandits, the attempted rape of both hero and heroine, and the enslavement of one or both.

The novels illuminate the values of the audience that enjoyed them—probably the Greek urban aristocracy. Their focus on romantic, heterosexual love leading to marriage, their equal attention to male and female protagonists, and the pervasive theme of class—the protagonists are from wealthy urban families but are forced to endure the humiliations of slavery—are just a few of their interesting features. Like the speeches of the Second Sophistic, they take place in the imaginary Greek past, and the Roman Empire is completely absent from the world they describe. Their characters often travel to foreign, "barbarian" lands or wander the countryside—which the novelists idealize or portray as dangerous and alien from the cities in which their protagonists grew up. The novels reflected, and helped to define, their audience's ideas about Hellenism and class.

Galen.   One Greek writer of the Imperial period who deserves special mention is Galen, best known as a doctor who treated the emperor Marcus Aurelius and his family and whose enormous body of work formed the foundation of medical knowledge through the medieval and early modern period. Born in Pergamum in A.D. 129, he studied medicine at Alexandria and began his career treating gladiators in his native city. He moved to Rome, where his successful and sometimes spectacular cures of prominent people—including Greek philosophers, sophists, and other doctors—made him famous.

Galen wanted others to see him not only as a doctor, but also as a master of many fields, especially mathematics, philosophy, and language (his longest work, now lost, was a dictionary of Attic words). Like the sophists, he most valued the writers of the classical past. Thus he champions the ideas of Hippocrates and Plato, while he tends to be critical of more recent authors.

Also like the sophists, Galen liked to perform before audiences, sometimes large ones; his most important performances were his anatomical demonstrations, where he would dissect or vivisect an animal. Galen dissected animals of all types—he thought apes and pigs were most similar to man, but also was interested in the anatomy of other creatures. Building on the work of Herophilus and others, he was especially proud of his thorough anatomy of the nervous system. He accepted and elaborated the Hippocratic idea of the four humors, which shaped Western medicine thereafter.

Life in the Provinces

While we have tried to generalize about some aspects of life in the Roman Empire, it is difficult to do this successfully because the Romans ruled a vast and very diverse territory. The Roman government's goals were mainly to collect taxes and prevent or suppress revolt; it was rare for an emperor to attempt to impose his own will on a province in other matters. The administration maintained only a small presence in most provinces. This is often true even if we count the army, which itself was not a homogeneous unit: It was recruited from all over the empire, distributed around it unevenly, and performed different functions in different regions. To the degree that the provinces became "Romanized"—culturally, socially, or economically—this seems to have taken place at the local level and was not dictated from above; there were regional differences in how Roman institutions were adopted.

For these reasons, although space prevents a discussion of all of the empire's individual provinces, it is helpful to look at a few specific examples. The discussion here focuses on three provinces about which we know a great deal (although we do not have the same kinds of information about each). This approach offers readers a deeper look at some aspects of provincial life and may also serve to point out the complexity and variety of the Roman Empire.

Imperial Rule: The Example of Judaea

How did the Romans rule their empire? What did they want from their subjects, and by what methods did they accomplish their aims? While it is tempting to imagine the Romans—or any imperial power—ruling by military force, on further reflection this idea seems impractical. The Roman army was relatively small—at most, less than half a million individuals among a population of perhaps 50 million, armed with weapons of no special technology. The Romans' rule depended on their ability to enlist the support of part of the native population. This might be its king, or any number of groups or classes who benefited in some way from Roman rule.

We know more about the mechanisms of Roman rule in Judaea (as the Romans called the kingdom of Judah after they conquered it) than most areas. This is partly because a substantial Jewish literary tradition existed, in Greek and also in Aramaic. Some of these writings survive, including two lengthy and detailed historical works by the same author, Flavius Josephus. One of them, called *The Jewish War*, recounts the causes and events of the disastrous revolt that broke out in A.D. 66 and resulted in the sack of Jerusalem and destruction of the temple in 70. His other major work, called *Jewish Antiquities*, traces the history of the Jewish people from creation through Josephus' own time.

Josephus was a Jewish general in the war against the Romans, who was taken prisoner by the future emperor Vespasian and lived out his days in Rome, where the emperor granted him citizenship and other privileges. In his works he is concerned not only with pleasing his patrons by emphasizing the power of the Romans but also with defending the priestly, aristocratic class to which he belonged by blaming the revolt on disreputable segments of the Jewish population. He also tries to exonerate himself from Jewish accusations of treason and collaboration that surfaced during and after the revolt. Modern historians must allow for all of these complicated goals when using his work.

Herod the Great: A Friendly King.   Josephus recounts the history of the Romans' relationship with Herod the Great, who ruled Judaea from 40 B.C. until his death in 4 B.C. The Romans maintained their empire partly by installing, supporting, and manipulating friendly native leaders, sometimes called "client-kings" by modern scholars. They did this throughout the empire's history, but Herod is the "client-king" about whom we know the most.

In 40 B.C., the Parthians invaded Judaea; they deposed Hyrcanus, the Hasmonaean ruler who had been appointed by Pompey, and installed Hyrcanus' brother and rival Aristobulus as king. In reaction, the Roman senate offered military support to Herod and declared him king. In 37 B.C. Herod captured Jerusalem and killed Antigonus, Aristobulus' son and successor.

Herod benefited as much from his relationship with the Romans as the Romans did. He helped Antony—then ruling the East—with troops, money, and supplies when Antony campaigned locally against the Parthians and later against Octavian. In turn, Antony and the Romans lent him military support against his Hasmonaean rivals, and also against the rebels and insurgents whom Josephus calls "bandits" and "trouble-makers."

Herod, who has a mixed reputation in Jewish sources, was mostly remembered for his bloody purges of anyone connected with the Hasmonaean dynasty, including his own wife and children. His most important legacy was his vast building program, including the famous city of Caesarea, which he founded and named after the emperor. Here he constructed an aqueduct, a Roman-style theater, an amphitheater (probably the first permanent amphitheater outside Italy), a temple dedicated to Augustus and the goddess Roma, and a large artificial harbor built with Italian hydraulic concrete. He also proclaimed a Greek-style festival to be celebrated every four years, complete with musical and athletic contests, but also with Roman entertainments such as gladiatorial games. Caesarea is an example of how a native ruler's desire to impress the Romans upon whose support he depended could transform local culture.

Herod's most important monument, however, was the Temple of Jerusalem, which he rebuilt on a magnificent scale (the whole project took at least seventy years and was never finished). The temple itself was destroyed in A.D. 70; today only the massive platform survives, the "Temple Mount," which measures about sixteen hundred feet by nine hundred feet. Its retaining walls were constructed of limestone blocks, some measuring over thirty feet long, and reached one hundred feet in height in some places.

Judaea Under Roman Rule. The political history of Herod's kingdom after his death seems very complicated, perhaps because we know more about it than the history of other Roman provinces. In A.D. 6, amid civil unrest that followed Herod's death, the Romans deposed his son and successor Archelaus. From then until A.D. 44 part of Herod's kingdom (including Jerusalem) was ruled by a Roman "prefect" of equestrian rank, subject to the governor of Syria. Herod's sons continued to rule the rest of it. In A.D. 41 Emperor Claudius made Herod's grandson, Agrippa I, king of the whole territory once ruled by Herod. But Agrippa died in A.D. 44; from then until the revolt of 66, Judaea was governed by procurators of equestrian rank, except for a part of Galilee, which was ruled by Agrippa's son Agrippa II.

Who were "the Romans" in Judaea? The answer depends on how we define this group. The only representative of the official imperial administration was the prefect or procurator, with his entourage of friends and household staff. There was also a small auxiliary army in Judaea, whose main function was to keep order; Josephus writes that it was recruited locally from Judaea's cities (but in an emergency, to suppress a major riot, reinforcements came from Syria under the command of its governor). The kings Herod, Agrippa I, and Agrippa II were all Roman citizens, as were some other aristocratic Jews and Greeks in Judaea and all retired auxiliary soldiers. It is impossible to draw a sharp distinction between the Romans and their subjects.

Josephus' account of the origins of the revolt of A.D. 66 emphasizes ethnic tensions within Judaea's diverse population. He describes very bloody conflicts between Greeks and Jews, where the Romans usually supported the Greeks, and sometimes between ethnically distinct Jewish populations. When Jews and Greeks clash, Josephus usually identifies the cause as an issue of sacred law—for example, a Greek mocks Jewish custom by sacrificing over a chamber-pot. According to Josephus, the Jewish population of Caesarea and some other cities was annihilated as a result of the rioting there.

The Romans' brutal suppression of such riots is one of the grievances he cites against them. Others include the corruption and rapacity of some procurators and, especially, a series of offenses to Jewish law by procurators and soldiers. When the emperor Caligula wanted to install an image of himself in the Temple of Jerusalem and sent a large army to do this, the province came

The fortress of Masada, in Israel. The remains of a palace that Herod the Great built on this site can be seen on the hill's flat top. It was the last place to be captured by the Romans in the Jewish revolt of A.D. 66; they besieged it and constructed a massive ramp, still visible to the right of the picture, finally storming the fortress in A.D. 73. According to Josephus, Masada's defenders all committed suicide rather than surrender. At the foot of the hill, to the right, the rectangular outline of two Roman camps can be distinguished. (New York Public Library Picture Collection)

close to a violent rebellion; only the emperor's death forestalled its outbreak for a while.

But while nationalism and resentment of Roman rule were important causes of the revolt, Josephus also describes profound class divisions and conflicts within the Jewish population. Not everyone was equally eager to rebel from the Romans. King Agrippa II supported them and fought with them in the revolt. Josephus also gives the impression that the Jewish aristocratic and

Relief sculpture on the victory arch of Emperor Titus at Rome portrays his triumph over Judaea in A.D. 70; the menorah from the Temple of Jerusalem is easy to distinguish among the spoils. (Photo by Susan P. Mattern-Parkes)

priestly classes—people like himself—opposed the rebellion until it actually broke out. According to him, it was the masses and the "bandits" who were most attracted by the arguments of nationalist leaders. While Josephus may be motivated by self-interest in his description of Jewish society, it was typical of the Romans to work together with local elites; because urban elites benefited from their rule in some ways, their loyalty could usually be relied upon.

But Roman administrative strategies did not always work; the Jewish revolt of A.D. 66 is an example of such a failure. The violence with which the Romans repressed it was legendary: Josephus tells us—although he is certainly exaggerating—that over a million people died in the siege of Jerusalem. Afterward, the province was put under the command of a legate with a legionary army, but this did not prevent another revolt from erupting in A.D. 131, under the leadership of Simon bar-Kochba. Emperor Hadrian repressed the revolt, expelled the Jews from Jerusalem and a wide area around it, and refounded the city as a Roman colony.

Babatha: A Rural Woman and the Roman Government. Other sources from Judaea illustrate better than Josephus the effects of Roman rule on ordinary people. These include an archive of documents belonging to a woman named Babatha, found in a cave near the Dead Sea.

Babatha and the others taking refuge in the cave were killed in the revolt of Simon bar-Kochba, when Babatha was probably in her late twenties. She was from a village in the adjoining province of Arabia. Although she was probably one of the richest landowners in the village, she did not live in a city and was not literate in any language.

Nevertheless, her documents show that Roman rule touched her life in several ways. Perhaps the most important of these was her obligation to pay tax: One document is a census return, registering Babatha's property with the governor's office. On each of her properties she pays a part of her crop and also cash.

Her contacts with the Roman governors of Arabia are especially interesting. Babatha appeared at least twice before the governor and sent him at least three written petitions, all of them about disputes over the property left by her two dead husbands. Both she and her family actively sought his intervention in their quarrels, and it was part of his job to listen to the complaints of this fairly ordinary rural woman. The other "Romans" that appear in the documents include two military officers (one signs her census return, and the other lends money to her second husband) and a Roman citizen woman, the guardian of her niece or nephew, who is literate in Greek.

Neither the Jewish kings, nor the landowning elites, nor even Babatha were passive victims of Roman exploitation. In the interactions between the "Romans" and their subjects, the subjects might be just as cannily manipulative as their conquerors. Some groups had more to gain from Roman rule than others, and circumstances might change over time; but the Roman empire could not have endured without the cooperation of parts of the native population.

The Army in Roman Britain

Britain was the province with the largest army. We know about its garrison from archaeology because many forts have been surveyed or excavated; also from inscriptions on stone, from bronze "diplomata" granting citizenship to retired auxiliary soldiers, and from another, unique source—documents on wooden tablets that were found at a fort at Vindolanda on Hadrian's Wall. Because we know so much about the Roman forces in Britain, this is a good place to discuss the role of the army in provincial society.

Britain was a difficult province to conquer and to retain. In A.D. 43, under emperor Claudius, the Romans invaded and then occupied the southern part of the island. It took a long time to subdue the tribes of Wales; and under Nero a famous and destructive revolt of the Iceni, in east-central Britain, broke out under the leadership of their queen Boudicca. This is the revolt that we know most about, but several others are attested. Although the Romans tried twice to conquer Scotland, they succeeded only briefly.

Troops were stationed throughout the province, especially in those areas with rebellious populations. Forts tended to be built near native settlements or tribal "capitals." In the late 70s and early 80s, the Romans moved more troops to the north, as the governor Agricola tried to conquer Scotland and temporarily succeeded. But when emperor Domitian recalled him and withdrew some of his troops for a war on the Danube frontier, the Romans abandoned Scotland and began to fortify the narrow (seventy-six-mile) isthmus

The remains of the fort at Vindolanda, just to the south of Hadrian's wall. The fort housed auxiliary units of the Roman army. (The Vindolanda Trust)

between the Tyne and Solway rivers. Under emperor Hadrian, they constructed a permanent wall of stone (in the east) and turf (in the west) along this line, known today as **Hadrian's Wall.** Eventually they built a series of forts along the wall to house the auxiliary units stationed there. Under Antoninus Pius, they built a new wall further north, which they occupied briefly and then abandoned.

The fort at Vindolanda on Hadrian's Wall was built in the 80s A.D., long before the wall itself. The wooden writing-tablets found there, dating from the 90s to about 120, tell us a great deal about everyday life in the forts of this remote frontier area, undeveloped except for its large military garrison. The tablets themselves are thin slabs of wood with writing in ink—the wood was being used like papyrus, which must have been difficult to get in that region. Besides official military records and accounts, they also include private letters, especially the correspondence of one of the fort's commanding officers, Flavius Cerialis.

The Vindolanda tablets illustrate the many ways in which the army was a vehicle for the "Romanization" of its own recruits. Like most of the soldiers in Britain and all of those on the wall, the inhabitants of the fort were auxiliaries rather than legionaries; its garrison included the Ninth Cohort of Batavians, the Third Cohort of Batavians, and the First Cohort of Tungrians. Batavians and Tungrians were Germanic tribes from northeastern Gaul, and some of the names preserved in the documents sound Germanic. (Still, it is not necessarily the case that all of the soldiers at Vindolanda were ethnically German, only that the units had been raised originally among those tribes.) None of the names is certainly Briton. Scholars debate the extent to which the army was recruited locally; this was possibly common practice but is not well attested at Vindolanda. The commanding officers, including Cerialis, have Roman names, indicating citizenship; they probably had equestrian status, as tradition demanded. Cerialis may have been an ethnic Batavian from an enfranchised family.

All of the texts are in Latin, which was the language of the army and its massive bureaucracy wherever it was stationed, even in the East. The level of literacy that they suggest is surprisingly high. Hundreds of different "hands" are attested; some of the writers hold the rank of centurion or lower, and some were probably common soldiers. The commander's wife and her female friends could also write. It appears that a certain level of literacy in Latin was characteristic of the army everywhere in the empire, even in provinces where writing was uncommon in the general population.

It is much more difficult to get a sense of the army's effect on native society. In general, the Vindolanda documents mention few civilians by name, but some records of the purchase of food and other items probably reflect transactions with natives. One of the documents refers to a census—as in Arabia, the army probably had a role in conducting it. Some documents are requests for leave; these soldiers may be going to visit civilian family members, friends, or girlfriends.

There is no doubt that the army had direct and indirect effects on Britain's economy, culture, and landscape. The work of military surveyors can be seen in the grid layout of Britain's towns and of its few colonies and in the straight, paved Roman roads, of which a few are still in use. The army imported supplies and also requisitioned them from natives. Items that had once been scarce in Britain (like wine) became common, and the economy changed as natives were forced to produce more of the goods that the army needed. Soldiers were paid partly in cash, which may have led to more use of money in the economy. The opportunity to trade with the army encouraged the development of towns near military forts. Retired soldiers married native women and acquired Roman citizenship; with their savings or pension allotments they became, by the standards of the marginal economy in which they lived, well-to-do members of their communities. However, the army's influence should not be exaggerated. Even in Britain it was only a small part of the population—perhaps 2 percent. Although Britain became much more urbanized after its occupation by the Romans, it is likely that most natives were still living in the countryside, speaking Celtic languages that were never written down and leaving few permanent traces for archaeologists to find.

Society in Roman Egypt

Because thousands of documents on papyrus have been preserved in Egypt's dry climate, we know more about the social history of this province than of any other part of the empire. Census records, wills, marriage agreements, records of court cases, accounts, and contracts tell us about the family, the economy, and also demography and mortality.

Writing and Literacy.   Most people in Egypt could neither read nor write. However, writing was very widely used, not only by the government but also by private individuals. Written contracts for common transactions involving people well outside the upper classes survive—transactions such as leasing land, hiring a wetnurse, or taking on an apprentice. Those who could not write found others to write for them—friends, relatives, "guardians" (of women), or the professional scribes found everywhere, even in small villages. It is common for documents to end with a clause stating that X wrote for Y because Y was illiterate or a "slow writer."

When discussing literacy in Egypt and everywhere in the empire, it is important to remember the problem of language. Egyptian was probably the main spoken language in Egypt, but although it was used for some documents and became an important literary language in the third century, the main written language was Greek. As everywhere in the empire, many of those who learned to write learned a different language from the one they spoke at home. Dozens or hundreds of languages spoken by millions of people in the Roman world were never written down at all.

Family.   One of the most interesting and convincing modern discussions of the family in Egypt (or anywhere in the Roman Empire) is a study of about three hundred census records that survive on papyrus, dating from the first through third centuries A.D.* Because male Egyptians over age fourteen paid a poll tax on their "heads," the census returns list all of the inhabitants of the subject's house (or fraction of a house), their ages, and their family relationships.

Egyptians, especially in rural areas, tended to form complex families; sons would remain in the house with their wives when they married, rather than moving out. Nevertheless, because of high death rates the average number of people per household was about 4.3. Women married young—most were married by their late teens—while men married somewhat later, in their mid-twenties. Virtually all free men and women married at least once. Remarriage after divorce or widowhood was common for both men and women; children of divorced parents usually lived with their fathers.

About one-sixth of the households had slaves, and slaves make up 11 percent of the population attested in the census records. The ages registered for slaves show that males tended to be freed in their twenties, but female slaves were kept longer, generally until they could no longer bear children. Female slaves outnumber male slaves by a wide margin for this reason and because they were preferred for domestic service.

High infant mortality probably explains why most families report only a few children even though women married young. Another reason may be infant exposure, which was practiced throughout the empire and also in Egypt. The customary place to leave an unwanted infant was the local

---

*Roger S. Bagnall and Bruce W. Frier, *The Demography of Roman Egypt,* Cambridge: Cambridge University Press, 1994.

This portrait of a youth from Egypt dates to the second century A.D. Portraits like these deco-rated the coffins that held the mummified bodies of deceased men and women in the Roman period. The mummies illustrate the blend of cultures in Roman Egypt: the stunning natural-ism of the portraits is typical of Hellenistic Greek art, while the method of burial reflects native Egyptian traditions, and Egyptian gods often were depicted on the same coffins. The inscription (in Greek) on the youth's tunic indicates that his name was Eutychides, freedman of Kasanios. (The Metropolitan Museum of Art)

manure pile. It was not unusual for infants to be rescued by people looking for a child to adopt or (more often) for a slave. Contracts hiring women to breastfeed rescued infants survive, and names derived from the Greek word for manure (*kopros*) were common. While we have very little evidence for the motives of those who exposed babies, extreme poverty was likely the most typical one.

One of the most striking features of the census returns is that they often mention marriages between brothers and sisters. About one-sixth of the mar-riages they record are of this type. Scholars have long debated why brother-sister marriage was allowed in Egypt, but one of the most important reasons was probably an economic one. Wills and other documents show that people in Egypt (even Greeks and Roman citizens) tended to follow an ancient Egyptian practice of dividing property equally among all their children, both male and female. The result is that over time, estates were divided into miniscule pieces; references to the ownership of small fractions of a house and of tiny acreages of land are not unusual. One way to counteract this trend was brother-sister marriage, which would combine some pieces of the family's property into larger, more useful units. While it may have had its roots in ancient Egyptian tradition, brother-sister marriage was practiced by both Egyptians and Greeks and was more common in cities than in the countryside. It was illegal in Roman law and Roman citizens were not supposed to practice it.

Mortality and Disease.   The census records paint a sobering picture of mortality in Egypt. Average life expectancy at birth was perhaps in the low twenties. Mortality was highest in the first few years of life; between one-third and one-half of all children probably died before they were five. If they survived past age five, women could expect to live into their mid-thirties and men into their late thirties. Because of Egypt's unusually dense population, epidemic diseases probably spread more easily there than in other parts of the empire, where mortality may have been lower. Leading causes of death were dysentery and other gastro-intestinal illnesses, typhoid fever and similar diseases, malaria, diphtheria, probably tuberculosis, and possibly bubonic plague, although major outbreaks of this disease are only attested later, in the sixth through eighth centuries. Beginning in A.D. 166 an epidemic, probably of smallpox, swept the Roman Empire including Egypt, and smallpox may have been endemic after that.* Rates of death in childbirth are hard to determine, but the Egyptians perceived it as risky and approached it with obvious anxiety. Scorpion bites, eye diseases (often causing blindness), worms, and rabies are frequently mentioned in magic spells, amulets, and medical papyri from Egypt.

City and Country.   We do not know accurately what proportion of Egyptians lived in cities, but it may have been as high as one-third. This was probably very high compared to the rest of the Roman world. The biggest city by far was Alexandria; with perhaps half a million inhabitants, it was the second largest city after Rome itself. Aside from Alexandria there were several dozen "metropoleis," or regional capitals; a typical metropolis might have twenty-five thousand inhabitants, although some were larger.

Roman rule favored the Hellenized urban classes. Citizens of Egypt's four "Greek" cities (including Alexandria) were exempt from the poll tax and were allowed to buy state-owned land at auction; in this way some of them

---

*On disease in Egypt see Walter Scheidel, *Death on the Nile: Disease and the Demography of Egypt*, Leiden: Brill, 2001.

acquired huge estates. Although this was the only class that was recognized as "Greek" in Roman law, the elites of the metropoleis also thought of themselves as Greek and cultivated a Hellenic lifestyle. The special "gynmnasial" class, which was established under Augustus, considered themselves descendants of Greco-Macedonian settlers (or "colonists"); membership in the gymnasium was limited to this class and defined it. Gymnasial status, like citizenship in the Greek cities, was restricted and jealously guarded; only people with two parents in this class could qualify for membership. They were taxed at a reduced rate and took turns holding civic offices, which brought great prestige and also involved paying for civic institutions, like festivals or maintenance of the baths.

In Egypt as elsewhere in the empire, guilds or trade associations were an important part of urban life. Practically every craft or profession had a guild. They were mainly social organizations: They collected dues, held meetings, gave banquets, elected officials, and offered aid to members in hard times and funerals for those who died. The guilds also provided a convenient way for the government to levy taxes in labor or in kind or supplies for the army.

Although Egypt was an unusually urban province, nevertheless most people lived in the countryside, in tiny villages of a few hundred people or substantial towns of a few thousand. Much of the agricultural land was owned by the imperial government or by the emperor himself and leased to tenants, at a rent much higher than the tax collected on private land. Both rent and tax were fixed amounts, not a percentage of the crop, so that in bad years it was difficult to pay them. Peasants often fled from state land and rich landowners had to be forced to undertake its cultivation and pay its rent. It is hard to tell what percentage of the land was state land, but one-third is a good guess. Privately owned land was often leased out, either because it was owned by people living in the cities or sometimes because a villager owned two or more small, scattered plots. Tenant farmers paid a fixed rent or a share of the crop (a typical share might be 30 or 50 percent).

Village landowners formed their own "councils," as in the cities, but with a much lower property requirement; farmers, shepherds, weavers, and so on had their own guilds, also like in the cities. Property was distributed unevenly; a few landlords (including some women) held much of the privately owned land, while most people farmed innumerable small holdings. Like most peasants throughout history, they worked with the help of a few animals (donkeys, camels, and oxen) and a few basic machines. The most sophisticated farm equipment by far was the "Archimedean screw" (see p. 111), but most farmers used simpler methods of raising water. They depended mainly on their own families to supply the necessary labor, and more so than in the cities, extended families clustered together in the villages' mud-brick dwellings. Many peasants barely produced enough to feed their families; often they were unable to save enough seed to plant the next year's crop, and numerous contracts lending seed survive (the normal rate of interest was 50 percent). Vulnerable to exploitation and strong-arm tactics from local "big men" or urban landlords, many of their complaints survive—

recorded by the village scribe and sent to the nome supervisor or even to the governor of Egypt, they sometimes succeeded in obtaining justice.

Crisis and Reform in the Third Century

Wars and Emperors

In A.D. 235, the emperor Severus Alexander was murdered by his troops on the Rhine frontier. The army proclaimed his successor: a Thracian named Maximinus, of only equestrian rank. His reign lasted three years before he, too, was killed in a mutiny.

The third century was a period of political and military crisis. The details of Severus Alexander's situation illustrate part of the problem: more aggressive foreign enemies and simultaneous attacks on separate parts of the empire. In the 220s a revolution had occurred in the East; a new dynasty of Persians called the Sasanians had taken control of the former Parthian Empire, proudly tracing their heritage to Cyrus and his descendants, and claiming dominion over Rome's eastern provinces. Under Severus Alexander they invaded northern Mesopotamia, which the Romans had recently conquered. The emperor was still waging that war when a group of Germans— a new federation of tribes called the Alamanni—crossed the Rhine in a very destructive invasion. It was too dangerous to entrust a major war to another general, who might then become a rival emperor; furthermore the army from the East was now needed in the West, so Severus undertook the long march to the Rhine.

For reasons that are not well understood, new, larger coalitions of Germanic tribes formed in Europe around this time; it is in the third century that we first hear of the great federations of Goths, Franks, and Alamanni. It is extremely difficult, however, to determine what was going on in barbarian Europe in this period. Archaeology is difficult to interpret; the barbarians themselves were illiterate and left no written records. Roman writers were not careful about the names they applied to foreign peoples, and their descriptions of barbarians often reflect literary tradition rather than contemporary reality. But for whatever reason, invasions on multiple fronts—which the Romans had avoided until now—became more frequent. Rome's relatively small and static army was ill-equipped to handle the situation. The problem was exacerbated by an imperial ideology in which all military power was vested in the emperor; any military success by a subordinate practically guaranteed an attempt at usurpation and civil war.

From 235 to 284 there were about thirty major emperors and dozens of usurpers. Most were proclaimed by the army; many were also murdered by the army, and most emperors lived only a short time after their accession. These emperors tended to come from the equestrian class and from the Danube provinces—such as Thrace and Pannonia—which also were the main recruiting-grounds for the Roman army. They were men of little culture but long military experience. They spent most of their time fighting in Rome's frontier provinces, and little or none in Rome.

This relief carved into rock at Naqsh-i-Rustam, Iran, depicts King Shapur I of Persia on horseback. It depicts his victories over the Romans. The figure kneeling before him is the emperor Philip the Arab, who surrendered to him in 244 B.C., paying a large ransom; the figure with raised arms represents emperor Valerian, whom he defeated and captured in 260. (SEF/Art Resource, NY)

Rome suffered military disasters that were previously unthinkable. The empire began giving up territory—including Dacia, the province of Mesopotamia (although Diocletian recovered this later), and some fortified land across the Rhine. In 260, the emperor Valerian was captured alive by Shapur, the Persian king. In 267 the Herulians (a Gothic tribe) invaded Greece, reached Athens, and sacked much of the city. The Athenians fought them off under the leadership of the historian Dexippus—the Roman army was nowhere in sight. They then hastily constructed a new wall with a small perimeter (it excluded the *agora*, for example), using the remains of devastated buildings as fill. Under Emperor Aurelian in the 270s a vast new defensive wall was constructed around Rome itself; much of it is well preserved today.

Huge parts of the empire broke off and formed separate kingdoms. Gaul revolted in the West; in the East, the provinces of Syria, Egypt, and much of Asia Minor rebelled under the leadership of the Syrian city Palmyra and its queen Zenobia. These kingdoms maintained their independence for years, until Emperor Aurelian finally reconquered them.

Economic Crisis

While the empire as a political structure was on the brink of collapse in the third century, it is much harder to determine whether there was also a widespread economic crisis, one that affected how most people lived. It is difficult to identify economic trends that affected all parts of the empire or even large parts of it; different places prospered and declined in different ways and at different times. Certainly people living in areas ravaged by civil war or foreign invasion suffered—not only because of the destruction caused by the wars themselves, but also because the burden of supplying the army fell on them. In some European provinces cities declined in size, wealth, and population; on the other hand, in some of these same provinces country estates did not decline or even became more prosperous.

One clear economic effect of the crisis was the collapse of the silver coinage. This had its roots in the early third century A.D., when Severus and his successors doubled and quadrupled military pay. They did this to buy the loyalty and support of the army, on which their rule increasingly depended. Because Severus could not afford the higher salaries, he mixed in more base metal with the silver in the *denarii* he issued—previous emperors had done this, but not so much. At first this had no clear effect on prices, but by the 260s hyperinflation had set in. By the end of the third century the *denarius* was a base-metal coin with a thin coating of silver, and prices had skyrocketed out of control.

But it is not clear that the fall of the *denarius* had important consequences in everyday life. People went on using coins, and do not seem to have changed their buying habits. The gold coinage survived the crisis unadulterated and could still be used for large transactions, and some provinces perhaps never had thoroughly monetized economies at all.

Many scholars have described a crisis in the urban propertied classes—the decurions who paid for most of the cities' buildings and held their political and religious offices. The strain on this class seems to have led to a decrease in public construction projects in African provinces and may have contributed to the decline of cities in Europe. More decurions complained of their burdens and tried to escape them; property requirements were gradually lowered to broaden the pool of candidates. Even here, however, the evidence is not unambiguous; in some Egyptian cities there was a resurgence of public-spirited munificence exactly at the height of the crisis, in the late third century.

Diocletian and the Later Roman Empire

Regardless of its economic health, the empire as a political institution in the late third century was in grave danger. It did not, however, collapse. Diocletian at first seemed like any other emperor when he was proclaimed by the army in 284; a rough soldier from Dalmatia (the modern Croatian coast) with a stubble beard, he assassinated his predecessor himself, to the cheers of the troops. But unlike other third-century emperors, Diocletian went on to rule

The tetrarchs were portrayed as tough, stocky, military types in stylized and geometric, almost crude sculptures like this one, now at St. Mark's cathedral in Venice. The sculpture emphasizes the harmony and cohesion of the imperial administration as the emperors, who all look alike, embrace one another.   (Scala/Art Resource)

for two decades until he retired in A.D. 305. The reforms he made, although all of them were problematic, saved the empire.

Diocletian's most interesting innovation was to abandon the idea of a single emperor. A few emperors had ruled jointly with their sons or brothers earlier in the Imperial period, but Diocletian tried to institutionalize the idea of a divided imperial office. He proclaimed one co-emperor or "Augustus," Maximian, and two junior emperors or "Caesars." The idea behind this reform is reflected in coins and portrait sculptures depicting the emperors of the "tetrarchy"—blocky, tough-looking men who all looked alike. One was supposed to be just as good as another, and since all could legitimately command the army, a war could be conducted on four fronts if necessary. This particular innovation of Diocletian's did not outlast his reign.

Diocletian addressed the problem of inflation with a reform of the coinage and his famous "price edict," which fixed prices for a long list of goods and services. Although the penalty for violating the price edict was death, neither this nor the coinage reform was very successful at stemming inflation.

But the new emperor's most sweeping reforms were to the imperial bureaucracy and its tax system. He divided the provinces into smaller, more numerous units and grouped them into twelve **dioceses** under equestrian officials, called *vicarii*; under Diocletian, the senate ceased to function as Rome's administrative class. He also divided up official responsibilities in a new way; *duces* commanded the provincial armies, while civilian tasks were handled by separate officials. The result was a vastly amplified administration that, he hoped, would be able to collect taxes more efficiently—but would also be more costly to maintain.

Much of what we know about taxes in the fourth century is based on the *Theodosian Code*, a codification of imperial rulings compiled by Theodosius II in A.D. 437. Diocletian apparently tried to create a more uniform and flexible taxation system by inventing the units of *iugum* and *caput*—very roughly, these were taxable units of land and of human and animal resources, but no precise definition of either term is possible. Each person or community owed a certain number of these units; the amount they were obligated to pay, and thus the total revenue received, could be adjusted by raising the amount due per unit. The Roman government had always collected taxes in kind and in labor as well as in cash, but Diocletian's reforms expanded this practice, although cash payment in gold is often mentioned in the *Code*. Virtually everyone with a job was required to produce something or perform some task for the government as part of his (or her) tax liability. The law also tried to pin people in place, to prevent them from squirming out of their duties and to ensure a stable supply of the goods and services the empire needed. The office of decurion was made hereditary; so was the profession of soldier and other professions and crafts, and people were not allowed to change jobs. Tenant farmers were not allowed to leave their land. These restrictions make the later Roman Empire sound like a totalitarian state, but they could be enforced only in a limited way, and many people did quite illegal things. Especially, Diocletian's reforms strengthened the position of large landowners by tying their tenants to their property, with the result that some landlords could run their estates like small kingdoms and ignore Roman authority.

The army of the late empire was divided into more numerous, smaller units than before; legionary forts of the fourth century A.D. tend to accommodate only about a thousand soldiers. Garrison troops stationed on the frontiers were commanded by *duces*, chosen from the equestrian class. Under Diocletian's eventual successor Constantine, the size and importance of the elite mobile army that traveled with the emperor increased; largely composed of cavalry, these troops were often recruited from tribes on the empire's fringes. By the mid-300s the mobile army contained one-fourth of the empire's total forces.

When Diocletian retired and forced his colleague Maximian to do the same in 305, his plan for an orderly succession to imperial office fell apart. After a prolonged series of civil wars in which he defeated several rivals, Constantine became sole emperor from 324 until his death in 337. But while Constantine ruled alone at the end of his reign, in general the later Roman Empire would be ruled by two emperors. There was an increasing tendency to divide it into eastern and western halves, until the last western emperor, Romulus Augustulus, was deposed in 476.

Rome remained the official capital at first, but emperors spent little time there. They were much more likely to be found in cities closer to the frontiers: Milan (in northern Italy), Trier (in Gaul), Sirmium (in Serbia), Thessalonica (in northern Greece), and Nicomedia (in Turkey) all flourished in the fourth century. In 330, Constantine officially moved Rome's capital to Byzantium on the Bosporus strait, which he renamed Constantinople ("Constantine city").

SUMMARY

The origins of Rome are lost in legend. In the seventh century B.C., under its semi-mythical kings, it developed from a collection of small villages into a city. After the kings were expelled, class struggle dominated the first few centuries of the Republic, as "plebeians" fought for, and achieved, political equality with "patricians." However, power in the Republic remained in the hands of a narrow aristocracy of rich, well-born families; these were Rome's military leaders, its office-holders, and its large landlords. Each commanded a vast and complicated social network of friends, dependents, slaves, and ex-slaves.

Under their leadership the Romans gradually conquered and absorbed the peoples of Italy. They annexed large tracts of land from defeated enemies and incorporated Italian troops into their army. By the end of the Republican period Italy had become "Romanized"; all Italians were Roman citizens and exempt from tribute, the main tax.

Beginning in the third century B.C. Rome began to fight overseas enemies in the East and West. They controlled the peoples they had defeated in various ways; often they left a native king in charge, but would depose him if he disobeyed Roman orders; some provinces needed permanent armies of occupation. Roman culture and the economy were transformed, as they imposed expensive indemnities on their defeated enemies, captured enormous quantities of treasure, and came into contact with Greece's more sophisticated civilization.

In the first century B.C. the Republican government collapsed amid increasingly violent clashes between powerful aristocrats. After almost two decades of civil war, Octavian (later Augustus) became sole emperor in 31 B.C. and established a standing, professional army commanded by senators who were appointed by him and acted under his authority. He founded overseas colonies for veterans, and in his reign the Roman system of ruling through local urban elites was extended throughout the empire. Civic constitutions established local senates of wealthy landowners, on whose loyalty and cooperation Roman rule largely depended.

The second half of the third century was a time of crisis. Parts of the empire were racked by foreign and civil war; new kingdoms broke off in the East and

West; emperors were assassinated in rapid succession; the currency collapsed. In A.D. 285, Emperor Diocletian made sweeping reforms; he broke the empire down into smaller administrative units, vastly expanded the bureaucracy, and reformed the way taxes were assessed. The new system depended on assigning everyone a very specific place in the economy; farmers were tied to the land, craftsmen to their professions, and local senators to their office, and all of these positions were made hereditary by law.

FOUR

Christianity and the Late Antique World

Paganism

Christians called those who followed traditional, polytheistic religious practices **pagans**. In this context the word *paganus* meant, roughly, "civilian" (in contrast to soldiers in the army of Christ); later its more usual meaning of "rustic" or "ignorant" also came into play. Pagans for the most part did not think of themselves as practicing a distinct religion; the gods permeated every aspect of ancient life and seemed fundamental features of their world. Before Christianity, the closest approximation to the modern concept of "paganism" was the idea of "ancestral custom"—in Greek, *ta patria*—for which the Romans professed respect and toleration; even Judaism could claim some protection on this basis. When Christians rejected the worship of the pagan gods and became committed to rooting them out wherever they could be found, they found them everywhere.

On the level of local and everyday experience were agricultural rituals, wedding ceremonies, and funerary customs; household gods and nature-cults of hills or streams could be found everywhere in the empire. There were also the great national gods—Greek and Roman, but also Egyptian, Syrian, Celtic, and so on. It was common to equate native gods with Greek or Roman counterparts. Thus the Roman Mercury, the most popular god on inscriptions from Gaul after Jupiter himself, was in fact the Celtic god Teutates, thinly disguised. Some native gods were worshipped only by their own people, but a few engendered cosmopolitan cults attested all over the empire; these included Isis (from Egypt), Cybele (from Asia Minor), and two gods especially popular with the army: Jupiter Dolichenus (from Syria) and Mithras (from Persia).

The gods might be honored with small shrines and altars or stone temples—the most common type of public building wherever one looked. Hymns and prose poems were written for them; statues, paintings, and relief sculptures were dedicated to them. They were honored with festivals that typically included music and singing, a dance or dramatic spectacle, a procession in which the god's statue was carried through the streets, and also feasts on the meat of sacrificed animals, drinking, and a day off for masters, workers, and slaves. The festivals of the East's Greek cities, and of some Western cities, attracted tourists and trade from all over the empire. They included contests in athletics, poetry, rhetoric, music, even medicine; in short, they featured every aspect of Hellenic "high culture." In a broader sense, the myths that surrounded the gods were the very fabric of art and literature; philosophy largely speculated about the nature of divinity; literature and philosophy, in turn, were the foundations of Greco-Roman education.

People communicated with the gods, first, through the rules and regulations posted in temple precincts. These explained the wishes of the deity about who might enter, and in what state of ritual purity (certain foods, sexual intercourse, childbirth, or contact with the dead might all contaminate). They described how the deity should be worshipped—whether he or she preferred sacrifices of wine, grain, incense, or animals, and if animals, which ones. The gods might address an individual more directly, through an oracle. One could travel to one of the famous sites, like Delphi in Greece, but a multitude of local deities also gave responses to simple questions through priests or priestesses or by a number of other methods. Gods and goddesses often appeared in dreams. Worshippers sought their favor or expressed their gratitude with gifts: Sacrifices of the god's favorite food or altars with inscribed dedications were popular gifts, but almost anything might be offered, from simple figurines to live snakes or fish for the temple's pond. Sometimes the gift was dedicated "in accordance with a vow," a promise made beforehand to compensate the god for some benefit, if it were received. The relationship was one of reciprocity: The god conferred favors, and received gifts and gratitude.

The favor most frequently attested on stone inscriptions is healing. Many gods could heal; but one god in particular who rose to great popularity in the Hellenistic and Roman periods was Asclepius, the Greek god of medicine. His temples could be found everywhere, especially in the East; his largest cult-centers, at Epidaurus (in the Peloponnese) and at Pergamum, attracted pilgrims from far and wide. Appearing to them in dreams as they slept in the temple precinct, he healed them himself or prescribed a therapy. His temple precincts were crowded with dedications from grateful patients, on display as proofs of his efficacy—from beautifully carved marble reliefs depicting healing scenes to humble terracotta models of body parts. At Epidaurus long inscriptions related stories of past miracles, complete with the names of those healed. From the second century A.D. come the diaries of the famous sophist and hypochondriac Aelius Aristides, relating the long history of his communication with the god and his experiences at the temple of Pergamum.

Other favors recorded in the offerings of grateful worshippers include rescue from shipwreck, natural disasters or the dangers of travel and war; victory in a contest; and sometimes fertility, although the latter not very often. It is possible that this and other universal needs—for a good crop, for example—were the province of household and agricultural gods whose worship has left fewer permanent traces.

The Written Record

ASCLEPIUS' MIRACLES

Grateful worshippers dedicated these models of body parts, excavated from the temple of Asclepius at Corinth, when they had been healed by the god. (Photo by Susan P. Mattern-Parkes)

> The following text is excerpted from a long inscription on marble found at Epidaurus, the site of Asclepius' most famous temple complex. It was probably inscribed in the fourth century B.C. but may incorporate earlier material. The marble slabs bearing the record of Asclepius' miracles were displayed in the temple precinct for everyone to read, along with the dedications of former suppliants who had been cured; the latter no doubt included Ambrosia's silver pig. Note how the god uses medical techniques (drugs and surgery) to cure the patient.

Ambrosia from Athens, blind in one eye. She came to the god as a suppliant. Walking around the sacred precinct she laughed at some of the cures as unbelievable and impossible, that the lame and the blind were healed after seeing a mere dream. Then she fell asleep, and saw a vision. It seemed that the god stood near her and said that he would heal her, but that as a fee she should make a dedication to the temple, namely a silver pig, as a memorial to her ignorance. He said these things, then cut open the eye that was diseased and poured in some medicine. The next day she left, healed.

Inscriptiones Graecae, IV², no. 121.

For a study and translation of the text, see Lynn R. LiDonnici, *The Epidaurian Miracle Inscriptions*, Atlanta, GA: Scholars Press, 1995.

IMPORTANT DATES IN THE LATE ANTIQUE PERIOD

A.D. 284–305	Reign of Diocletian
A.D. 312	Constantine's conversion to Christianity
A.D. 324	Council of Nicaea
A.D. 330	Dedication of Constantinople as the empire's new capital
A.D. 356	Death of Saint Antony
A.D. 361–363	Reign of Julian, the last pagan emperor
A.D. 378	Battle of Hadrianople
A.D. 410	Sack of Rome by Alaric and Visigoths
A.D. 429	Vandals invade Africa
A.D. 527–565	Reign of Justinian
A.D. 622	Flight of Muhammad to Medina; year 1 of Muslim calendar

This emphasis on the gods' power to grant benefits is not meant to imply that paganism offered no deeper, more subtle rewards. Pagan philosophers gave moral guidance—not only in their written works, but also in the public teachings of the Cynics, Sceptics, and sophists found in every city. One could feel an emotional or spiritual connection to a god—as Aelius Aristides with Asclepius, or Lucius, the hero of Apuleius' novel *The Golden Ass*, with the goddess Isis. The gratitude expressed by dedicants of all classes for the gods' help and protection, although formulaic, was no doubt sincere. Some cults offered "mysteries" including secret rituals, initiation into a select group, and perhaps the promise of a better life after death—although this last idea was never central to any pagan cult. Most importantly, pagan gods and traditions linked people with their heritage, their community, their family, and their ancestors. The idea that Christianity eventually succeeded in displacing paganism because it offered more spiritual satisfaction is too simplistic. Pagan religions developed over centuries to encompass a full range of human needs, both mundane and exalted, artistic, intellectual, emotional, and social. The price of converting to Christianity was very high.

The Rise of Christianity

Because of the way that ancient works were preserved in the West—copied and recopied in European monasteries—early Christian writings survive in large numbers. Historians, familiar with the outcome of the struggle between paganism and Christianity, tend to focus on the new religion's rise and inevitable triumph. But until the middle of the fourth century, only a small minority of the Roman world was Christian. Paganism remained a vital force for centuries after that, and Christianity never succeeded in completely displacing it: Western civilization is a mixture of Greco-Roman and Judeo-

Christian influences. In studying the early history of Christianity, especially before its legalization in the fourth century A.D., it helps to remember its character as a marginal sect.

The New Testament and the Gospels

The **gospels** are the four books of the New Testament—the Christian part of the Bible—that record the words and deeds of Jesus, a Jewish carpenter's son who became a prophet and teacher. They were written down in the second half of the first century A.D. Besides the gospels, the New Testament contains the Acts of the Apostles, which tells the story of the early church after Jesus' death, and especially the deeds of Paul, who is discussed later in this chapter. It also contains some of Paul's letters and a few other letters; and the book of Revelation, an apocalyptic work describing the end of the world and the "last judgment" that ushers in a new age. Other gospels, letters, and apocalypses circulated in antiquity and many survive today, although they did not become part of the canonical New Testament.

All of the texts in the New Testament were written in *koine* Greek, but Christian writing, especially from the third century A.D. onward, was not only composed in the languages of the ruling elite. In the twentieth century a large collection of papyrus texts was discovered near the town of Nag Hammadi in Egypt, written in Coptic Egyptian, containing works associated with a mystical Christian sect—the Gnostic sect. Many Christian texts in other languages survive, especially Syriac, Armenian, and Slavonic. Some popular works survive in several languages. Christians also produced translations of the Bible, both the Hebrew Bible (or the Septuagint) and New Testament. Syriac translations are attested already in the first and second centuries, and by A.D. 400 there was a good, stable text of the Bible in Syriac. In the late 300s, Saint Jerome produced a Latin translation of the Bible, not from the Septuagint but from the original Hebrew, called the "Vulgate." Also in the fourth century, Ulfilas made a famous translation of the Bible into Gothic. Translations into several other ancient languages, including Coptic, Ethiopic, Armenian, Georgian, Slavonic, and Arabic, survive; and many of them are still used in church ceremonies today.

Three of the New Testament's four gospels (Matthew, Mark, and Luke) are "synoptic," which means "seeing together": They all tell similar stories. Matthew and Luke both contain more material than the shortest and possibly earliest gospel, Mark. The gospels are the main historical sources for Jesus' life, but they are problematic in this regard. They were composed well after his death and based on material that probably circulated orally for decades before it was written down. Jesus himself wrote nothing. Basic facts such as the year of his birth are hard to pin down.* Nevertheless, while they

---

*Jesus' birth took place in the year of Augustus' notorious census (A.D. 6, Luke 2:1) but also while Herod the Great was still alive (Matt. 2; Herod died in 4 B.C.). The elements of folktale in the birth narrative are very prominent; for example, the story that Jesus narrowly escaped Herod's massacre of infant boys recalls the story of Moses' birth and that of many other folk heroes.

should not be pressed too hard for specific facts, the gospels provide a wealth of information about the nature of early Christianity.

Miracles. Jesus' miraculous deeds account for much of the content of all three synoptic gospels. Of the miracles he performs, most are healings and exorcisms. Jesus heals blindness, deafness, paralysis, leprosy, and a woman suffering from chronic bleeding, whom doctors have failed to help; he raises a young girl from the dead, an extreme type of healing miracle. Typically these cures take place in front of crowds of onlookers, although Jesus some-times deliberately tries to escape the crowd. Sometimes there are skeptics among the spectators who criticize Jesus or laugh at him until they witness his impressive deeds. He cures by touching the patient's affected part, or patients touch him; in one case, he spits; in some cases, he speaks a few words. The effect of his cure is usually obvious to the spectators (someone who is carried in, paralyzed, on a stretcher picks it up and walks away), and his reputation grows until he is besieged everywhere by crowds of the sick.

Some patients are possessed by demons. Many symptoms of demonic pos-session would today be interpreted as signs of mental illness, and one victim of possession has seizures like those that doctors in antiquity and today asso-ciate with epilepsy ("grand mal" seizures). Jesus **exorcises** the patient—expels the demon—usually with a short command (such as "Be silent, come out").

Parables and the Apocalypse. Jesus often taught using parables—stories about ordinary things with an allegorical meaning. In the gospels he explains the meaning of some parables to his "disciples" (which means "students"). Many of them are allegories about the last judgment and the kingdom of heaven, to which only a select group will be admitted. The parables convey a sense of urgency, as they emphasize the need to be prepared at all times—the event seems imminent, and there is no way of knowing when it will happen.

Several passages in the Hebrew Bible look forward to a time when Yahweh will reverse the disasters suffered by Israel and a new, better age will begin. But the idea of a day of judgment, complete with punishment for evildoers, the salvation of a chosen group, and the resurrection of the dead, is more typ-ical of noncanonical Jewish literature, especially a genre called "apocalyptic" literature. (While the resurrection of the dead is not a major theme in Jesus' parables, his own resurrection is the climax of the story.)

Jesus considered himself a prophet like those of the Hebrew Bible. It is not clear that he thought of himself as the "son of God" or as the *messiah*—a sav-ior king whose future reign is predicted by some Hebrew prophets—but the gospels certainly present him this way. His epithet "Christus" is a Greek translation of the word *messiah*, which means "the anointed one."

Jesus and Society. The gospels portray Jesus as an authority on Jewish law, debating Pharisees and "scribes" (also legal scholars) on several of its points. Some passages suggest that he rejects their tradition of interpreting the law and seeks the true law in the Torah itself and especially in the Ten Com-mandments. On the subject of divorce, he rejects one part of the Torah (from

Deuteronomy), which permits it, citing another passage (from Genesis) in support of his argument against it. Jesus does not reject Jewish law, but, on the contrary, offers authoritative opinions about it.

The gospels are full of stories of Jesus' interactions with marginal, under-privileged, or despised groups of people. Jesus helps and associates with women as well as men, slaves, eunuchs, a non-Jew (by special exception), and even soldiers, tax-collectors, and thieves. Some of the people he heals—such as lepers and the woman with chronic bleeding—were ritually unclean in Jewish law. He urges one rich man to sell everything he has and give it to the poor if he wants to enter the kingdom of heaven. His appeal to the poor also emerges in his parables that reflect everyday rural life—they are about farming, vine growing, and sometimes about fishing (two of the twelve dis-ciples were fishermen). The gospels' social message is one of inclusion and equality, and could probably be described as unconventional or even radical, although Jewish law had always had a strong egalitarian strain.

Jesus' attitude toward the Romans is difficult to pin down. The gospels con-tain many references to Roman rule—soldiers, the census, tax collectors, and a "legion" of demons all play important roles. Jesus is tried and condemned by Pontius Pilatus, the Roman prefect of Judaea from A.D. 26 to 36; he is exe-cuted by crucifixion, a typical and extremely painful Roman punishment. Apocalyptic literature, whose ideas lie behind many of Jesus' parables, was usually very political: It anticipated the overthrow of a kingdom of evil oppressors, in this period the Romans. (In the New Testament apocalypse, Revelation, Rome is depicted as a slavering seven-headed monster.) But the gospels seem to play down any political message that Jesus may have pro-claimed. While he is accused before Pilate of inciting the Jews to revolt and opposing the payment of tribute, the gospels suggest that he was not guilty of these charges. They place most of the blame for his execution on the Jewish council of elders, called the Sanhedrin, as well as the Jewish priests and peo-ple. All of this probably reflects the atmosphere in which the gospels were writ-ten: They seem to be aimed at a gentile audience,* at a time when the extension of the mission to the gentiles was the main controversy that the church faced.

Paul

Christianity began as a Jewish sect. At first, its members were the followers of Jesus and after that, of the **apostles**—which means, roughly, "deputies" or "messengers." In the gospels, the apostles are disciples of Jesus who travel around, casting out demons, spreading the news about Jesus and his deeds, and carrying out the purification ritual of baptism, which marked one's entrance into the ranks of Jesus' followers. But at first it was not clear who the audience for the apostles' message should be. Was salvation available only to God's chosen people, Israel, or could non-Jews be admitted to the kingdom

---

*The word **gentile** comes from a Latin root meaning "tribe" or "nation"; depending on the context it could mean either "non-Jewish" or "non-Christian" (i.e., pagan).

of heaven? This question dominated the early church, but Christianity gradually died out among the Jewish population and by the middle of the second century A.D. was mainly a gentile religion. The extension of the mission to the gentiles was perhaps the most important thing to happen to Christianity, and its most prominent advocate was Paul.

Paul was born in Tarsus, a city in Asia Minor. According to tradition, he was a tentmaker by profession. But his family was prominent enough to have Roman citizenship; like many Roman citizens he had two names, a Hebrew one (Saul) and Paul, his Roman name. Paul was a Pharisee, educated in Jewish law at Jerusalem, and he also may have had some Greek education, as he seems familiar with the rhetorical style of Greek philosophy and with many of its ideas. He wrote in Greek, but could also speak Aramaic.

At first, Paul opposed Christianity and joined those who were trying to stamp it out. His conversion was the result of a singular, vivid experience in which he saw and heard Jesus, who had died years before. After that, although he had never met Jesus when he was alive, Paul considered himself an apostle (and when Christian authors mention "the Apostle" they are referring to Paul). He traveled far and wide with tireless enthusiasm, preaching the gospel and founding new churches in cities such as Ephesus, Corinth, and Athens. He preached mainly in synagogues and most of his converts were Jewish. But he also believed that it was his mission to convert non-Jews and he was instrumental in making Christianity acceptable to gentiles. Few would have embraced the new religion if it had required conforming to Jewish law; dietary restrictions and the practice of circumcision were especially difficult barriers. But Paul argued for a much simpler dietary code that, at most, only banned blood and the meat of animals that had been strangled or sacrificed to pagan gods. He also argued that circumcision was unnecessary and instead advocated a strict code of sexual behavior, which idealized sexual abstinence and condemned sex outside of marriage for men as well as women. Paul's emphasis on sexuality was an early sign of the important role it would play in defining the Christian community.

The Acts and also Paul's letters or "epistles," of which some are preserved in the New Testament, are among the best sources for early Christian practices. In their mission to convert people, the apostles emphasized the same themes found in the gospels: the imminent end of the world, the miraculous resurrection of Jesus, and the fulfillment of Jewish prophecy. They healed and exorcised demons and also "spoke in tongues," a new kind of miraculous phenomenon. In Acts, baptized converts are supposed to sell all their personal property and share it in common; this recalls the practices of the Jewish community that produced the Dead Sea Scrolls. But Paul's letters are full of references to rich and poor Christians, suggesting that the rule about selling one's property was not universal by that time. Christians met to pray and to share a meal, and both of these rituals acquired formulae at an early stage; a simple prayer called the "Lord's prayer," universal among Christians today, and the "Lord's supper," in which bread and wine represented the body and blood of Christ, are attested in the first century.

Certain persistent themes in Paul's letters may reflect tensions in early church society. Paul repeatedly advocates harmony between gentiles and Jews; he also exhorts slaves to be obedient to their masters and wives to their husbands. I Corinthians, which Paul wrote in response to a lost letter asking his advice on several issues, perhaps gives the most detailed picture of problems in an early congregation. The community is divided on several points which they ask Paul to clarify: Is sex desirable or permissible within marriage, and is marriage a good idea? Regarding Jewish law, is it permissible to eat meat sacrificed to pagan gods (yes), to eat with gentiles (yes), or to marry one's former stepmother (no)? Regarding the resurrection, is it really necessary to believe that the physical body will be raised? (Paul does little to clarify this particular issue in his eloquent but mystifying discussion.) Church meetings have become raucous: Ecstatic prophecy and speaking in tongues are dominating the agenda, and some people are overindulging in food and drink at the communal meals. Women are also prophesying, with their heads uncovered: At one point Paul advises that women should be silent in church, but elsewhere he only states that they should pray and prophesy with their heads veiled as a symbol of their submission to men.

Persecution and Martyrs

The Roman government had no official policy either of religious tolerance or of the enforcement of religious conformity. In general, conflicts over religion were rare, but there were some exceptions. A series of incidents regarding Jewish law led up to the revolt of A.D. 66; in Britain and Gaul the Romans deliberately destroyed the priestly class of Druids; and the Bacchic cult, a cult of the Greek god Dionysus, had been illegal since 186 B.C. Christians rejected the festivals, sacrifices, and rituals in which everyone else participated. They struck others as eccentric and possibly dangerous extremists and were sometimes treated as criminals. The earliest known persecution of the Christians was under Nero, who found them a convenient scapegoat for the fire that consumed Rome in A.D. 64 and made a public spectacle of torturing them cruelly to death. Tradition holds that Paul and also Peter, Jesus' disciple and the founder of the church in Rome, died in this event. About thirty-five years later, Pliny the Younger, traveling through one of the more remote districts of his province in northern Asia Minor, encounters Christians in the town of Amastris. In a letter to Trajan he asks whether he is doing the right thing by ordering the execution of confessed Christians who refuse to sacrifice to the emperor; he explains that the cult includes women, children, and the elderly and that he can find no evidence of the depraved behavior supposedly practiced in the cult. (Later sources indicate that pagans associated Christianity with sexual indulgence, incest, and cannibalism, among other moral outrages, and these were perhaps what Pliny had in mind.) Persecutions occurred sporadically after this—major events are attested at Smyrna in the 160s, at Lyons in 177, and at Carthage in 202–203. In 249, Emperor Decius decreed that everyone in the empire must obtain a certificate of sacrifice to

The Written Record

PLINY AND THE CHRISTIANS

Here, Pliny the Younger writes to emperor Trajan from his post as governor of the provinces of Bithynia and Pontus, around A.D. 110. This letter and accounts of trials of Christian martyrs, which survive in large numbers, are some of the best sources for criminal procedure in the Roman Empire.

Pliny to Emperor Trajan:

It is my custom, lord, to refer to you all things about which I am in doubt. For who is better able to resolve my hesitation and instruct my ignorance? I have never taken part in trials of Christians; therefore I do not know whether and to what extent they are usually punished or sought out. And I have serious concerns about whether some distinction should be made according to age, or whether children should be treated no differently from adults; whether clemency should be granted for repentence, or whether no one who has ever been Christian should benefit from having ceased; whether the name itself, in the absence of vices, or the vices associated with the name should be punished. In the meantime, this is the method I have followed with those who were denounced to me as Christians. I asked them whether they were Christians. If they confessed, I asked them again and a third time, threatening punishment; if they persevered, I ordered them to be led to execution. I had no doubt that no matter what they were confessing, their stubbornness and inflexible obstinacy surely ought to be punished. There were others similarly demented, whom, because they were Roman citizens, I noted to be sent to the city [of Rome].

Now, as often happens, my attention to the problem has led to more widespread and various accusations. A pamphlet has been produced anonymously, containing the names of many people. I thought it best to release those who denied that they were Christians or ever had been, when they had invoked the gods in my presence and offered incense and wine to your image (which I had ordered to be brought in for this purpose, together with statues of the gods), and besides that had cursed Christ—none of which things, supposedly, those who are really Christians can be forced to do. Others who were named by an informer, said that they were Christians and then denied it; some said that they had been Christians and had ceased, either three years previously, or longer than that, and sometimes even twenty years previously. All of these worshipped your image and the images of the gods, and cursed Christ. But they affirmed that the sum total of their vice and error was only that they were accustomed to meet before dawn on a fixed day, and to sing a song to Christ as though to a god, and to bind themselves to one another with an oath, not for the purposes of some crime, but promising not to commit theft or banditry or adultery, nor to betray a trust, nor to refuse to return a deposit when asked for it. And when they have done these things it is their custom to disperse and to meet again later to take a meal, but an ordinary and harmless one; and they had ceased to do even this after my edict, in which I prohibited clubs according to your orders. For this reason I thought it was all the more necessary to seek out the truth from two slave-women, called deaconesses, by torture. I discovered nothing but a perverse and immoderate superstition.

Therefore, I have postponed the hearings and hastened to ask your advice. It seems to me that the matter is worthy of referring to you, most of all because of the number who are in danger; for many of all ages and classes and both sexes are being accused, and will continue to be accused. The taint of this superstition has pervaded not only the cities, but also the villages and the fields; but it seems possible to stop and correct it. Certainly it is clear that the temples, formerly almost deserted, have now begun to be crowded again; and the sacred ceremonies, long interrupted, have been revived, and everywhere the meat of sacrificial animals is being sold, for which previously very few buyers could be found. From this it is easy to imagine what a multitude of people could be reformed, if given a chance to repent.

Trajan's answer to Pliny:

You have followed the right course of action, my Secundus, in investigating the cases of those who have been denounced to you as Christians. It is not possible to make a ruling in fixed form that would apply to all situations. They are not to be sought out; if they are denounced and proved guilty, they should be punished; but anyone who denies that he is a Christian and makes this clear by his actions—that is, by worshipping our gods—will obtain mercy for his repentance, however suspect he may have been in the past. Pamphlets published anonymously should have no place in any indictment. For it sets the worst possible example and is out of keeping with our times.
(Pliny the Younger, *Letters* 10.96–97)

the gods. Many Christians were killed in this persecution; but most performed the sacrifices to save their lives or obtained forged certificates. The largest-scale persecution of Christians was the last one, which occurred under Diocletian and his successor Galerius, from 303 to 311. Not all governors pursued Christians with equal enthusiasm and the number of Christians killed, in the low thousands, was a small percentage of the Christian population. But psychological impact of the "Great Persecution" was substantial, and stories of its martyrs circulated in large numbers.

Bishops and Theologians

Much early Christian literature circulated anonymously or pseudepigraphically (that is, under a false name) and was unsophisticated in style and narrative in character: gospels, acts, and similar works. Beginning especially in the second century A.D., Christian writers in Latin and Greek produced a large quantity of more theoretical writings. These include "apologies" (formal defenses of Christianity); theological works on the nature of God and Christ; tracts on other points of Christian doctrine, ethics, or behavior; commentaries on Biblical texts; and (beginning in the fourth century) histories of the church. The authors of these works, sometimes called the **church fathers,** were highly educated men (not women), trained in Greco-Roman philosophy and rhetoric. While they rejected paganism and its influences (or tried to), they used the style and conventions of classical literature.

The writings of the church fathers do not seem to have reached much of an audience outside the church, and they circulated mainly among other Christian intellectuals. But the early Christian fathers, and their ideas, were influential in other ways. Many were leaders of important churches, called *episkopoi* or "supervisors" (today, we use the word **bishops** to translate this Greek term). Some of their works, particularly the letters of Cyprian of Carthage (died 258) and the letters and sermons of Saint Augustine of Hippo (died 430), address practical issues of church administration and are good sources for everyday problems in the church. Through their congregations their ideas might reach a wide audience, far beyond the narrow aristocracy that could read and understand them. Their disputes on points of theology and doctrine sometimes caused major rifts in the church and gave rise to "heresies," which are discussed later in this chapter.

Christianity in the Later Roman Empire

The Conversion of Constantine

Perhaps the most important date in the history of Christianity was 312: the year in which Emperor Constantine converted. According to one version of the story, the event occurred near Rome, as Constantine prepared for battle with his rival Maxentius, who was occupying the city. That night, he had a vision or dream instructing him to paint a Christian symbol on his soldiers' shields. Constantine followed these directions, and the next day he and his troops demolished Maxentius' forces at the famous battle of the Milvian Bridge.

Constantine's conversion was in some ways a typical one. It was not unusual for gods, both pagan and Christian, to appear to humans in visions or dreams. The result of a supernatural event that proved the power of god to bestow benefits—in this case, victory—it recalls episodes from the gospels, Acts, and numerous early apocryphal Christian works. While a few intellectuals were converted by the arguments of Christian philosophers or theologians, most people were introduced to Christian ideas only after they had been drawn into the church in some other way. Ancient sources usually emphasize the role of healings, exorcisms, and other miracles. Miracle stories circulated widely and reported details designed to enhance their credibility—references to the number of witnesses, the humiliation of skeptics, the dramatic results that the miracle produced, and specific names and places.

While ancient accounts tend to describe mass conversions in response to miracles, parallels with other religious movements suggest that most people converted because others in their social circle were Christian too: They were convinced not by the theology or the miracle-story itself, but because of their

The Later Roman Empire

This colossal portrait of Constantine is over 8 feet high. It was originally part of a 30-foot seated statue of the emperor, portrayed bare-chested like the god Jupiter, located in the Basilica of Maxentius and Constantine in Rome. (Credit: Scala/Art Resource, NY)

relationship with the ones professing it. The pervasive network of patronage and dependence that turned Roman society into a densely interconnected web was well suited to the spread of a new religion: One convert of high status could influence his or her whole entourage of slaves, freedmen, friends, and dependents. While the church remained a small community at first, in this model conversion grows by a certain percentage per year and accumulates momentum exponentially.

One of the keys to Christianity's early growth is the commitment it demanded. After all, pagan gods could work miracles too (those of Asclepius were particularly well advertised) and pagan cults offered many of the other benefits of Christianity, such as membership in a select group or a sense of spiritual connection with a god. But they did not make converts at the same exponential rate simply because they did not require "conversion" at all: Asclepius did not demand that his devotees cease worshipping the gods of their people, city, village, club, or family and become, to the exclusion of everything else, "Asclepians" (or that they try to convince their friends to do the same). The Christian god did, and in this way was able to shoulder out the competition. Once the emperors became Christian, new laws favoring

Christians and outlawing pagan practices followed naturally from the exclusive nature of the new religion.

But the effects of Constantine's conversion were not instantaneous, perhaps not even on the emperor himself. He continued to portray himself together with the sun-god, Sol, on coins; some of the church's subtler moral teachings he absorbed late, or never. Infant exposure, banned in Jewish law and Christian doctrine, remained legal (and although a law of Valentinian in 374 eventually criminalized it, exposure continued to be widely practiced until modern times). Gladiatorial contests were permitted until 325 (when Constantine banned them in a law that seems to have had little effect), and criminals still suffered gruesome deaths. He addressed doctrinal conflicts within the church hesitantly and ineffectively, relying on his advisors; they were matters which he did not understand. However, the legal position of Christianity changed right away. In 313 Constantine and Licinius, with whom he shared imperial power for a time, legalized Christianity when they proclaimed general religious toleration in the "Edict of Milan." Laws of about the same time also exempted church land from taxation and granted relief to Christian clergy from the heavy burden of serving as decurions. Constantine preferred Christians for appointment to high office; the proportion of pagans in imperial service gradually decreased until, after 400, very few pagans in these positions are known. In the fifth century laws required all imperial appointees to be Christians.

Formerly confined to meeting in private homes or out-of-the-way places, Christianity now developed its own public architecture; Constantine himself sponsored the construction of churches in Rome, Jerusalem, and Constantinople. The **basilica,** a kind of civic building typical of Roman towns in the West, was well-adapted to the purposes of the church, which required large interior spaces for services.

By the end of the fourth century most pagan practices, including animal sacrifice, were illegal; the penalties for infraction were hideous. Violent confrontations between Christians and pagans were not unusual. Wandering gangs of monks and urban mobs destroyed temples, defaced pagan works of art, and committed murder; among their victims was Hypatia, a renowned female philosopher, lynched at Alexandria in 415. Many pagans, especially from the upper classes, converted for practical reasons, for the tax advantages or the career opportunities; many others were converted by force or through terror.

After Constantine, surviving literary sources are mainly Christian; the works of pagans were not preserved. The emperors who made law were Christian, with the exception of Julian, who reigned briefly, from 361 to 363. The laws themselves, which survive in the *Theodosian Code* and the *Corpus Juris Civilis,* promote Christianity and criminalize paganism with increasing vigor. Dependent mainly on these sources, as historians are, it is easy to get the impression that the empire was mostly Christian after Constantine. But the main nonliterary source of evidence—inscriptions on stone, including epitaphs—suggests that Christianity was still a minority religion in many

The brick basilica at Trier, constructed under Constantine. Like other emperors of this period, Constantine spent most of his time in cities near the empire's frontiers. The basilica was a part of his palace, where he heard cases and received embassies. (Vanni/Art Resource)

areas well into the fifth century A.D. In the mid-500s, Emperor Justinian was still trying to stamp out paganism with new laws.

Heresy and Schism

When Constantine's conversion made Christianity a legitimate religion in 312, the church was already plagued by internal conflicts. Pagan philosophy tolerated, even thrived, on its diverse intellectual traditions—schools or *haireseis*—but Christianity did not. In the church, *hairesis* or **heresy** was a disease to be stamped out.

Heresy was any doctrine rejected by that part of the church that was in a position to enforce its views. The definition of **orthodoxy** (literally, "straight thinking") and its opposite, heresy, thus depended on the shifting dynamics of power within the church. Doctrine was often decreed by a council of bishops; which bishops were invited would depend on which were preferred by whoever called the council, often the emperor. True doctrine was arrived at by consensus among bickering parties, in which dissenting voices might be suppressed, or even by vote. "Heretics" might call their own councils, and the decrees of any council might be rejected by some or most bishops. Some heresies were very widespread and strong contenders for orthodoxy.

The most important conflict within the church in 312 was the Donatist controversy, which arose in Africa in the wake of the "Great Persecution" that began in 303. Donatists rejected the authority of those bishops who had agreed to hand over sacred writings for destruction; by 311 there were two rival bishops of Carthage. Technically Donatism is called a "schism" today rather than a "heresy" because the original dispute was not so much an issue of doctrine as of church leadership. But Donatism quickly developed its own institutions, cults and martyrs, and purist ideology.

The emperor called a church council, which rejected the Donatist position. Violence ensued, and the Donatists claimed new martyrs for their cause, but the sect remained strong in Africa and even flourished there. It was still thriving in the early fifth century when Augustine, bishop of Hippo, set about eradicating it with the Roman army's help; it only disappeared with the Islamic conquest of Africa.

Another conflict arose around the doctrines of a priest named Arius: Originating in Alexandria, it quickly spread over the entire Eastern Empire. Like other heresies of the fourth and early fifth centuries, the Arian controversy involved ideas about the nature of Christ and his relationship to God. The idea of the "Trinity" of God, Christ, and Holy Spirit was reconciled to monotheism only by the subtle arguments of the church's most able theologians, and they disagreed on the exact terms of this reconciliation. Roughly (although the ideas involved were extremely complicated) Arius erred on the side of making Christ too different from God, while other heresies (such as the "Monophysite" heresy of the fifth century) strayed in the other direction. After Emperor Constantine conquered the East from Licinius in his final round of civil wars, he tried to resolve the Arian problem with an "ecumenical" church council—that is, a council of bishops from all over the Christian world. They met at Nicaea in 325 and produced a short list of church rules and a creed, or statement of belief, in which the controversial word *homoousios*, or "of the same substance," described the relationship between Christ and God (Constantine is supposed to have contributed this word himself). But this was hardly the end of the conflict; Arianism in various forms remained strong throughout the East and achieved ascendancy there in the mid-fourth century. Council after council revisited the same theological problems until "orthodox" Nicene theology was reinstated under Theodosius I in 381 at the Council of Constantinople. Most German tribes had been converted to Arianism through the influence of Ulfilas, a missionary who had translated the Bible into Gothic, and remained Arian until the sixth century.

Heresy was not a problem that only involved bishops and theologians; it penetrated every level of society. Doctrines were popularized in songs and jingles, sung by masses in urban processions, or preached, in simplified form, by monks and other popular leaders. In the course of the fourth century heresies were defined and labeled with increasing precision and were made illegal. Emperors confiscated church property and exiled bishops or forced them to pay huge fines. Bishops incited riots in which thousands perished—either at the hands of the rioters or slaughtered by imperial troops sent to keep the peace. They died in numbers that exceeded the total of all Christians martyred in the persecutions of the past.

Why was heresy important? Why did a government that for hundreds of years had avoided meddling in local affairs now attempt to dictate the beliefs of all its subjects with great specificity? Why did many people sacrifice their lives for highly abstract, seemingly trivial articles of faith? These questions are very difficult to answer. Some doctrinal conflicts may reflect deeper ethnic or class divisions, an issue that scholars have long debated. Donatism was strong in the hinterlands of Numidia and had an important following among the province's poor, rural, and possibly Punic-speaking classes (although it also had wealthy, educated, and urban converts and produced a sophisticated literature in Latin). Monophysitism especially thrived in the inland, Syriac-speaking regions of Syria and among some Arab tribes. Rivalry for power—especially, for the position of bishop—among influential men of high status also played a crucial role. But explanations of this type account for only part of the evidence, nor do such rationalizing interpretations explain why doctrine or ideology, and not something else, was so important.

For whatever reason, doctrine was the main test of membership in what had become the empire's dominant political power, the Christian church, and, moreover, in the true or orthodox or "catholic"—meaning "universal"—church, whatever one believed that to be. But the resources available to the Roman Empire for the enforcement of its laws were limited, and this is important to remember. Heresies proliferated and endured; some survived the Islamic conquests of the seventh century, and some survive today.

Monks and Ascetics

Monks were distinguished by their way of life. This involved dramatic, sometimes spectacular restrictions on food, sex, material comforts, and social interaction. The Greek word **askesis** was sometimes used to describe the monastic way of life; it was a term borrowed from athletics, and meant "training." The monk, like the martyrs of earlier times, was an athlete, and the source of his—or her—power and mystique was the body.

By tradition, the first monk was Saint Antony, who lived from 251 to 356 (he was 105 when he died). A story of his life circulated in antiquity under the name of Athanasius, renowned bishop of Alexandria; immensely popular in antiquity and later, it survives in several languages. It describes how Antony, born into a well-to-do Egyptian family, refused education, renounced wealth, and took to living first in a tomb outside his village, and later in the deep desert. There he survived on simple, very meager rations and battled demons in noisy struggles overheard by numerous witnesses. Pursued by throngs of visitors despite his best efforts to escape to solitude, he heals and exorcises, resolves disputes, and advises judges on their legal decisions. He defends orthodox doctrine against the Arian heretics and the poor against the depredations of corrupt Roman soldiers. He defends Christianity against Greek philosophers, but through an interpreter (the *Life* insists that Antony spoke only Egyptian, although highly literate letters in Greek also circulated in his name). The *Life of Antony* illuminates not only the struggle with the body that was the heart of the ascetic movement, but also the function of the monk in society. He is a healer, an arbiter, and also a champion in a world full of tensions: not only the invisible, violent conflict between pagan and Christian deities, but also a more subtle tangle of ethnic, ideological, and class tensions.

Some monks lived, like Antony, in dramatic isolation and deprivation. Very striking is the example of Simeon Stylites, who lived on a pillar in a Syrian village for forty-five years. Others formed communities and lived according to rules dictating a simple, rigorous way of life. Pachomius, an ex-soldier, founded several monasteries in southern Egypt in the first half of the fourth century; the "Rule" that he published is the earliest one that survives. The most influential rules were those of Saint Basil of Caesarea, written in the mid-300s, which became the basis for monastic life in the Greek East; and the rule that Saint Benedict wrote in 540 for his monastery at Monte Cassino in Italy, which was used by most orders of monks in the medieval West. Stories and *Lives* of female monks survive along with those of their male counterparts, and some early monastic communities (including two founded by Pachomius) were for women.

Christianity and Social Change

The long-term effects of the rise of Christianity on Mediterranean civilization were profound—this seems beyond doubt. Yet, because of the scarcity and patchiness of evidence and because of the size and diversity of the areas involved, it can be difficult to measure these effects; where changes did occur, it is hard to prove that Christianity was responsible for them. Christianity did not displace pagan civilization; that, it was not possible to do.

Public Architecture.   The heart of the Roman Empire was the city, and the Greco-Roman city was its public buildings and spaces, its class of decurions, its roll of citizens, its civic festivals. By A.D. 600, after several episodes of bubonic plague, barbarian invasions, and perhaps for other reasons, cities in many areas of the Roman world were in decline. Some cities were abandoned or shrank in size, as the population moved to more defensible, fortified sites. Many cities rebuilt their walls or built new ones in the late antique period, and Constantinople was fortified with a triple wall and moat in the early 400s, under Emperor Theodosius II. In some cities, monumental public buildings, streets, and squares were allowed to decay, their spaces occupied by private workshops, bazaars, and houses.

It is possible that Christianity caused some of these changes. Christian bishops fulminated against the entertainments of the theater and amphitheater, and the baths, which they associated with sexual depravity. Christian aristocrats gradually redirected their spending on public projects away from theaters, baths, porticoes, temples, and spectacles to churches, which were constructed in great numbers, especially in the 400s and 500s. They also left large legacies to churches in their wills, by which means some of them accumulated huge amounts of land and wealth. But this change took a long time. Emperors and aristocrats were still funding fora, porticoes, circuses (for

This small bronze statuette portrays an episode from Homer's Odyssey, where Odysseus asks his crew to tie him to the mast so that he can hear the alluring song of the Sirens without changing course and wrecking his ship. Christian writers sometimes interpreted the story as an allegory: Like Odysseus, a good Christian should cling to the cross and maintain a true course, resisting temptations to stray. The object atop the ship's mast is a dove, a Christian symbol for the Holy Spirit, suggesting that the statuette has a Christian meaning. (Virginia Museum of Fine Arts, Richmond [The Adolph D. and Wilkins C. Williams Fund]. (Photo by Ron Jennings. © Virginia Museum of Fine Arts.)

horse races), baths, and other traditional buildings in some parts of the empire into the fifth century. Saint Augustine's works from about this time tell us that crowds in Africa were still flocking to the theater, the arena, and the circus to enjoy the popular entertainments against which he warned his congregation repeatedly and ineffectively. Not all pagan temples were destroyed; some, including the Parthenon in Athens, were converted into churches and survived that way.

Christian Charity and the Poor.   Christian values inherited from Judaism an emphasis, not nearly as characteristic of pagan sources, on helping the very poor. This was precisely the category of people most vulnerable and most neglected in the Greco-Roman system of patronage and euergetism—its foundations, handouts, and distributions of grain benefited large but circumscribed groups of people, often the citizens of a town. Greco-Roman values placed status above everything—it was better and more prestigious to help people of citizen status or of some social status than those of no status whatsoever. In contrast, the Christian virtue of charity meant almsgiving— gifts for distribution to the poorest and neediest Christians. Every church had an alms fund; wealthy Christians donated hospitals, orphanages, and homes for the aged, institutions virtually unknown in the pagan world. Whether these institutions actually alleviated the suffering of society's poorest members cannot be known. But although late antique Christianity did not decree the abolition of poverty by the redistribution of property (as some Jewish and early Christian communities did), it placed a high value on aid to the poor.

Women and Marriage.   The church had always explicitly included women in its mission. Whether Christianity was especially appealing to women, and whether it changed the position of women in society for the better, is more difficult to determine. The church fathers enjoined women to be obedient to their husbands; they did little to alter the social position of women or slaves except for encouraging husbands and masters to be nice to them. While these moral injunctions, often repeated, may have had some effect, this is impossible to measure. Women could not hold any church office higher than the lowly rank of deaconess (while it was not unusual for pagan cults to be headed by a priestess). They could be martyrs and saints (see the next section); but the number of these in the general population was small, and they exercised most of their influence after their deaths. Biographies of female monks emphasize that they overcame their femininity and dressed, looked, or thought like men.

Christian bishops insisted that divorce was wrong, without exception; under some Christian emperors divorce became more difficult legally, especially if it was the woman who wanted the divorce. But emperors waffled on this issue, and documentary evidence from Egypt suggests that neither the new laws nor Christian morality had a measurable effect on practice. Christian moralists condemned adultery and the double standard of sexual behavior that punished women, but not men, for infidelity, but in doing so they acknowledged that the double standard still existed.

Perhaps the main effect of Christianity on women's lives was that it legitimized (and idealized) celibacy. This had mixed consequences. On the one hand, women were viewed as dangerous temptresses, and there is a strong misogynistic strain in some Christian literature. On the other hand, young women and widows could now choose to remain unmarried (and not subordinated to a husband) without social stigma or legal penalty, and an increasing number of homes and monasteries accommodated them. The life of chastity was perceived as a way for women to escape the drudgery of marriage and housework and live a more spiritual life devoted to God—which might include learning to read and some education in Christian writings.

Festivals and Saints.   The cult of the saints transformed Christianity, especially after the mid-300s. At the center of the cult was the body of a martyr, or of a holy man or woman: A tomb, shrine, or church housed a piece of the dead body, a "relic," which sanctified the place and had the power to perform miracles. These sites sprang up in cities and villages everywhere in the empire. The saints were more approachable and more local than the remote, all-powerful Christian god. They found lost animals, cured infertility, answered questions in oracles, and healed every affliction of man, woman, child, and beast. It was the saints to whom people turned for solutions to their urgent, everyday problems—they filled the space left by the ubiquitous pagan gods. Sometimes this was literally true; sites once sacred to Isis or some other divinity might be converted to a martyr's shrine, and people would continue to go there for healing and to dedicate their tokens of gratitude. At local festivals the saint's statue might be carried in a procession, with dancing, feasting, and singing. Bishops, recognizing old pagan modes of worship, occasionally spoke out against some or most of these things; others approved as long as it was clear that the object of worship was a Christian saint, not a pagan god. Some features of the cult of saints were uniquely Christian—most obviously, its central focus on the saint's dead body. But Christianity was also shaped by the old traditions of the environment in which it spread.

Gradually the Christian year, like the Roman one, filled with holidays—mostly festivals in honor of the saints. In some ways the calendar and its cycle of festivals distinguished Christians from the rest of society, at first from Jews and later from pagans. But it was difficult to get Christians to abstain from some pagan celebrations. Everyone enjoyed the festivities of the Roman New Year on January 1; many Christians seem to have perceived this festival as essentially secular and therefore harmless. Pagans celebrated the birthday of the Unconquered Sun at the winter solstice on December 25; Christians easily adapted by celebrating Jesus' birthday on the same day.

Literature: Saint Augustine and the Classics

From the beginning, Christianity's attitude toward Greco-Roman literature and education was ambivalent. Monks, especially, were often portrayed as anti-intellectual heroes. In Athanasius' *Life of Antony*, the saint is depicted (probably inaccurately) as an illiterate man who only speaks Egyptian and refutes the verbal arguments of Greek philosophers with simple deeds, performing exorcisms that they are unable to do. Christian intellectuals, especially those from the West who wrote in Latin, denounced the pagan classical tradition; the Bible was the main source of their quotations and examples and the subject of their commentaries. At the same time, classical Greco-Roman literature was still the foundation of higher education. Nearly all of the "church fathers" of the second, third, and fourth centuries were well educated in classical literature, and most had converted to Christianity as adults. They had grown up thinking of the classics as their cultural heritage; they knew them by heart, had studied them word by word, and also loved them. Although Christianity proposed replacing the old canon of classical Greco-Roman works with a new canon of sacred scriptures, this is not exactly what happened. Many classical works survived along with the Christian writings of the first through fourth centuries, and the Greco-Roman classics had a place at the heart of Western education and civilization until recent times.

The works of Saint Augustine illustrate the church's relationship to classical culture. Bishop of the town of Hippo in modern Algeria from 395 until his death in 430, he became one of the most influential authorities in the Western church. He left a vast quantity of writing, of which most survives—from abstract theology and biblical commentary to sermons and letters reflecting the real, practical problems that he faced as leader of his congregation. Much of his work is polemical, arguing against different heresies. These included the Manichean heresy, which he had joined in his youth; the Donatists; and later the followers of Pelagius, an ascetic sect that believed that people could achieve salvation by their own efforts. In fact, Augustine's was one of the main voices that defined heresy and orthodoxy in the early church. His intellectual legacy is in some ways a grim one: It was Augustine who made the most influential and convincing argument for the use of force against heretics; and he developed the doctrine of "original sin" (the belief that even newborn infants inherit the sin and guilt of Adam) in its most complete form. He articulated the doctrine of predestination, in which salvation is reserved for a few, selected by God before time began, and everyone else is irredeemably condemned to hell. But Augustine was one of the most perceptive observers of the human condition and one of the most intelligent minds of the late antique world, and his vision, while dark, is compelling.

We know about Augustine's life from one of his most famous works, a spiritual autobiography called *Confessions*. He grew up in a village called Thagaste, the son of a pagan father and a devoutly Catholic mother, whose religion he was later to deplore for its unsophisticated character. He received a typical classical education, but did not like Greek and never learned it well—his understanding of Greek philosophy, which influenced his later thought, was based on Latin translations. At age sixteen he moved to Carthage, where he studied and taught rhetoric. There he met the woman who became his concubine, lived with him for fifteen years, and had a son with him. At age nineteen he joined the Manichean heresy; originating in Persia and illegal since Diocletian, it described the universe as an eternal conflict between forces of light and darkness and emphasized the role of esoteric knowledge and ascetic practices in achieving salvation. The Manichees also rejected the Old Testament, which Augustine had found intensely distasteful on a first reading.

Eventually Augustine moved to Rome and then to Milan, where he was appointed to a prestigious post as professor of rhetoric. There he met Saint Ambrose, the bishop of Milan, who was to become a friend and a major intellectual influence; he also joined a group of students of Platonist philosophy. His mother arranged a marriage for him to a twelve-year-old girl from a good family. He was forced to abandon his concubine and his son; this, together with the new intellectual influences he had encountered, touched off a spiritual crisis. In 386 he converted to Catholic Christianity and was baptized, resigned his professorship, and decided on a life of celibacy. He returned to Africa, where he founded an ascetic community with his friends and lived quietly until 391, when he was forcibly ordained priest, against his will, on a visit to Hippo. This practice was not unusual; qualified, educated Catholics were in short supply, and many congregations lacked leaders. Four years later he became assistant bishop, then bishop after his predecessor's death.

Two of Augustine's greatest and most influential works, the *Confessions* and his last major work, the *City of God*, illuminate his relationship to classical culture and are in fact largely about that. He had spent his youth as a student and teacher of classical literature. As a young man, Vergil's *Aeneid* moved him to tears; he wept for Dido, queen of Carthage, abandoned by the hero on his way to Italy. In the *Confessions*, written when he was forty-three, he recalls the emotions that Vergil's poem evoked with censure and shame.

But the pagan classics remained an important part of Augustine's intellectual armature. Quotations from Vergil pervade his works. The parallels between his spiritual journey to Catholic Christianity and Aeneas' wandering journey to the shores of Latium are an important theme in the *Confessions*; like Aeneas, he was distracted by love for a woman at Carthage and found his destiny in Italy. But Augustine also interpreted his conversion in the light of contemporary readings of Plato (by the "Neo-Platonist" philosophers of the third and fourth centuries). These focused especially on the idea of the immortal soul's fall from the realm of divinity and its quest to return. Relying on Plato's dialogues about love, they argued that *eros* (in Latin, *amor*) was really the desire to return to God, which is accomplished by turning inward, to contemplation. Augustine's constant invocation of *amor* in the *Confessions* and the eroticism of the feelings he describes for God, his meditations on memory and beauty in the later books of this work, and its pervasive theme of spiritual and geographic wandering are examples of the importance of Neo-Platonism in his thought.

City of God was written over the course of thirteen years, from 413 to 425, partly in response to those pagans who blamed Christianity for the Visigoths' catastrophic sack of Rome in A.D. 410 (see p. 211). But it goes far beyond an explanation of Rome's fall—it is, in fact, a brick-by-brick demolition of the entire edifice of pagan religion and philosophy (including Plato, the Neo-Platonists, and Augustine's favorite Latin philosopher, Cicero). It also attacks the Romans' understanding of their own history, especially in the *Aeneid* of Vergil. Augustine proposes a new vision of history by tracing the story of two cities: the "city of man" with its earthly empires and the sacred "city of God" (not identical with the Christian community on earth).

On the other hand, *City of God* attacks pagan poets and philosophers on a very sophisticated level, using techniques Augustine learned as part of his classical education. Had he not shared many basic assumptions with the authors whose ideas he rejects, he could have dismissed them in a much shorter work, and had pagan literature not remained important in late antique culture, it would hardly have been necessary to write *City of God* at all. It was through pagan authors that Augustine arrived at his understanding of Roman history; if he rejected its inheritance, along with Vergil's poems and Cicero's philosophy, this was only with great effort. Augustine did not read or interpret the classics in the same way that pagans did; nevertheless, his thoughts in many ways were shaped by his classical heritage.

In 429, the barbarian Vandals invaded Africa from Spain. They encountered little resistance as they crossed north Africa. Everyone who could fled to the fortified towns from the countryside, to escape the violence and devastation of the invaders. Augustine died as the Vandals besieged Hippo in 430; although they burnt the town, his library and his written legacy survived.

The Decline of the Western Empire

In retrospect, it seems safe to say that the western half of the Roman empire collapsed in the fifth century A.D. It is less clear how developments appeared to the people actually involved in them, especially since contemporary historical sources from the period between 378 and the mid-500s are scarce and problematic. The empire's deterioration was not the result of a sudden series of violent invasions, but of changes that took place over a long time. In the late third century and especially in the fourth century, the Roman army began relying more and more on ethnic units recruited from tribes on the empire's fringes. Emperors sometimes settled whole populations of prisoners or refugees on Roman territory, often in return for military service. By the end of the fourth century most of Rome's high military offices were occupied by men of Germanic background. Most of its fighting was being done by barbarian troops, with the paradoxical result that they sometimes fought to defend the empire against other branches of their own tribe. Civil wars also might pit barbarian armies against other barbarian armies, both led by barbarian generals. One barbarian of Vandal origin, Stilicho, wielded virtually unchecked power over the entire Roman army and married Theodosius I's daughter. Guardian of the young and weak Emperor Honorius, he was the real power behind the throne until his execution in 408.

Almost none of the barbarians who ruled the new, virtually independent kingdoms of western Europe in the fifth and sixth centuries entered the Roman Empire as invaders; they were invited to settle in Roman territory, in return for military service. Whether a given barbarian commander was an independent king of his own country, or a general in the Roman army, could be open to interpretation. It is likely that at least until the sixth century, and perhaps until much later, most barbarian kings in Europe considered their lands part of the Roman Empire.

The Roman emperors for centuries had practiced the policy of relocating barbarian tribes on Roman soil. Why this was done on such a grand scale in the late imperial period is the heart of the problem of the Western Empire's

The Western Mediterranean, circa A.D. 500

decline. Had the economy deteriorated so that huge tracts of land in Europe had been abandoned and were now lying uncultivated? Had the population declined? Had recruits for the army become scarce for other reasons, perhaps because the imperial government could not afford to pay them? Had attitudes toward military service changed? Whatever reasons we postulate for the empire's decline—and scholars have proposed literally hundreds of them—must account for the fact that it fell in the West but not in the East. While the empire gave up huge tracts of territory to the Islamic conquests of the seventh century, it survived until Constantinople fell to the Ottoman Turks in 1453. Even then, the Turkish rulers thought of themselves as successors of the Roman emperors.

Franks

Frankish troops had fought in the Roman army since the third century, and Frankish units were prominent in the Roman army of the fourth century. Some

Franks reached the highest levels of the Roman military command. In the mid-300s a group of Franks was allowed to settle in a northern region of Roman Germany. It was from this population, which later called itself the "Salian Franks," that the Merovingians—a dynasty of kings that expanded and consolidated Frankish power in western Europe—emerged in the late 400s.

When did the Frankish kingdom become an independent entity? Most scholars would date this to the reign of Clovis, in the early 500s, following the account of Gregory, bishop of Tours, who wrote several decades later. But Clovis was the first Catholic king of the Franks; Gregory wants to idealize him, and his interpretation of Clovis' defeat of the last "Roman" general in Gaul, Syagrius, seems too simplistic. How Clovis regarded his own relationship to Rome is simply not known. Another sixth-century source, Procopius, seems to describe Clovis' people as descendants of a population of Roman soldiers living among the Germanic tribes (*Gothic Wars* 5.12.13–19); he is not necessarily well informed, but his account shows how confusing the situation in Europe was at the time. Clovis and his descendants may have portrayed themselves to the people they ruled as legitimate representatives of Roman authority.

When the Merovingian kings achieved domination in Gaul, they preserved some of the administrative structure of the Roman Empire. They appointed nobles from the Gallo-Roman population, as well as Franks, to rule the territories under their control; they gave them the Roman titles of count (*comes*) and duke (*dux*). At first they continued to collect some of the traditional Roman taxes from their Gallo-Roman subjects, although they granted immunity to the privileged class of Franks. They minted coins, but throughout the sixth century they continued to put the Roman emperor's image on them. Education in the Latin classics and the ability to compose speeches and poetry in Latin still were the hallmarks of high culture, even if few people could be found with such skills.

At some time during his life, Clovis converted to Catholic Christianity, either from paganism or from Arianism. It is difficult to tell what part of the Frankish population, or of the people they ruled, was Christian either before or after Clovis' conversion. The Frankish king Charlemagne was still legislating against some forms of paganism in the late eighth century.

Visigoths

In the middle of the sixth century a Goth, Jordanes, wrote a history of his people, tracing their origins back thousands of years to a primeval homeland on the island of Scandza. Some scholars have taken Jordanes literally and searched for traces of Gothic culture in Scandinavia, but most historians now agree that it is not productive to investigate the history of the Goths prior to the third or fourth century A.D. No meaningful biological or cultural continuities extend back further than that, nor could the Goths, an entirely oral culture until the fourth century, have preserved the memory of their own history accurately. Jordanes' history is the result of the Goths' growing awareness or creation of themselves as a people in the late antique period.

The story of the Visigoths seems to begin around 375, when a new, semi-nomadic people, the Huns, appeared in Europe (see box, p. 212). Scholars have long speculated about their origins, without arriving at a consensus; like the Goths or the Franks, they were perhaps a loose, multiethnic confederacy of tribes. While they defeated or absorbed some Goths, others sought refuge in the Roman Empire and were granted it, crossing the Danube in a mass in 376.

Like the Franks, Goths had served in the Roman army throughout the fourth century and reached the highest levels of military command. But the mass migration of 376 led to a crisis. In 378, the refugees rebelled, together with some other immigrant barbarians and disaffected groups; combined, they became the Visigoths. They defeated Emperor Valens at the fateful battle of Hadrianople, in European Turkey, and killed him. In the late fourth century the Visigothic leader Alaric both fought for, and revolted against, Roman emperors both in the East and West. In 408 he besieged Rome, and in 410 he sacked it. The psychological consequences of the sack of Rome were widespread and well attested, especially because many of the city's nobles were forced to become refugees.

But although Alaric wanted land for his followers, his aim was not to establish an independent barbarian kingdom on Roman territory. His main demand as he besieged Rome was to be granted the high imperial office of *magister militum*, which would give him command over a large part of the Roman army. Unsuccessful, he died shortly after the assault on Rome. His successors surrendered to the Romans and fought against their enemies; in 418, Emperor Constantius III granted the Visigoths territory in southwestern Gaul. In the early sixth century this Gothic kingdom was defeated and absorbed by the Franks.

Another Visigothic kingdom emerged in Spain, where some Visigoths had already settled in the 450s. We know little about this kingdom in the fifth and sixth centuries, but in the seventh century the learned works in Latin of Isidore, bishop of Seville, shed light on its society and culture. The kingdom survived until it was conquered by Muslims in the early eighth century.

Ostrogoths

Like those of the Visigoths, the origins of the Ostrogoths seem to lie in the traumatic arrival of the Huns in Europe. It seems that those Goths who joined the Huns' empire in the late fourth century emerge later as the Ostrogoths, after the death of the Huns' leader Attila and the dissolution of his empire in the 450s. At this time the emperors allowed several different groups and waves of Goths to migrate into the Roman Empire, and they were eventually unified under a single leader, Theodoric, in the 480s.

In the 470s a Roman general named Orestes had revolted against the Western emperor, Julius Nepos, and installed his son Romulus (nicknamed Augustulus, "the little Augustus") at Ravenna, now the Western Empire's capital. Romulus—usually described as the last of the Western emperors of Rome—was deposed in 476 by Odoacer, the son of a Hunnic general who had risen

---

The Written Record

THE HUNS

The following is an extract from the historian Ammianus Marcellinus, writing in Latin in the late 300s A.D. It is the earliest description of the Huns in Western sources. This vivid account owes much to a long tradition of Greco-Roman ethnography—writing about foreign peoples—and many themes can be traced back to Greek descriptions of the nomadic Scythians in the fifth century B.C. (see p. 77). In fact, other ancient writers often referred to the Huns as Scythians.

The historian Brent Shaw has traced the history of the portrayal of nomads by agricultural civilizations, especially in the West, from ancient Mesopotamia to the present day.* He argues that deep-seated, traditional stereotypes have always shaped how farming populations perceive nomadic peoples.

The tribe of Huns, hardly mentioned in earlier histories, who live near the frozen ocean beyond the waters of Maeotis [the Sea of Azov, north of the Black Sea], transgress all bounds of savagery. They furrow the cheeks of their infants with iron blades from the very first days of life, so that when the beard eventually emerges, it is blunted by the ridged scars; so they grow old without beards and without any attractiveness, like eunuchs. They all have firm, compact limbs and thick necks, and are unnaturally ugly and crooked, so that you would think they were two-legged animals. . . .

Their way of life is so harsh that they use neither fire nor seasoned food, but eat the roots of wild plants and the half-raw meat of any kind of animal, which they warm briefly between their thighs and the backs of their horses. No buildings shelter them; they avoid these, just as we are accustomed to avoid tombs and set them apart; not even a reed-thatched hut can be found among them . . . . They wear clothes made of linen or sewn from the skins of wild mice; and they wear the same clothes in public and at home. Once they have put their necks into some faded undershirt they never take it off or change it, until it gradually decays and falls to pieces. . . .Their shoes are made without a last, and prevent them from walking easily. For this reason they are poorly suited to infantry battles, and in fact are practically affixed to their horses, which are tough but ugly; sometimes they sit on them like women to perform their daily chores. . . .When important matters arise for deliberation, they all consult together in this manner [i.e., on horseback]. They are subject to no royal authority, but content with the haphazard leadership of their chiefs they demolish whatever opposes them. . . .

None of them farms or ever touches the handle of a plow. They all lack fixed homes, and wander around without hearth or law or a stable way of life, like fugitives, with the wagons in which they live—where their wives weave their disgusting clothes, and copulate with their husbands, and give birth, and raise the children to the age of puberty. None of them can tell where he is from when asked; he was conceived in one place and born far off, and raised even farther away than that. They are faithless and untrustworthy in truces; they are easily swayed by every breath of favorable news that reaches them, and they are entirely overcome by the most excited frenzy. Like irrational animals they are completely ignorant of right and wrong; they speak in deceptive ambiguities, constrained by no reverence for religion or superstition; they burn with an immense desire for gold, and are so fickle and easily angered that they sometimes break with their allies several times in one day without provocation, and make up with them again when no one has tried to conciliate them. (Ammianus Marcellinus 31.2.1–7, 10–11).

*Brent Shaw's articles "'Eaters of Flesh, Drinkers of Milk': The Ancient Mediterranean Ideology of the Pastoral Nomad" and "Fear and Loathing: The Nomad Menace in Roman North Africa" are both reprinted in *Rulers, Nomads, and Christians in Roman North Africa*, Collected Studies Series vol. 497, Aldershot, Great Britain: Variorum.

through the ranks of the Roman army and rebelled with the troops under his command. Odoacer is usually described, in ancient and modern sources, as Italy's first barbarian king. He maintained an ambiguous relationship with the Eastern emperor, Zeno, until 489, when Zeno asked Theodoric and his Goths to march on Italy against Odoacer. Once he had established himself in Italy, Theodoric's position there was just as ambiguous as Odoacer's—he called himself "king," but the Eastern emperors continued to appoint consuls for the West and he did not interfere with this, or usurp other powers traditionally belonging to the emperor, such as granting Roman citizenship. It was only in the reign of Justinian that the Eastern emperor tried to reconquer Italy.

Vandals

In 406, perhaps because of conflict with the Huns, several barbarian tribes crossed the Rhine and devastated the Western provinces in a violent invasion. They reached Spain in 409 and settled there—possibly as allies with the permission of the emperors. In 429, under their king Geiseric, they invaded north Africa, and ten years later they captured Carthage. Christian historians who suffered under the Arian Vandals' persecution of orthodoxy in Africa painted them as cruel, violent, and anti-Roman. But even the Vandals did not insist on independence from the Roman Empire; rather, they wanted the emperors to acknowledge their dominion over parts of it, which they did in a series of treaties, until Justinian destroyed the Vandal kingdom in 535.

Barbarian Legal Codes

In the late fifth and early sixth centuries the Visigoths and the Franks both issued law codes; so did the Burgundians, another Germanic tribe whose territory was located in south-eastern Gaul and absorbed into the Frankish kingdom under Clovis. These were the earliest, but codes from the seventh century published by the Anglo-Saxons (in Britain) and the Lombards (in Italy) also survive. The texts make fascinating reading, but in many ways they raise more questions than they answer. The purpose of these documents remains obscure and may be different in each case.

Were the barbarian codes codifications of Germanic custom or adaptations of Roman law? This is a difficult question to answer for some of them, because we do not know how much German custom was influenced by Roman law before the codes were written down. All of the codes, except for that of the Anglo-Saxons, were written in Latin, probably with the help of Roman scribes and advisors. The Visigoths and the Burgundians each issued two laws—a "Roman" law for their subjects and a separate code for the class of overlords. Clovis published only one law, which seems especially Germanic in character, but its scope is limited fairly narrowly to torts and it may have been intended as a supplement to Roman law rather than a replacement for it. The Frankish, Burgundian, and Visigothic codes all distinguish between Romans and Germans, but do not offer a definition of either class.

All of the barbarian codes are brief compared with the Roman codifications of Theodosius II and, later, of Justinian. While the vast bulk of Roman law concerns property and inheritance, loans, and other economic transactions, the barbarian codes focus largely or mainly on torts—theft, homicide, assault, and so on, all treated as offenses against individuals and remedied by compensation to the victim. These are areas to which Roman law had devoted comparatively little attention.

Justinian

The long reign of Emperor Justinian, from 527 to 565, was an era of ambitious imperialism and momentous events near the end of the antique world's history.* Justinian repressed the bloody Nika Riots, which began as a conflict between circus factions, at Constantinople in 532, and nearly died in an epidemic of bubonic plague, the first on record, which swept the Mediterranean world in 542–543. He sponsored a vast building program, including the great basilica of Saint Sophia (Hagia Sophia) in Constantinople, which survives largely intact as one of antiquity's most impressive monuments (although the dome collapsed in 558 and had to be rebuilt). He ordered the compilation of the massive legal code that became Rome's judicial legacy to the medieval world (see p. 160). Deeply religious, he persecuted heretics and pagans and tried to heal what was then the major division in the church, between orthodoxy and the Monophysite movement in the East. But his most ambitious project was his reconquest the barbarian kingdoms of the West. His general Belisarius succeeded in recovering north Africa from the Vandals and Italy from the Ostrogoths and in displacing the Visigoths from southern Spain, which he occupied. But Justinian held these territories only with great difficulty, bloodshed, and expense; shortly after his death, Italy was conquered by the Lombards.

---

*Whereas our knowledge of events in the fifth and seventh centuries is patchy, Justinian's reign is illuminated by the works of Procopius, who wrote a history of the emperor's wars and also a vicious, derogatory *Secret History* of the same period.

Art and Society

EMPRESS THEODORA

This mosaic from the Church of San Vitale, Ravenna, dates to the early 6th century and portrays the empress Theodora and her entourage.   (Scala/Art Resource)

This mosaic from the Church of San Vitale at Ravenna dates to the sixth century and is the only certain image that survives of Justinian's wife, Empress Theodora. The mosaic shows stylistic features typical of some late antique art: The figures are more frontal, more symmetrical, and more stylized than in earlier works in the Greek naturalistic tradition. The centrality of Theodora—who is slightly larger than the other figures—and the orderly ranks of her attendants may reflect late imperial society's greater emphasis on hierarchy and authority.

The most important literary source for Theodora is Procopius' *Secret History*, a racy and cynical work that portrays her, prerhaps inaccurately, as a former actress from a lower-class family. She is best known for her generosity in financing churches, hospitals, and other religious institutions and for her support of the Monophysite heresy.

Muhammad and the Rise of Islam

Muhammad, the prophet of a new religion called Islam, was born in Mecca—an almost exclusively pagan oasis city in the western part of the Arabian peninsula, a relatively undeveloped and isolated part of the Mediterranean world. At the time, the peninsula was populated mainly by tribal peoples, except for Yemen in the south, where a sophisticated culture had flourished for centuries.

In antiquity the Semitic word "Arab" referred to the nomadic tribesmen of the Near Eastern deserts in Syria, Mesopotamia, Arabia, and Egypt. Called "Saracens" in Greek (they are now called Bedouin), they were herdsmen able to navigate the desert by camel. In the summer, their search for pasturage brought them to the villages and cultivated lands of the desert's edge. This transhumance could take the form of terrifying and destructive raids, but the Arabs also traded with the farmers, and even settled among them. Like other "barbarians," some Arab tribes served in the Roman army or made alliances with the Romans or with the Persians; some of these tribes converted to Christianity, although not normally to the orthodox version of it. Pre-Islamic Arab poetry, as it was transmitted by later Muslim sources, seems to reflect the values of Bedouin society; its heroic ideal is the brave and skilled warrior, generous host, and ruthless avenger of injuries.

Inscriptions show that the peoples of the desert Near East spoke several different Semitic dialects. The earliest inscription in Arabic dates to A.D. 328 and comes from Namara, in modern Syria; it is the epitaph of Imru' al-Qays, here called "king of all the Arabs"—but scholars disagree on how this should be interpreted. Arabic is the language in which the Islamic sacred book, the Qur'an, was written, and it became the language of Islamic high culture.

Around 610 the angel Gabriel of Jewish tradition began to speak to Muhammad in dreams. He repeated what Gabriel had said; the transcription of his words became the Qur'an, or "recitation." Like Christianity, the new religion he founded rejected pagan gods and customs; the status of Judaism and Christianity was more ambiguous, since Islam recognized Jesus as a prophet in the Jewish tradition and Muhammad as the last of the prophets. Jews and Christians were "protected peoples," subject to special taxes and sometimes to other forms of oppression, but not the same as pagans.

In 622, Muhammad was driven out of Mecca by conservative pagans and fled to Medina; this event marks the beginning of the Muslim calendar.* But he already had a substantial following; he soon became master of Medina and, through conquest and alliance, leader of the peoples of Arabia. Shortly after his death in 632 the combined forces of Islam conquered Roman Syria and the entire Persian Empire. By the end of the seventh century they had conquered Egypt and all of Roman north Africa, and in 711 they invaded Visigothic Spain.

---

*Because the Muslim year is shorter than the Western solar year, charts or mathematical calculations are required to covert Muslim to Christian dates.

East and West

By the middle of the seventh century, an empire that had once dominated the entire Mediterranean world was reduced to a small fraction of its former extent. But the Roman Empire was, after all, only one in a series of great multicultural empires in the region—including those of the Persians, the Greco-Macedonians, and the Muslims. None of them erased the cultures they conquered, but all influenced the peoples subject to them and were influenced by them. With all this in mind, it can be difficult to understand the traditional parameters of "western civilization": Why is the Near East part of the West prior to Islam but not after? Why does the study of the West after 600 primarily focus on what the Romans—for the empire centered on Constantinople survived—called "barbarian" Europe?

It is unquestionable that profound cultural and economic changes occurred in the late antique period in both West and East. These changes are significant but difficult to track; they took place over a long time and for reasons that are not always clear. They did not always result from the coming of barbarian or Arab invaders, who were always a small minority among the mass of former Roman subjects. The "fall of Rome" was a process, not an event, and in some ways one that never ended. The Roman Empire—its laws; its geography and provinces; its languages, literature, science, and philosophy; its cults and religions; and the almost mythic power of the memory of the emperor—remained part of the shadowy background against which European and Near Eastern history unfolded for centuries and, in some ways, until the present day.

The difference between "East" and "West" is not a precise one that can be objectively measured and mapped; it is simply a way of viewing the world that has existed for a long time. Virtually all peoples define themselves partly by constructing traditional ideas of the alien or foreigner; Western ideas of the East can be traced back to the Greeks of the fifth century B.C., in the wake of the Persian wars. It is not surprising that western Europeans choose to claim Greco-Roman culture—so much more sophisticated and "civilized" than that of the European kingdoms that followed it—as their own, nor that they also identify an alien Eastern civilization, the Islamic world, with which to contrast their own culture. But the distinction, no matter how clearly perceived on both sides, is in some ways an artificial one. The Islamic Mediterranean arguably preserved the cultural legacy of the Greco-Roman world as much as the European West did, or more. And as always, many local traditions remained undisturbed or evolved independently, regardless of what kingdom or empire claimed dominion over them.

SUMMARY

Christianity arose among the followers of Jesus, a Jewish prophet and teacher. Through them it spread throughout the Jewish diaspora and eventually to gentiles, until finally it became mainly a gentile religion. At first it was illegal, but after Emperor Constantine converted to Christianity in 312 the laws changed to favor Christians. Christian emperors and also bishops, monks, and crowds tried to eliminate paganism, but this took a long time, and Christianity succeeded only by changing to accommodate many of the needs that paganism had once filled. At the same time, Christianity itself was divided among different sects who called one another "heretics." Emperors persecuted heretics and tried to unite the empire under a single version of Christianity, but they were not successful.

Once it became legal, Christianity won vast numbers of converts and a rich Christian culture developed. A huge quantity of literature was produced in Greek, Latin, and several other languages, much of it biographical in nature—stories of Christ or his followers or of martyrs and saints. Upper-class Christians with classical educations wrote profusely on theology, church history, and the Bible. The works of Saint Augustine show how deeply they were indebted to the classical tradition, even those who tried to reject it. Christianity developed its own architectural traditions, such as the basilica, a form that was especially useful for Christian worship. A whole new range of themes from the Bible and the lives of Jesus, Mary, and the saints suffused late antique art.

Beginning in the early fifth century, the empire weakened and toppled in the West. New barbarian kingdoms were established in Europe and North Africa. These barbarians were not usually invaders; they settled in Roman territory as military allies, and most of their kings did not claim independence from Rome, but sought recognition of their authority from the Roman emperors. Although Emperor Justinian conquered some of these kingdoms in the mid-sixth century, the cultural and political distance between the West and the empire centered in Constantinople gradually increased. It is not, however, possible to say when any part of Europe became independent from the Roman Empire.

Suggested Readings

CHAPTER 1:   The First Civilizations

Sources

One of the most important literary sources for early Near Eastern history is the Hebrew Bible. Many good translations of the Bible are widely available, including the New Revised Standard Version and the *New Jerusalem Bible*. *The Oxford Study Bible* (ed. M. Jack Suggs et al., Oxford: Oxford University Press, 1992) is also an excellent resource.

Writings from the Ancient World (Atlanta: Scholars Press, 1991–1999; Leiden: Brill, 2002–) is an excellent series of translated texts from the Bronze Age Near East, including Mesopotamian, Egyptian, Ugaritic, and Hittite works.

William W. Hallo and K. Lawson Younger, eds., *The Context of Scripture*, 2 vols., Leiden: Brill, 1997– . Extensive collection of ancient Near Eastern literature and inscriptions in English translation.

Miriam Lichtheim, *Ancient Egyptian Literature*, 3 vols., Berkeley: University of California Press, 1973–1980. Egyptian literary sources in English translation.

A. G. McDowell, *Village Life in Ancient Egypt*, Oxford: Oxford University Press, 1999. Select documents from Deir el-Medina, a workmen's village in New Kingdom Egypt, with introduction and commentary.

James B. Pritchard, *The Ancient Near East: Anthology of Texts and Pictures*, 2 vols., Princeton, N.J.: Princeton University Press, 1965.

Studies

Piotr Bienkowski and Alan Millard, *Dictionary of the Ancient Near East*, Philadelphia: University of Pennsylvania Press, 2000. Up-to-date, one-volume encyclopedia.

Trevor Bryce, *The Kingdom of the Hittites*, Oxford: Clarendon, 1998. Detailed, up-to-date political history of the Hittites.

Aubrey Burl, *A Guide to the Stone Circles of Britain, Ireland, and Brittany*, New Haven, Conn.: Yale University Press, 1995. Detailed discussion of individual sites intended for travelers, but also useful for scholarly purposes.

Oliver Dickinson, *The Aegean Bronze Age*, Cambridge: Cambridge University Press, 1994. Difficult to read, but offers the most up-to-date survey of the subject.

Robert Drews, *The End of the Bronze Age: Changes in Warfare and the Catastrophe ca. 1200 B.C.*, Princeton, N.J.: Princeton University Press, 1993. Military interpretation of the crisis of 1200 B.C.; also provides a good overview of theories that attempt to explain it.

Brian Fagan, ed., *The Oxford Companion to Archaeology*, Oxford: Oxford University Press, 1996. Reference work in encyclopedia form.

Kenneth L. Feder, *The Past in Perspective: An Introduction to Human Preshistory*, 2nd ed., Mountain View, Calif.: Mayfield Publishing Company, 2000. An up-to-date introduction; be sure to read the latest edition.

Israel Finkelstein and Neil Asher Silberman, *The Bible Unearthed: Archaeology's New Vision of Ancient Israel and the Origin of its Sacred Texts*, New York: Free Press, 2001. Two leading scholars skeptical of the traditional, biblical version of early Israelite history offer an influential alternative.

O. R. Gurney, *The Hittites*, 2nd ed., London: Penguin, 1990. Brief, readable introduction to Hittite history, culture, and society.

William W. Hallo and William Kelley Simpson, *The Ancient Near East: A History*, 2nd ed., Fort Worth, Pa: Harcourt Brace College Publishers, 1998. Survey emphasizing the political history of Mesopotamia and Egypt, but including a chapter on Mesopotamian culture as well.

Amélie Kuhrt, *The Ancient Near East: 3000–330 B.C.*, 2 vols., London: Routledge, 1995. Detailed political history of Mesopotamia, Egypt, the Hittites, and the kingdoms of Syria and the Levant.

Thomas E. Levy, *The Archaeology of Society in the Holy Land*, New York: Facts on File, 1995. The Levant from the Paleolithic to the twentieth century, emphasizing material culture and social history.

James Mellaart, *The Neolithic of the Near East*, New York: Scribner's, 1975. An excellent survey, but outdated in some respects.

Bruce M. Metzger and Michael D. Coogan, eds., *The Oxford Companion to the Bible*, Oxford: Oxford University Press, 1993. Excellent one-volume encyclopedia.

Marc van de Mieroop, *The Ancient Mesopotamian City*, Oxford: Oxford University Press, 1999. In-depth look at the social, political, and economic structure of Mesopotamian cities; also discusses architecture and city planning.

Leo G. Perdue et al., *Families in Ancient Israel*, Louisville, Ky.: Westminster John Knox Press, 1997. Social history of Israel through the first century A.D.

J. N. Postgate, *Early Mesopotamia: Society and Economy at the Dawn of History*, London: Routledge, 1992. Survey emphasizing social and economic history, but also providing a useful, concise discussion of political history.

Gay Robins, *Women in Ancient Egypt*, Cambridge, Mass.: Harvard University Press, 1993. Excellent study covering a wide range of topics, but also offering in-depth analysis of the primary evidence.

Jack M. Sasson, ed., *Civilizations of the Ancient Near East*, multiple vols., New York: Scribner's, 1995–. Comprehensive reference work on the history and culture of the ancient Near East.

Denise Schmandt-Besserat, *Before Writing*, vol. 1: *From Counting to Cuneiform*, Austin: University of Texas Press, 1992. Convincingly solves a crucial puzzle in the history of early civilizations by tracing the origins of cuneiform writing to a system of accounting by tokens that developed in the Neolithic period.

Orin C. Shane and Mine Küçük, "The World's First City," *Archaeology* 51.2 (March/April 1998), 43–47. A brief but accessible summary of recent excavations at Çatalhöyük.

Hershel Shanks, ed., *Ancient Israel: From Abraham to the Roman Destruction of the Temple*, 2nd ed., Washington, D.C.: Biblical Archaeological Society, 1999. The standard introduction to the subject.

Daniel C. Snell, *Life in the Ancient Near East*, New Haven, Conn.: Yale University Press, 1997. Survey of Mesopotamian social and economic history, with some discussion of Egypt as well.

Emily Vermeule, *Greece in the Bronze Age*, Chicago: University of Chicago Press, 1964. This classic work is still the best survey of Mycenaean Greece, exploring social, cultural, and economic aspects of Bronze Age civilization.

Websites

Abzu: A Guide to information related to the study of the Ancient Near East on the Web (http://www.etana.org/abzu/). Comprehensive index of links to resources and scholarship in the Ancient Near East, maintained by the University of Chicago's Oriental Institute.

Çatalhöyük: Excavations of a Neolithic Anatolian Höyük (http://catal.arch.cam.ac.uk/catal/catal.html). Excellent source of bibliography and information on the site.

Internet Ancient History Sourcebook (http://www.fordham.edu/halsall/ancient/asbook.html). Comprehensive site for sources, bibliography, and links. Maintained by Paul Halsall of Fordham University.

CHAPTER 2:   Greek Civilization: Hellas and Hellenism

Sources

English translations of most surviving Greek literary works are widely available. The most complete series of translations is the Loeb Classical Library, now published by Harvard University Press. The following are useful collections and translations of material not found in the Loeb series.

James H. Charlesworth, ed., *The Apocrypha and Pseudepigrapha of the Old Testament in English*, 2 vols., Oxford: Clarendon, 1913. Essential texts for the study of Second Temple Judaism.

Russel Meiggs and David Lewis, eds., *A Selection of Greek Historical Inscriptions to the End of the Fifth Century B.C.*, 2nd ed., Oxford: Clarendon, 1988.

Jane Rowlandson, ed., *Women in Greek and Roman Egypt: A Sourcebook*, Cambridge: Cambridge University Press, 1998. Translates hundreds of otherwise inaccessible documents on Egyptian papyri.

Heinrich von Staden, *Herophilus: The Art of Medicine in Early Alexandria*, Cambridge: Cambridge University Press, 1988. Collection and translation, with extensive commentary and analysis, of the fragments of the great physician's work.

Marcus Niehbur Tod, ed., *A Selection of Greek Historical Inscriptions*, 2 vols., Oxford: Clarendon, 1933–1948.

Géza Vermès, ed., *The Complete Dead Sea Scrolls in English*, New York: Allen Cane/Penguin, 1997. These texts created a sensation when they were discovered in caves in Israel beginning in 1947. At long last, they have been published and translations have become available. Essential texts for the study of Second Temple Judaism.

Ronald F. Willetts, *The Law Code of Gortyn*, Berlin: De Gruyter, 1971. Translation and study of a code inscribed in the fifth century B.C. at Gortyn, on Crete.

Studies

William R. Biers, *The Archaeology of Greece: An Introduction*, 2nd ed., Ithaca, N.Y.: Cornell University Press, 1996. The standard introduction to Greek archaeology.

Alan K. Bowman, *Egypt After the Pharaohs: 332 B.C.–A.D. 642, from Alexander to the Arab Conquest*, Berkeley: University of California Press, 1986. Excellent discussion of the history, society, and culture of Greco-Roman Egypt, based on extensive study of documents on papyrus.

Claude Calame, *Choruses of Young Women in Ancient Greece: Their Morphology, Religious Role, and Social Functions*, 2nd ed., Oxford: Rowman & Littlefield, 2001. Calame changed the way we read lyric poetry by using it as a source for social history, exploring the world of the aristocratic girls who danced in lyric choruses.

David Cohen, *Law, Sexuality, and Society: The Enforcement of Morals in Classical Athens*, Cambridge: Cambridge University Press, 1991. Cohen uses comparative evidence from other Mediterranean societies to argue that women had more power in the Athenian family than was previously thought.

David Cohen, *Law, Violence, and Community in Classical Athens*, Cambridge: Cambridge University Press, 1995. Uses ancient Greek oratory to reconstruct the competitive, honor-obsessed value system of classical Athens.

Shaye J. D. Cohen, *From the Maccabees to the Mishnah*, Philadelphia: The Westminster Press, 1987. Introduction to the cultural and intellectual history of Judaism in the Second Temple Period.

Francis M. Cornford, *Thucydides Mythistoricus*, London: Arnold, 1907. Classic study of the structure and artistry of Thucydides' work. Cornford was the first to identify tragic themes in Thucydides.

K. J. Dover, *Greek Homosexuality*, 2nd ed., Cambridge: Harvard University Press, 1989. Explores the Greeks' concept of love between mature men and adolescent youths. Classic work on an important aspect of Greek culture.

Elaine Fantham et al., *Women in the Classical World: Image and Text*, Oxford: Oxford University Press, 1994. An up-to-date survey of its subject based on a wide variety of primary sources (not only literature, but also inscriptions and artifacts).

Peter Green, *From Alexander to Actium: The Historical Evolution of the Hellenistic Age*, Berkeley: University of California Press, 1990. Detailed political, cultural, and economic history of the Hellenistic period.

Erich S. Gruen, *Heritage and Hellenism: The Reinvention of Jewish Tradition*, Berkeley: University of California Press, 1998. Gruen demonstrates how Jews of the Hellenistic period adapted Greek ideas to create a rich and uniquely Jewish literature in Greek.

Edith Hall, *Inventing the Barbarian: Greek Self-Definition Through Tragedy*, Oxford: Clarendon, 1989. Explores Greek ideas of national identity and the emergence of the "barbarian" in classical literature.

Jonathan M. Hall, *Ethnic Identity in Greek Antiquity*, Cambridge: Cambridge University Press, 1997. Difficult to read, but important work that challenges traditional views about Greek ethnic categories.

Victor Hanson, *The Western Way of War: Infantry Battle in Classical Greece*, New York: Knopf, 1989. Brings hoplite battle to life and explores the role of warfare in Greek society and culture.

Simon Hornblower and Antony Spawford, eds., *The Oxford Classical Dictionary*, 3rd ed., Oxford: Oxford University Press, 1996. Excellent one-volume reference work.

G. E. R. Lloyd, *Early Greek Science: Thales to Aristotle*, New York: Norton, 1970. Classic introduction to the subject.

Albert B. Lord, *The Singer of Tales*, 2nd ed., ed. Stephen Mitchell and Gregory Nagy, Cambridge, Mass.: Harvard University Press, 2000. Originally published in 1960, this book revolutionized Homeric studies by synthesizing the insights of Lord's teacher, Milman Parry, on the nature of oral composition. Updated with a new introduction and audio-visual materials on CD-ROM.

Oswyn Murray, *Early Greece*, 2nd ed., Cambridge: Harvard University Press, 1993. Classic, well-written introduction to the Archaic period.

Lisa C. Nevett, *House and Society in the Ancient Greek World*, Cambridge: Cambridge University Press, 1999. Nevett studies the remains of houses on the Greek mainland and elsewhere to learn about the Greek family.

Josiah Ober, *Mass and Elite in Democratic Athens: Rhetoric, Ideology, and the Power of the People*, Princeton, N.J.: Princeton University Press, 1989. Ober draws attention to inequalities in wealth, education, and social status at Athens while arguing that the rich never formed a "ruling elite"—power was ultimately in the hands of the people.

Robin Osborne, *Greece in the Making, 1200–479 B.C.*, London: Routledge, 1996. Up-to-date social and economic history of Dark Age and Archaic Greece.

J. J. Pollitt, *Art and Experience in Classical Greece*, Cambridge: Cambridge University Press, 1972. Introductory text that integrates art, history, and culture to produce an illuminating view of classical Greece.

J. J. Pollitt, *Art in the Hellenistic Age*, Cambridge: Cambridge University Press, 1986. Lucid, insightful survey.

Sarah Pomeroy et al., *Ancient Greece: A Political, Social, and Cultural History*, Oxford: Oxford University Press, 1999. A good introductory textbook.

R. B. Rutherford, *The Art of Plato: Ten Essays in Platonic Interpretation*, London: Duckworth, 1995. Rutherford examines the literary aspects of Plato's work, a fascinating but neglected subject.

Graham Shipley, *The Greek World after Alexander: 323–30 B.C.*, London: Routledge, 2000. Up-to-date introduction to the Hellenistic world.

Andrew Stewart, *Greek Sculpture: An Exploration*, 2 vols., New Haven, Conn.: Yale University Press, 1990. Integrates art history with broader social and cultural themes. The standard reference work.

Rosalind Thomas, *Literacy and Orality in Ancient Greece*, Cambridge: Cambridge University Press, 1992. Thomas investigates the different ways in which the ancient Greeks used writing and argues that Greek culture remained fundamentally oral through the Classical period.

R. E. Wycherley, *The Stones of Athens*, Princeton, N.J.: Princeton University Press, 1978. This survey of Athenian archaeology combines discussion of material remains and literary evidence to show how the Athenians lived and thought.

Websites

Ancient Medicine/Medicina Antiqua (http://www.ea.pvt.k12.pa.us/medant/).

Diotima (http://www.stoa.org/diotima/). Bibliography, sources, and links for the study of women and gender in antiquity.

The Internet Ancient History Sourcebook (http://www.fordham.edu/halsall/ancient/asbook.html). Comprehensive site for sources, bibliography, and links. Maintained by Paul Halsall of Fordham University.

The Perseus Digital Library (http://www.perseus.tufts.edu/). Website for the study of Greek civilization (and now other areas as well) has Greek texts online, as well as images from Greek art and archaeology and numerous reference aids.

CHAPTER 3:   The Romans and Their Empire

Sources

English translations of most surviving Greco-Roman literary works are widely available. The most complete series of translations is the Loeb Classical Library, now published by Harvard University Press. The following are useful translations of material not found in the Loeb series.

Aelius Aristides, *Complete Works*, ed. C. A. Behr, 2 vols., Leiden: Brill, 1981. The works of one of the leading figures in the "Second Sophistic."

Roger S. Bagnall and Bruce W. Frier, *The Demography of Roman Egypt*, Cambridge: Cambridge University Press, 1994. Groundbreaking study of the Egyptian population based on about three hundred census declarations surviving on papyrus.

It contains a "Catalogue of census declarations" that summarizes the data about each household and can be used as a primary source for some purposes.

Hans Dieter Betz, ed., *The Greek Magical Papyri in Translation, Including the Demotic Spells*, 2nd ed., Chicago: University of Chicago Press, 1992.

K. Bowman and J. D. Thomas, *The Vindolanda Writing-Tablets (Tabulae Vindolandenses II)*, London: British Museum Press, 1994. Edition, English translation, and discussion of the military documents from Vindolanda, on Hadrian's Wall in England. Bowman has also published a more accessible translation of selected documents, aimed at students rather than scholars (*Life and Letters on the Roman Frontier: Vindolanda and Its People*, New York: Routledge, 1994).

P. A. Brunt and J. M. Moore, *Res Gestae Divi Augusti: The Achievements of the Divine Augustus*, Oxford: Oxford University Press, 1967. Augustus' self-composed, first-person epitaph.

The Documents from the Bar Kokhba Period in the Cave of Letters, vol. 1: *Greek Papyri*, ed. Naphtali Lewis, and vol. 2: *Hebrew, Aramaic, and Nabataean-Aramaic Papyri*, ed. Yigael Yadin et al., Jerusalem: Israel Exploration Society, 1989–2002. Invaluable sources for life and society in Roman Arabia and Judaea.

Naphtali Lewis and Meyer Reinhold, eds., *Roman Civilization: Selected Readings*, 2 vols., 3rd ed., New York: Columbia University Press, 1990. Many otherwise inaccessible documents are translated here.

Jacob Neusner, *The Mishnah: A New Translation*, New Haven, Conn.: Yale University Press, 1988. The Mishnah is an excellent source for Jewish thought and society in the Roman period. Another good English translation by Herbert Danby (*The Mishnah*, London: Oxford University Press, 1977) is also available.

Clyde Pharr, *The Theodosian Code and Novels, and the Sirmondian Constitutions*, New York: Greenwood Press, 1952. Codification of imperial edicts beginning with Constantine; excellent source for society and economy of the late empire.

P. Reardon, ed., *Collected Ancient Greek Novels*, Berkeley: University of California Press, 1989. English translations of all the surviving Greek novels, including fragments, and some related works.

Jane Rowlandson, ed., *Women and Society in Greek and Roman Egypt: A Sourcebook*, Cambridge: Cambridge University Press, 1998. Translates hundreds of otherwise inaccessible documents on papyrus.

Oswei Temkin, tr., *Soranus' Gynecology*, Baltimore: The Johns Hopkins University Press, 1956. Good translation of a second-century Greek medical text.

Alan Watson, ed., *The Digest of Justinian*, 4 vols., Philadelphia: University of Pennsylvania Press, 1985. Latin text and English translation of Rome's most important and influential legal text. A two-volume version (1998) containing the English translation only is also available.

Studies

E. Badian, *Publicans and Sinners: Private Enterprise in the Service of the Roman Republic*, 2nd ed., Ithaca, N.Y.: Cornell University Press, 1983. Illuminates the world of high finance and corruption in the late Republic.

Alan K. Bowman, *Egypt After the Pharaohs: 332 B.C.–A.D. 642, from Alexander to the Arab Conquest*, Berkeley: University of California Press, 1986. History, society, and culture of Greco-Roman Egypt, based on extensive study of documents on papyrus.

Keith Bradley, *Slavery and Society at Rome*, Cambridge: Cambridge University Press, 1994. Covers broad historical, demographic, and economic issues, but also tries to reconstruct what it was like to be a slave.

David J. Breeze and Brian Dobson, *Hadrian's Wall*, 4th ed., New York: Penguin, 2000. Up-to-date study of the wall's history, archaeology, and function, and of the Roman troops that were stationed there.

Raymond Chevallier, *Roman Roads*, tr. N. H. Field, London: Batsford, 1976. Still the best study of Roman roads; well-written and easy to read.

T. J. Cornell, *The Beginnings of Rome: Italy and Rome from the Bronze Age to the Punic Wars (c. 1000–264 B.C.)*, London: Routledge, 1995. Thorough, up-to-date survey of Rome's early history. Cornell argues against an Etruscan "conquest" of Rome.

Michael Crawford, *The Roman Republic*, 2nd ed., Cambridge, Mass.: Harvard University Press, 1992. Concise but sophisticated textbook; emphasizes themes in social, political, and economic history.

J. A. Crook, *Law and Life of Rome, 90 B.C.–A.D. 212*, Ithaca, N.Y.: Cornell University Press, 1967. Outdated on some topics, but still a useful survey of social and economic issues in Roman law and a good introduction to Roman law.

Harriet I. Flower, *Ancestor Masks and Aristocratic Power in Roman Culture*, Oxford: Clarendon, 1996. This study of the Roman tradition of ancestor portraits sheds light on aristocratic culture and self-definition.

Adrian Keith Goldsworthy, *The Roman Army at War: 100 B.C.–A.D. 200*, Oxford: Clarendon, 1996. Many surveys of the Roman army are available, but this one brings the subject to life by debunking the image of a perfect, machine-like force and focusing on the real experiences of soldiers and generals in war.

Erich S. Gruen, *Culture and National Identity in Republican Rome*, Ithaca, N.Y.: Cornell University Press, 1992. Explores Rome's encounter with Greek civilization, emphasizing that the Romans did not just copy the Greeks in a superficial way, but transformed Hellenic culture to suit their own needs.

William V. Harris, *War and Imperialism in Republican Rome: 327–70 B.C.*, Oxford: Oxford University Press, 1979. Examines the motives for Roman imperialism; emphasizes the aristocracy's appetite for glory and the economic benefits of conquest for all classes.

Ramsay MacMullen, *Roman Social Relations, 50 B.C. to A.D. 284*, New Haven, Conn.: Yale University Press, 1984. Compelling, well-written synthesis of a vast and complicated topic.

Ramsay MacMullen, *Soldier and Civilian in the Later Roman Empire*, Cambridge, Mass.: Harvard University Press, 1963. Groundbreaking study of the army's varied, everyday functions in peacetime.

Fergus Millar, *The Emperor in the Roman World (31 B.C.–A.D. 337)*, 2nd ed., Ithaca, N.Y.: Cornell University Press, 1992. Explores how the emperor interacted with his peers and subjects; emphasizes the personal nature of Roman authority.

Robert Morstein Kallet-Marx, *Hegemony to Empire: The Development of the Roman Imperium in the East from 148 to 62 B.C.*, Berkeley: University of California Press, 1995. Changed the way we understand Roman imperialism by arguing that the Romans of the Republican period perceived their empire as a sphere of authority rather than a collection of territorial provinces.

Claude Nicolet, *The World of the Citizen in Republican Rome*, tr. P. S. Falla, Berkeley: University of California Press, 1980. Explores what it meant to be a Roman citizen; illuminating study of politics and society.

Nancy H. Ramage and Andrew Ramage, *Roman Art: Romulus to Constantine*, 3rd ed., Upper Saddle River, N.J.: Prentice Hall, 2001. A good introductory survey.

Heinrich von Staden, "Anatomy as Rhetoric: Galen on Dissection and Persuasion," *Journal of the History of Medicine and Allied Sciences* 50 (1995), 47–66. Brilliant discussion of Galen's anatomical demonstrations in their cultural context and a good, brief introduction to the Second Sophistic.

Susan Treggiari, *Roman Freedmen During the Late Republic*, Oxford: Clarendon, 1969. Illuminating study of one of Rome's most interesting social classes.

Paul Veyne, *Bread and Circuses: Historical Sociology and Political Pluralism*, tr. Brian Pearce, New York: Penguin, 1990. This abridged translation of a longer book in French is an engrossing introduction to the ancient system of euergetism—the obligation of the rich to give to their communities.

Colin Wells, *The Roman Empire*, 2nd ed., Cambridge, Mass.: Harvard University Press, 1992. Offers social, economic, and cultural history as well as political narrative and a useful bibliography.

Websites

De Imperatoribus Romanis (http://www.roman-emperors.org). Online encyclopedia of emperors, with links to coins and maps.

Diotima (http://www.stoa.org/diotima/). Bibliography, sources, and links for the study of women and gender in antiquity.

The Duke Papyrus Archive (http://scriptorium.lib.duke.edu/papyrus/). Duke University has contributed enormously to the study of Hellenistic and Roman history by creating a digital database of documents on papyrus. Although some applications of the database will be too advanced for students, this website also has links to introductory discussions and bibliographies.

The Internet Ancient History Sourcebook (http://www.fordham.edu/halsall/ancient/asbook.html). Comprehensive site for sources, bibliography, and links, maintained by Paul Halsall of Fordham University.

The Perseus Digital Library (http://www.perseus.tufts.edu/). Although its main focus is on Greek civilization, Perseus now has many resources for the study of the Roman period.

ROMARCH: Roman Art and Archaeology (http://acad.depauw.edu/romarch/).

CHAPTER 4:   Christianity and the Late Antique World

Sources

An enormous quantity of literature, more than many people realize, survives from the late antique period. In general it is not as easily accessible as classical literature, and much of it has not been translated into English. Following is a select (not comprehensive) list of English translations of some important late antique sources and earlier sources on pagan and Christian religion.

Series

Many pagan and some Christian sources from late antiquity have been translated in the Loeb Classical Library series, now published by Harvard University Press.

Translated Texts for Historians (Liverpool: Liverpool University Press, 1979–) translates many otherwise inaccessible works, including some hagiographies, panegyrics, and historical sources not listed here.

The writings of some of the "church fathers" are available in *The Ante-Nicene Fathers*, eds. Alexander Roberts and James Donaldson, 1890 (repr. 1978) and *A Select Library of the Nicene and Post-Nicene Fathers of the Christian Church*, ed. Philip Schaff, 1890 (repr. 1956–1957). These can be downloaded online at www.ccel.org/fathers2 or www.newadvent.org/fathers/. Another important series is *The*

Fathers of the Church: A New Translation (New York: Cima and Washington, D.C.: Catholic University Press of America, 1947–).

The New Testament and Apocrypha

The New Testament is an important source for early Christianity. Many excellent translations into English are widely available, such as the New Revised Standard Version or the *New Jerusalem Bible*. Other early Christian writings circulated without becoming part of the canonical New Testament; scholars use the word "apocrypha" to designate some of these. Many have been translated and published individually, and collections of some of them have been made, including those listed here.

J. K. Elliott, *The Apocryphal New Testament: A Collection of Apocryphal Christian Literature in an English Translation*, Oxford: Clarendon, 1993.

Edgar Hennecke, *New Testament Apocrypha*, ed. William Schneemeleher, tr. R. McL. Wilson, 2 vols. Philadelphia: Westminster Press, 1964.

Henry Musurillo, *The Acts of the Christian Martyrs: Introduction, Texts and Translations*, Oxford: Clarendon, 1972.

James M. Robinson, ed., *The Nag Hammadi Library in English*, 4th ed., Leiden: Brill, 1996. Translates a large archive of Egyptian documents, many associated with the Gnostic Christian heresy.

Roman Law

Clyde Pharr, *The Theodosian Code and Novels, and the Sirmondian Constitutions*, New York: Greenwood Press, 1952. Imperial edicts and rulings from Constantine through 437.

Alan Watson, ed., *The Digest of Justinian*, 4 vols., Philadelphia: University of Pennsylvania Press, 1985. Latin text and English translation of Rome's most important and influential legal text. A two-volume version (1998) containing the English translation only is also available.

Panegyric

Speeches praising Roman emperors were produced on a routine basis in late antiquity, and many have survived. They provide information on some historical events and are good sources for values and expectations of rulers. A collection of Latin panegyrics is translated in C. E. V. Nixon and Barbara Saylor Rodgers, eds., *In Praise of Later Roman Emperors: The Panegyrici Latini*, Berkeley: Univeristy of California Press, 1994. Some panegyrics are translated in the series *Translated Texts for Historians*, mentioned earlier.

Hagiography

The genre of hagiography ("saints' lives") is especially vast; a few accessible collections in translation are listed here, but they represent only a small percentage of the total that survive. An excellent online collection of saints' lives is available from the Internet Medieval History Sourcebook (http://www.fordham.edu/halsall/sbook3.html).

John Binns, ed., *Lives of the Monks of Palestine*, by Cyril of Scythopolis, tr. R. M. Price, Kalamazoo, Mich.: Cistercian Publications, 1991.

Sebastian P. Brock and Susan Ashbrook Harvey, *Holy Women of the Syrian Orient*, 2nd ed., Berkeley: University of California Press, 1998.

Gregory of Nyssa, *Life of Gregory the Wonderworker*, in *St. Gregory Thaumaturgus: Life and Works*, tr. Michael Slusser, The Fathers of the Church: A New Translation, vol. 98, Washington, D.C.: Catholic University Press of America, 1998.

John of Ephesus, *Lives of the Eastern Saints*, tr. E. W. Brooks, 3 vols., Paris: Firmin-Didot, 1923–1925.

Norman Russell, *The Lives of the Desert Fathers: The Historia Monachorum in Aegypto*, London: Mowbray, 1980.

Helen Waddell, *The Desert Fathers*, Constable & Co., 1936; reprinted by the University of Michigan Press, 1957. Includes lives of some female monks.

Benedicta Ward, *The Sayings of the Desert Fathers: The Alphabetical Collection*, London: Mowbray, 1975.

Carolinne White, *Early Christian Lives*, New York: Penguin, 1998. Includes Athanasius' life of Antony.

Barbarian Europe

Bertram Colgrave and R. A. B. Mynors, eds., *Bede's Ecclesiastical History of the English People*, Oxford: Clarendon, 1969.

Katherine Fischer Drew, ed., *The Burgundian Code*, Philadelphia: University of Pennsylvania Press, 2nd ed., 1972.

Katherine Fischer Drew, ed., *The Laws of the Salian Franks*, Philadelphia: University of Pennsylvania Press, 1991. Besides a translation of the Salian Laws, this is also a good introduction to Frankish history.

Gregory of Tours, *The History of the Franks*, tr. Lewis Thorpe, New York: Penguin, 1974.

Charles Christopher Mierow, *The Gothic History of Jordanes in English Version*, Cambridge: Speculum Historiale and New York: Barnes & Noble, 1960.

S. P. Scott, ed., *The Visigothic Code*, Boston: Boston Book, 1910; repr. Littledon, Colo.: Rothman, 1982.

Studies

G. W. Bowersock, Peter Brown, and Oleg Grabar, eds., *Late Antiquity: A Guide to the Postclassical World*, Cambridge, Mass.: Harvard University Press, 1999. Encyclopedia that also contains up-to-date essays on important aspects of late antique history.

Peter Brown, *Augustine of Hippo: A Biography*, 2nd ed., Berkeley: University of California Press, 2000. Brown updates his classic biography of one of the church's most influential "fathers" with an epilogue discussing recent scholarship.

Peter Brown, *The Body and Society: Men, Women, and Sexual Renunciation in Early Christianity*, New York: Columbia University Press, 1990. Discussion of the ascetic tradition that illuminates some of the complexities of Christian attitudes toward the body.

Peter Brown, *The Cult of the Saints: Its Rise and Function in Latin Christianity*, Chicago: University of Chicago Press, 1981. Classic work on an important feature of late antique religion.

Averil Cameron, *The Later Roman Empire, A.D. 284–430*, Cambridge, Mass.: Harvard University Press, 1993. A concise survey of the period.

Averil Cameron, *The Mediterranean World in Late Antiquity, A.D. 395–600*, London: Routledge, 1993. A concise survey of the period.

Gillian Clark, *Women in Late Antiquity: Pagan and Christian Life-Styles*, Oxford: Clarendon, 1993. A good survey of women's life and status.

Everett Ferguson, ed., *The Encyclopedia of Early Christianity*, 2 vols., 2nd ed., New York: Garland, 1997. Excellent reference work.

Robin Lane Fox, *Pagans and Christians*, New York: Knopf, 1987. While histories of the early church abound, this one also includes a good discussion of pagan religion and explores the interaction between the two systems.

W. H. C. Frend, *The Early Church*, 2nd ed., Philadelphia: Fortress, 1982. Well-written survey.

W. H. C. Frend, *Martyrdom and Persecution in the Early Church: A Study of a Conflict from the Maccabees to Donatus*, New York: New York University Press, 1967. Outdated in some respects, but still the best survey of the subject.

Peter Garnsey and Caroline Humfress, *The Evolution of the Late Antique World*, Cambridge, England: Orchard Academic, 2001. Up-to-date social and cultural survey of the period.

Peter Heather, *The Goths*, Oxford: Blackwell, 1996. Survey that addresses the problem of defining the "Goths" and the development of Gothic ethnic identity.

Edward James, *The Franks*, Oxford: Blackwell, 1988. A good analysis of the scanty evidence for the early Franks.

Alexander P. Kazhdan, ed., *The Oxford Dictionary of Byzantium*, 3 vols., Oxford University Press, 1991. Excellent reference work.

Sabine MacCormack, *The Shadows of Poetry: Vergil in the Mind of Augustine*, Berkeley: University of California Press, 1998. Argues that Vergil's formative influence from Augustine's school days remained important throughout his life, although he used Vergil differently from pagan writers.

Ramsay MacMullen, *Christianity and Paganism in the Fourth to Eighth Centuries*, New Haven, Conn.: Yale University Press, 1997. Emphasizes the length and difficulty of the Christian struggle against paganism and the degree to which Christianity adapted to incorporate pagan elements.

Ramsay MacMullen, *Christianizing the Roman Empire, A.D. 100–400*, New Haven, Conn.: Yale University Press, 1984. Important study that draws attention to the overwhelming emphasis on miracles as instruments of conversion in early Christian sources.

Ramsay MacMullen, *Constantine*, The Dial Press, 1969; reprinted by Croom Helm, 1987. Well-written biography aimed at students and nonspecialists.

Ramsay MacMullen, *Paganism in the Roman Empire*, New Haven, Conn.: Yale University Press, 1981. Concise, vivid discussion of a difficult and often misunderstood subject; conveys the cultural richness and variety of paganism.

R. A. Markus, *The End of Ancient Christianity*, Cambridge: Cambridge University Press, 1990. Explores how Christianity redefined itself in the fourth century as it became a mainstream religion.

Bruce M. Metzger and Michael D. Coogan, *The Oxford Companion to the Bible*, Oxford: Oxford University Press, 1993. Useful reference in encyclopedia form.

Graham Stanton, *Gospel Truth? New Light on Jesus and the Gospels*, London: HarperCollins, 1995. Discusses Jesus as a historical subject, challenging some previous conclusions by incorporating recently discovered evidence and non-Christian sources.

Rodney Stark, *The Rise of Christianity: A Sociologist Reconsiders History*, Princeton, N.J.: Princeton University Press, 1996. While many of his arguments about ancient society are questionable, Stark's application of models based on modern studies of religious conversion to suggest that Christianity spread mainly through social networks is convincing.

Kurt Weitzmann, *Age of Spirituality: Late Antique and Early Christian Art, Third to Seventh Century*, New York: Metropolitan Museum of Art, 1979. Exhibit catalog with scholarly essays introducing each chapter and detailed text entries on each item. Especially interesting for interactions between pagan and Christian culture. Includes essays on architecture at the end of each chapter.

Websites

Diotima (http://www.stoa.org/diotima/). Bibliography, sources, and links for the study of women and gender in antiquity.

Internet Medieval History Sourcebook (http://www.fordham.edu/halsall/sbook2.html). Excellent resource for primary source material in translation.

The Online Reference Book for Medieval Studies (http://orb.rhodes.edu/index.html).

Index

Boldface page numbers indicate citations contained in maps. *Italic* page numbers indicate citations contained in illustrations.

Charity, 204
Charlemagne (Frank), 210
Chattel slavery, definition, 21
Chauvet Cave, 5
Cheops. *See* Khufu
Chersonesus (peninsula, Turkey), **61**
Childbirth, 33, 175, 185
China, 110n.
Chios (Aegean island), **61**
Choruses, 65, 68–69, 82–84, 93; definition, 82
Christ. *See* Jesus
Christianity, Christians, 184–208; and chronology, 3; and Franks, 210; and Greco-Roman culture, 112, 187, 205–8; and Hebrew Bible, 47, 206; and Islam, 216–17; and Justinian, 214; and Theodora, 215
Christmas, 205
Chronological charts, of early Roman history, 120; of Egyptian history, 30; of Greek history, 56; of Mesopotamian history, 17; of late antiquity, 187; of Roman emperors, 150
Chronology, 3, 19. *See also* Chronological charts
Church Fathers, 194–95, 206
Churches, 198, 202–3, 215
Churchill, Sir Winston, xiv
Cicero, Marcus Tullius, 119, 120, 141–42, 144, 207–8
Cincinnatus, 118
Cinna, Lucius Cornelius, 140
Circe (Greek myth), 57
Circumcision, 191
Circus, **151**, 202–3, 214
Cities: in the Bronze Age Levant, 34; and civilization, 15; in early Israel, 49; and elite classes, 15, 106; Etruscan, 121; in Greek world, 62–64, 74; Hellenistic, 105; of Hittites, 36; in late antiquity, 202–3; in Mesopotamia, 17–20; origins of, 8, 16; personifications in sculpture, *114*–115; in Plato, 91; in Roman Egypt, 175–77; in Roman provinces, 158–60; and sieges, 18, 32, *43*; in third century crisis, 179. *See also* Polis; *Politeia*; and individual cities
Citizenship: Athenian, *see* Athenian citizenship; Caracalla's edict, 147; Greek, in Roman Egypt, 175–76; in Hellenistic world, 105; in *poleis*, 62–64; Roman, *see* Roman citizenship; Spartan, 64–66. *See also Politeia*
City Dionysia (Athenian festival), 67

City of God (by Augustine), 207–8
Civil engineering. *See* Architecture
Civil War: Caesar vs. Pompey, 120, 142–44; Constantine vs. Licinius, 200; Constantine vs. Maxentius, 195; Octavian vs. Antony, 144, 153; in Roman Empire, 146, 152
Civilization, definition, x-xii, 13–15
Class. *See* Social class; Economic class; Elite classes
Claudius (Roman emperor), 150, 151, 156, 167, 170
Claudius Marcellus, Marcus, *See* Marcellus
Cleisthenes (of Athens), 56, 67
Cleopatra VII (of Egypt), 56, 105, *107*, 144
Clientela. *See* Patronage
Clients, dependents, 124–25; and Christianity, 197; client-kings, 134, 166; freedmen as, 139; and gang violence, 137, 142, 143; in household, 137
Climate: in Egypt, 26; Greek theory of, 110; in Mesolithic, 7; in Mesopotamia, 15–16; in Paleolithic, 5
Clodius Albinus (Roman emperor), 150
Clothing: and Greek sculpture, 71, *71*, 86–87, 99; of Huns, 212; manufacture of, *See* Textiles; of Roman rural slaves, 138; toga, *135*
Clovis (Frank), 210, 213, 214
Cnidus (Turkey), **61**, 86
Coates, John, 78
Code of Hammurabi, 19, 21, 23, 25
Cognomen, 119
Coinage: in Athens, 67; and Constantine, 198; Diocletian's reforms, 181; in Frankish kingdom, 210; Hellenistic kings on, 106, 115; in Roman economy, 172, 179, 181; Roman emperors on, 146, 180, 198, 210
Colonies: Greek, 59, 118; Hellenistic, 105, 176; Minoan, 39; Phoenician, 35; Roman, 127, 138, 169, 172
Colosseum, **151**, *152*, 153
Colossus of Nero, 151–52
Columbus, Christopher, xiv, 110n.
Column of Trajan, *154*
Comedy, 77, 82–84, 94, 113, 132
Comes (pl. *comites*), 210
Comitia centuriata (Roman assembly), 123
Comitia tributa, 126, 138, 140; definition, 126
Commodus (Roman emperor), 150